AF695990

FITNESS TO STAND TRIAL

Fitness to Stand Trial

FAIRNESS FIRST AND FOREMOST

The Honourable Justice Richard D. Schneider

ONTARIO COURT OF JUSTICE

CHAIR, ONTARIO REVIEW BOARD

ADJUNCT PROFESSOR, FACULTY OF LAW & DEPARTMENT OF PSYCHIATRY, FACULTY OF MEDICINE, UNIVERSITY OF TORONTO

Hy Bloom

CONSULTANT IN FORENSIC PSYCHIATRY, THE PSILEX GROUP

ASSISTANT CLINICAL PROFESSOR, PSYCHIATRY AND BEHAVIOURAL NEUROSCIENCES, McMASTER UNIVERSITY

ASSISTANT PROFESSOR, FACULTY OF MEDICINE & ADJUNCT FACULTY, LAW UNIVERSITY OF TORONTO

IRWIN LAW

Fitness to Stand Trial

Published in 2018 by

Irwin Law Inc
Suite 206, 14 Duncan Street
Toronto, ON M5H 3G8
www.irwinlaw.com

ISBN: 978-1-55221-497-8 ebook ISBN: 978-1-55221-498-5

Cataloguing in Publication available from Library and Archives Canada

Printed and bound by CPI Group (UK) Ltd, Croydon, CR0 4YY

1 2 3 4 5 22 21 20 19 18

Summary Table of Contents

Detailed Table of Contents

RICHARD SCHNEIDER

With love to Ruth, Lan, Ann, Laura, Heidi, Erik, Nils, Michael, Leif, and Vera (current count), who keep me fairly fit.

HY BLOOM

To Resa and Sam, with love, affection, and my endless appreciation. They keep me fit to stand the trials and tribulations of authorship.

And, to my canine companions, Otis and Talullah ... what can I say except "keep up the good work."

Introduction

A central objective in the criminal trial process is fairness. The guarantee of a fair trial is and should remain a court's paramount concern, especially in light of the risks the accused faces. These include deprivation of liberty, penal sanctions, and a criminal record, as well as potential psychological consequences such as harm to self-esteem and damage to one's dignity. The rules regarding fitness to stand trial are in place to help ensure that the accused receives a fair trial. "Fitness" varies as a function of an accused's mental state and its determination therefore constitutes a fundamental mental health issue in the criminal trial process. In fact, the issue of fitness is the most common matter that brings mental health professionals and the courts together. While a statistical figure for the frequency with which the issue of fitness to stand trial is raised in criminal proceedings in Canada is not available, it is raised considerably more often than lack of criminal responsibility. In the United States, a defendant's "competence to stand trial" is raised as a concern by defence counsel in 10 to 15 percent of cases.[1]

The need for an accused to be fit at the time he or she faces trial is an entrenched principle of common law, born of the demand for fairness. It may be trite to say that fairness has always been a foundational principle of law at most any time in the evolution of judicial

1 Steven K Hoge et al, "Attorney-Client Decision-Making in Criminal Cases: Client Competence and Participation as Perceived by Their Attorneys" (1992) 10:3 *Behavioural Sciences and the Law* 385; Norman Poythress et al, "Client Abilities to Assist Counsel and Make Decisions in Criminal Cases: Findings from Three Studies" (1994) 18:4 *Law and Human Behavior* 437.

institutions, and in most any civilized legal system. That said, we suggest that nothing operationalizes that concept better than the fitness rules, without which mentally compromised individuals could enter what some critics have termed a "den of inequity."

Insistence that an accused be fit to stand trial also ensures the maintenance of the integrity of the justice system and, from a practical point of view, keeps the ever-expanding volume of trials moving. And, importantly, as we discuss later, while the fitness rules are typically seen as protective in nature, they should not operate unreasonably as an obstacle to the trial process and thus unnecessarily prevent the accused from obtaining closure.

Commencing in the early 1990s, we have seen in Canada an unprecedented increase in the number of mentally disordered accused entering the criminal justice system in respect of whom the issue of "fitness" is in question. Statistics show that, since that time, the number of such accused entering the criminal justice system has been escalating by as much as 10 percent annually while overall arrest and prosecution rates have been declining.[2] There have been a number of hypotheses offered to explain this growth, including (1) cutbacks in mental health care (civil) spending; (2) a perception that the "new" Part XX.1 of the *Criminal Code* is less harsh and is therefore inviting challenges based on fitness; (3) inadequate civil legislation; and (4) a climate of "zero tolerance" regarding criminal activity, whether or not it is the product of mental disorder. As well, it may be that fewer accused with mental disorder are slipping through the system unnoticed. These explanations are speculative and, if valid, may be complementary and overlapping. What is very clear is that the criminal justice system has been left to deal with mentally disordered accused in volumes that are difficult to accommodate. Also clear, as set out in the following pages, is the fact that, while the broad objectives of the fitness rules can be traced to antiquity, there remains considerable uncertainty with respect to their scope and application.

---

2 See Richard D Schneider, *Statistical Survey of Provincial and Territorial Review Boards* (Ottawa: Department of Justice, 2002); Canadian Centre for Justice Statistics, *Crime Statistics in Canada, 2001* (Ottawa: Canadian Centre for Justice Statistics, 2002).

CHAPTER 1

A Brief History of the Fitness Rules

The requirement that an accused be "fit to stand trial" stems from the ancient notion that an accused must be present to respond to accusations of the state. That basic requirement developed into a more refined view that the accused must be present not only physically but mentally as well. In Canada, rules originally developed at common law were codified in 1992 and are contained in section 2 of the *Criminal Code* of Canada[1] as follows:

> *unfit to stand trial* means unable on account of mental disorder to conduct a defence at any stage of the proceedings before a verdict is rendered or to instruct counsel to do so, and, in particular, unable on account of mental disorder to
> (a) understand the nature or object of the proceedings,
> (b) understand the possible consequences of the proceedings, or
> (c) communicate with counsel

The procedures for dealing with the issue of unfitness to stand trial, and with mental disorder in general, are set out in Part XX.1 of the *Criminal Code*. Within the *Criminal Code*, Part XX.1 can be seen as a "mini *Code*" that deals exclusively with the mentally disordered accused.

1 RSC 1985, c C-46 [*Code*].

A. THE EVOLUTION OF THE FITNESS RULES

The fitness rules have evolved over millennia. And the same general notions of "fairness" as requiring an accused's presence can be found in most Western legal systems. Canadian, Commonwealth, and American jurisdictions can naturally trace their rules to older British law.

Limitations in an accused's physical well-being, intellect, and/or mental stability have historically resulted in special dispensations of one kind or another. Protections against trying a physically unwell or physically "un-present" accused preceded recognition that, while an accused may be physically present, intellectual and/or emotional compromise would render his presence meaningless, and that subjecting him to legal process in these circumstances was unfair.[2] And, while the disadvantaged mentally ill accused had to be protected, at the same time, she was not to be unnecessarily prevented from moving forward and disposing of the criminal allegations in a timely manner.[3]

The earliest English statute dealing with fitness to stand trial was passed in the thirty-third year of Henry VIII's reign.[4] Of interest, *An Act for Due Process to Be Had in High Treasons, in Cases of Lunacy or Madness*[5] concerned itself not only with whether the accused was mentally unwell, but whether his uncommunicative presentation was authentic ("mute by visitation"—i.e., based on mental disorder) or contrived/deliberate ("mute of malice") to evade prosecution.

The concept of fitness to stand trial (or "insanity upon arraignment,"[6] as it was originally known)[7] was fairly well established in England by

---

2 It is for similar reasons that individuals under a certain age are statutorily exempt from the criminal law process and sanctions. See, for example, Arlie Loughnan, "Dynamics of Inclusion and Exclusion: Unfitness to Plead and Infancy" (May 2012), *Oxford University Press Online*: DOI:10.1093/acprof.oso/9780199698592.003.0004. Loughnan refers to "infancy" as the minimum age upon which criminal responsibility can be imposed.

3 *R v Penny*, 2010 NBCA 49; *R v LSC*, [2003] AJ No 388 (CA).

4 Ralph Slovenko, "Competence to Stand Trial for Crime in the United States" (1998) 11 *Security Journal* 191.

5 (UK), 33 Henry VIII, c 20.

6 Originally, there was no clear conceptual distinction between "insanity" at the time of trial and at the time of the otherwise criminal act. Hence, the same term was used in both circumstances. The only distinction pertained to the point along the prosecutorial timeline at which the condition was recognized.

7 Eventually, the notion of "unfit to plead" (or "insanity upon arraignment") was merged with the related notion of inability to participate in the trial process.

the eighteenth century and was included in Lord Hale's *Pleas of the Crown* published in 1736,[8] and later, in Blackstone's treatise on English law.[9] According to Hale,

> If a man in his sound memory commits a capital offence, and before arraignment for it, he becomes mad, he ought not to be arraigned for it: because he is not able to plead to it with that advice and caution that he ought. And if, after he has pleaded, the prisoner becomes mad, he shall not be tried: for how can he make his defence? If, after he be tried and found guilty, he loses his senses before judgment, judgment shall not be pronounced; and if, after judgment, he becomes of nonsane memory, execution shall be stayed: for peradventure, says the humanity of the English law, had the prisoner been of sound memory, he might have alleged something in stay of judgment or execution.
>
> . . .
>
> And, further, a man who becomes "absolutely mad"' before arraignment "ought not by law to be arraigned during such a phrenzy but be remitted to prison until that incapacity be removed."[10]

One of the earliest elaborations of the principle occurred in *Frith's Case*[11] in 1790. Frith, a forcibly retired military man with persecutory and messianic delusions, threw a stone at King George III's coach, to draw attention to his cause. Frith's inability to make sense, however, resulted in him being declared unfit to plead by reason of insanity.

During this era, in which monarchs were portrayed as tolerant and forgiving of the mentally afflicted, the court in *Frith* stated:

> No man shall be called upon to make his defense at a time when his mind is in that situation as not to appear capable of so doing, for however guilty he may be, the inquiring into his guilt must be postponed to that season, when by collecting together his intellects, and have them entire, he shall be able so to model his defense as to ward off the punishment of the law.[12]

8 Sir Matthew Hale, *Historia Placitorum Coronae*, vol 1 (London: E and R Nutt, and R Gosling, 1736) at 34.

9 Sir William Blackstone, *Commentaries on the Laws of England*, 9th ed (1783) at 94.

10 Hale, above note 8 at 34 and 74.

11 *Frith's Case*, 22 How St Tr 307 (1790).

12 *Ibid* at 318.

It must also be recognized that trials of that era were exculpatory processes where the accused was presumed to be guilty unless his response proved his innocence. Refusal to plead ("mute of malice") or inability to plead ("mute by visitation") at the time of arraignment on the part of the accused created an impasse to the trial process. Today, the reverse is true. The accused is presumed to be innocent until the state has proven guilt beyond a reasonable doubt. Indeed, counsel may take the position that the state must prove a *prima facie* case before the issue of fitness is considered.

In their review of the historical background to the law and procedure relating to competence to stand trial in the United States, Zapf and Roesch[13] reference the importance of two particular cases. In the first, *United States v Lawrence* (1835),[14] the defendant was found incompetent to stand trial following his attempt to assassinate President Andrew Jackson and spent the rest of his life in mental institutions. In the second, *Youtsey v United States* (1899),[15] the Court of Appeal reversed the finding of a trial court and found the accused incompetent due to its doubts about his capacity to *appreciate* his legal predicament and *intelligently* instruct his lawyer about his defence.

The modern jurisprudential threads relevant to the issue of fitness to stand trial in Canada begin with the English case of *R v Pritchard* (1836).[16] In the context of considering whether a potentially mentally ill accused should proceed to trial, and after considering the writings of Hale, the trial judge suggested that three issues be considered:

> First, whether the prisoner is mute of malice [i.e. wilfully mute] or not; secondly, whether he can plead to the indictment or not; thirdly, whether he is of sufficient intellect to comprehend the course of the proceedings on the trial, so as to make a proper defence—to know that he might challenge any of you to whom he may object—and to comprehend the details of the evidence, which in a case of this nature must constitute a minute investigation.[17]

---

13 Patricia Zapf & Ronald Roesch, *Evaluation of Competence to Stand Trial* (New York: Oxford University Press, 2009).

14 *United States v Lawrence*, 4 Cranch, CC 518 (1835).

15 *Youtsey v United States*, 97 F 937 (6th Cir 1899).

16 *R v Pritchard* (1836), 7 Car & P 303, 173 ER 135.

17 *Ibid* at 304 (Car & P).

B. THE EVOLUTION OF THE FITNESS RULES IN CANADA

The above glimpse of the historical evolution of the fitness rules makes clear that it is fundamental to our system of criminal justice that an accused be able to participate in the judicial process in a meaningful way. In *R v Taylor*,[18] generally considered to be the most authoritative case on point in Canada to date,[19] Lacourcière JA of the Court of Appeal for Ontario articulated the issue in this way:

> In order to ensure that the process of determining guilt is as accurate as possible, that the accused can participate in the proceedings or assist counsel in his/her defence, that the dignity of the trial process is maintained, and that, if necessary, the determination of a fit sentence is made possible, the *accused must have sufficient mental fitness to participate in the proceedings in a meaningful way.*[20]

While this excerpt appears to capture the spirit of the common law, the same court went on to articulate the so-called limited cognitive capacity test, which, as we shall discuss below (see, in particular, Chapter 2, Section B), does not require that an accused have a rational understanding of their legal predicament, and, consequently, seemingly detracts from the need for "*meaningful*" participation Justice Lacourcière saw fit to specifically mention.

1) The 1973 Law Reform Commission of Canada and the Present Law

As with many topics in criminal law, a number of issues pertaining to fitness to stand trial have been around a long time but, every few decades, are discussed as if new. Quoted at length below is the introductory section of a study paper[21] produced for the Law Reform Commission of Canada in 1973. We have deliberately extracted a substantial portion

18 *R v Taylor*, [1992] OJ No 2394 (CA).

19 Though not without its controversies, as we shall see later in the text. See Chapters 2 and 3 in particular.

20 *Taylor*, above note 18 at para 50 [emphasis added].

21 Law Reform Commission of Canada, General Principles of the Criminal Law Project, "Fitness to Stand Trial," Study Paper (May 1973). Copyright Government of Canada. Reproduced with the permission of Library and Archives Canada (2018). Source: Library and Archives Canada/Criminal Law, General Principles, Fitness to Stand Trial: A Study Paper/Pages 1-3/AMICUS 482595.

of that introduction as it provides a valuable backdrop for the discussion that follows. The authors—eminent legal and medical scholars of the day—begin with a statement of the common law as it stood in 1973. Much of what was ultimately recommended by the commission found its way into the amendments to the *Criminal Code* with Bill C-30 (4 February 1992), which now, for the most part, makes up Part XX.1 of the *Code*. However, much of what was identified as problematic was not solved with Bill C-30 and, from the authors' perspective, remains problematic. In particular, while indicators are that Bill C-30 purported to merely "codify" the common law regarding fitness to stand trial, we argue later that it failed to do so in some important ways (see Chapter 2).

> The *Criminal Code* of Canada provides that a person may not be tried if he is unable to understand the purpose and meaning of the trial or if he is unable to rationally present his defence because of some mental disability. This exemption from trial, derived largely in both substance and form from the common law, has been widened by an increasing judicial concern for the mentally disordered accused. The present study memorandum examines the fitness rule as it has been developed in Canada in relation to mental disorder and makes recommendations for its reform.
>
> Reappraisal of the fitness rule is one part of a review of the law and mental disorders which the Project on the Principles of the Criminal Law has undertaken. Other study papers which consider the defence of insanity and the mentally disordered prisoner are being prepared. These and the present paper are closely related to each other and to collateral subjects such as civil commitment and the court's powers to remand for psychiatric examination. As a result, the Project has considered the potential impact which suggested changes in the fitness rule might have on related areas of the law. Nevertheless, as it is always difficult to foresee every consequence which may flow from the implementation of a given reform, the Project would appreciate comments concerning the effect of its recommendations on related procedures and practices.
>
> The study memorandum is being distributed for two reasons: to present the problems and principles of the fitness rule as they have been perceived by the Project, and to elicit comment and criticism which will be helpful in the formulation of the recommendations

which will eventually be submitted to the Law Reform Commission. We are hopeful that the memorandum will accomplish these ends.

The Present Law

At common law an accused who was unable to act rationally in his own defence or to understand the nature and object of the proceedings against him could not be tried. This exemption from trial was a result of the ban against trying a person in his absence; the accused's mental awareness was considered to be as important to the fairness of the proceedings as his physical presence. As well as the mentally disordered, persons with physical handicaps, such as the deaf and dumb, and even persons with linguistic and cultural differences could be found unfit. As technological and social developments improved the participation at trial of physically handicapped and culturally different persons, the disabilities which caused unfitness were restricted to mental impairment. This narrowing of the scope of the fitness rule was accompanied by a corresponding broadening of its application to mental disorders because of increased concern for mental illness.

In Canada, the *Criminal Code* codifies the fitness rule in section 543(1), which states in part:

> A court may, when it appears that there is sufficient reason to doubt that the accused is, on account of insanity, capable of conducting his defence, direct that an issue be tried whether the accused is then, on account of insanity, unfit to stand trial.

The issue of fitness may be raised by the prosecutor or the defence, despite the objections of the other party; or by the court despite the objections of either party. The fitness of the accused may be brought into question more than once at trial and again on appeal, and the party alleging unfitness must prove it on a balance of probabilities.

Fitness is determined by the trier of fact, whether a judge sitting alone, or the jury in a trial by jury. The same jury usually tries both fitness and guilt, but the jurors are re-sworn for the fitness hearing and a different oath is administered. If, however, the issue arises before the accused is given in charge of the jury, a separate jury is empaneled to decide it alone. These initial jurors, if they find the accused fit, do not in practice sit on the jury which decides guilt.

The presiding judge or magistrate decides whether an inquiry into the accused's fitness is warranted. He may refuse to hold a hearing if he concludes that the allegations are unfounded. But, if a hearing is necessary, trial on the merits is delayed and does not continue unless the accused is declared fit.

Prior to 1969, the accused's fitness was considered as soon as it was brought into question. However, an amendment in that year to section 543 of the *Criminal Code* empowered the presiding judge or magistrate to defer consideration of the matter up to the close of the case of the prosecution. The defence may, therefore, test the validity of the charges against the accused and, if he is acquitted, no inquiry as to fitness is made.

A decision by the trial judge to hold a fitness hearing is usually accompanied by an order made pursuant to section 543(2), remanding the accused to a medical facility up to 30 days for observation. If the accused has shown symptoms of mental disorder at arraignment or preliminary inquiry, he may be remanded for up to 60 days for observation under sections 465(c) and 738(5). Although the *Code* does not prescribe the procedure to be followed after the accused has undergone the required observation, the report of the examining doctor usually forms the basis of the court's decision concerning the accused's fitness.

If the accused is found fit, trial on the merits resumes, if the accused is found unfit, the judge sets aside the plea of the accused, discharges the jury, and orders the accused detained until "the pleasure of the lieutenant governor is known." The accused has a statutory right to appeal a finding of fitness or unfitness. Once the avenue of appeal has been exhausted, the courts have nothing further to do with the unfit accused until such time as he is returned to trial by the lieutenant governor.

The discretion of the lieutenant governor has usually been exercised by committing an unfit accused to a mental institution for an indeterminate period. As a result of a recent amendment to the *Criminal Code*, however, an unfit accused may now be discharged either absolutely or subject to conditions where the lieutenant governor thinks that such an action would be in the best interests of the accused and not contrary to the interests of society. The *Criminal Code* also empowers the lieutenant governor to create a Review Board which systematically considers the case of all persons detained in the province under

> Executive Warrant. The Board reports the progress of accused detained as unfit and makes recommendations concerning their return to trial or the need for further treatment. Such recommendations are not, however, binding upon the lieutenant governor, and not all provinces have Review Boards.

Much of what the commission recognized as the common law of the day—that is, in 1973—remains the same today; yet much has changed. Much of the common law as recognized by the commission was captured with Bill C-30 in 1992; some considerations were not. In particular, we will argue that the common law prior to the proclamation of Bill C-30 in 1992 required that an accused remain "fit" throughout the criminal proceedings (including the sentencing portion, if convicted) and that "fitness" required an ability to *meaningfully* participate in the legal proceedings.

Ten-Point Review

1) The requirement that an accused be "fit to stand trial" stems from the ancient notion that an accused must be present to respond to accusations of the state.
2) The rules originally developed at common law were codified in 1992 and are contained in section 2 of the *Criminal Code* of Canada.
3) An historical review of the fitness rules makes clear that an accused must be able to participate in the judicial process in a "meaningful way" or instruct counsel "rationally."
4) A person may not be tried if they are unable to understand the purpose and meaning of the trial or if they are unable to rationally participate because of some mental disability.
5) At common law, an accused who was unable to act rationally in their own defence or to understand the nature and object of the proceedings against them could not be tried.
6) The issue of fitness may be raised by the prosecutor or the defence or by the court, despite the objections of either party.
7) The fitness of an accused may be brought into question more than once at trial and again on appeal, and the party alleging unfitness must prove it on a balance of probabilities.
8) Fitness is determined by the trier of fact, whether that is a judge sitting alone or, in a trial by jury, a jury.

9) The presiding judge or magistrate decides whether an inquiry into the accused's fitness is warranted.
10) Where an accused is found unfit, the trial on the merits is delayed and does not resume until the accused is declared fit.

CHAPTER 2

"Unfit to Stand Trial": The Test

As discussed in Chapter 1, the common law regarding the test of whether someone was unfit to stand trial was codified in Canada with Bill C-30 in 1992. That test is now contained in section 2 of the *Criminal Code*. We will come back to this section many times throughout the text. As well, we will return to discuss the extent to which the common law was captured with this codification.

A. SECTION 2 OF THE *CRIMINAL CODE*

As noted in Chapter 1, "unfit to stand trial" is defined in section 2 of the *Criminal Code* as

> *unable* on account of *mental disorder* to *conduct a defence at any stage of the proceedings before a verdict is rendered* or *to instruct counsel to do so*, and, in particular, unable on account of mental disorder to
> (a) understand the nature and object of the proceedings,
> (b) understand the possible consequences of the proceedings, or
> (c) communicate with counsel[1]

Traditionally, the criteria set out in section 2 have been explored through a set of questions put to the accused, such as, but not limited to, the following:[2]

1 RSC 1985, c. C-46, s 2 [emphasis added].

2 Some clinicians/practitioners refer to these as the "*Taylor* Questions," a reference to *R v Taylor*, [1992] OJ No 2394 (CA) [*Taylor*]. These questions, in fact, really have nothing to do with the decision in *Taylor*. They came from an early Law Reform

- What are the roles of the various people in the courtroom?
- What are the charges the accused is facing?
- What are the available pleas?
- What are the consequences of a conviction?
- What is the meaning of an oath?
- What is perjury?
- What are the consequences of perjury?

In the following sections, we deconstruct the statutory definition and consider its elements.

1) Ability

The test is not whether the accused *knows* their legal situation, and so on, but whether they are *able* to understand the concepts and communicate with counsel. The accused's *capacity* is the central concern. Simple ignorance does not render an accused unfit. An accused is unfit to stand trial only if they are *unable* on account of mental disorder to conduct a defence. A declaration of inability should be made only after didactics have unequivocally failed.

2) Mental Disorder

"Mental disorder" is defined in section 2 of the *Criminal Code* as "a disease of the mind," a phrase preserved and retained from previous caselaw. A disease of the mind is broadly defined in Canada; it includes "any illness, disorder or abnormal condition which impairs the human mind and its functioning."[3] The definition from the perspective of criminal law is broad and includes, for example, mental retardation.[4] Indeed, according to caselaw, an accused who is deaf and unable to speak could not be said to suffer from a mental disorder.[5]

Commission report as questions that might guide a determination of whether the accused had sufficient wherewithal to conduct a defence. See Law Reform Commission of Canada, General Principles of the Criminal Law Project, "Fitness to Stand Trial," Study Paper (May 1973) [Criminal Law General Principles].

3 *R v Cooper*, [1980] 1 SCR 1149 at 1159.

4 For example, *R v Rouse*, [1996] OJ No 4688 (Gen Div).

5 *R v Isaac*, [2009] OJ No 5804 (Ct J).

Mental disorder *simpliciter* does not, by itself, render an accused unfit: it is a necessary but not sufficient condition. Two findings are necessary: (1) that a mental disorder is present, and (2) that the mental disorder prevents the accused from conducting a defence. It is the impact of the mental disorder upon the accused's abilities that is in question.

3) Conduct a Defence

The inclusion of the ability to "conduct a defence" suggests that any dysfunction caused by a mental disorder that would render the accused unable to understand and manage the exigencies of the criminal charge(s) (or unable to instruct counsel to do so) is conceptually broader than the examples contained in section 2. The operative consideration is the accused's ability "to conduct a defence." The three particulars listed in subsections (a), (b), and (c) of the definition of "unfit to stand trial" are examples of the most common domains of inquiry bearing on an accused's ability to conduct a defence. In addition, given that a "defence" may require competence over some, if not a considerable, period of time, depending on the nature of the litigation, fitness arguably contemplates a prospective component to the test. Whether minutes or months later, the trial will be an event held in the future.

Even where the accused appears to understand the nuts and bolts of the trial process, delusions caused by a mental illness may cause the accused to believe they have no part in the process, as occurred in *R v King*, where the accused believed that he was "Captain Rod Malak Yah-Wah" and not "Rodney King" (his real name).[6] The same result obtained where an accused saw the trial process as a vehicle for demonstrating that she was not mentally ill. In the circumstances, it was not possible to move the accused on to relevant dimensions of her case even though, in an abstract sense, she understood the nature and object of the proceedings.[7]

4) Before a Verdict Is Rendered

While much of what is contained in the "new" section 2 definition of "unfit to stand trial" set out in the *Criminal Code* was taken from the

6 *R v King*, 2007 ONCA 713.

7 *R v Xu*, [2007] OJ No 5796 (Ct J).

draft legislation proposed by the study paper prepared for the Law Reform Commission of Canada in 1973, there were two curious omissions. First, subsection 1(1) of the draft provided:

> (1) A person who is unfit to stand trial shall not be convicted *or sentenced* so long as such unfitness endures.

In addition, subsection 1(2) of the draft provided:

> (2) A person is not unfit to stand trial if he suffers from a disorder, mental or otherwise, whose sole effect is to deprive him totally or partially of *recollection of the circumstances* of the offence alleged against him.[8]

We will return to both of these issues below.

A strict reading of the statutory provisions dealing with unfitness to stand trial makes clear that they pertain only to the point of a verdict. In Ontario this "end point" has in some cases been modified by the courts to include sentencing. A fuller discussion of this issue appears in Chapter 3, Section D.

B. THE LIMITED COGNITIVE CAPACITY TEST

The court in *R v Taylor* states that the test for fitness to stand trial is to be the "limited cognitive capacity test."[9] This test requires that the accused have, at minimum, only a rudimentary factual understanding of their legal predicament.[10] A "rational" understanding is specifically not required, nor is it necessary that the accused be able to act in their own best interests.[11] To the best of the authors' knowledge, no court prior to

8 Criminal Law General Principles, above note 2 at 31 [emphasis added].

9 *Taylor*, above note 2 at para 52.

10 *R v Stojanovic*, [2014] OJ No 4823 (Ct J); *R v Eisnor*, [2013] NSJ No 584 (SC).

11 For a critique of the *Taylor* decision, see Richard D Schneider & Hy Bloom, "*R v Taylor*: A Decision Not in the Best Interests of Some Mentally Ill Accused" (1995) 38 *Criminal Law Quarterly* 183; *R v Ejigu*, [2012] BCJ No 910 (SC); *R v Fortune*, [2009] OJ No 5135 (SCJ); *R v Stojanovic*, above note 10; *R v Williams*, [2012] OJ No 4974 (SCJ); *R v Wisniewski*, [2012] AJ No 1010 (Prov Ct). Curiously, the court in *Taylor* also states that the inquiry as to an accused's ability to communicate with counsel is limited to an inquiry into whether or not an accused can recount to their counsel the necessary facts relating to the offence in such a way that counsel can properly present a defence. *Taylor*, above note 2 at para 21. An inability to recount or remember facts has typically not been accepted as a basis for a finding of unfitness.

Taylor had held that an accused need not have a rational understanding of their legal predicament to be fit to stand trial. As we contend, and expound in the remainder of this chapter, repudiation of the need for an accused to have a rational understanding of their legal predicament is counterintuitive in the presence of mental disorder and is anathema to the existence and evolution of the fitness rules.

A requirement of "rationality" was specifically articulated in the United States in the widely known and relied on US Supreme Court case of *Dusky v United States*.[12] According to Felthouse, however, the inherent wisdom behind the requirement that an accused bring rational understanding to bear on the criminal proceedings and dealings with counsel has been incrementally lost by courts—"slipping into oblivion with nary a word"—over time.[13]

The limited cognitive capacity test sets the knowledge and understanding bar quite low. In determining fitness, it is required that the accused must: understand the nature and object of the proceedings (the accused needs only a basic factual understanding of their legal predicament—i.e., an awareness of what is happening to them in the criminal process); understand the possible consequences of the proceedings (this amounts to a basic understanding of the potential outcomes in a criminal trial); and be able to communicate with counsel. This third element is limited to whether the accused can recount to counsel the necessary facts related to the offence in such a way that counsel can then properly conduct a defence[14] (or, if there is no memory of the event(s) to communicate with respect to tactical/process options). In Canada, a lack of memory for the events in question is not, by itself, a basis for a finding of unfitness (see the discussion of *R v Morrissey* in Section B(4), below in this chapter).

The Ontario Court of Appeal in *R v MAW*[15] considered once again the appropriate test for fitness to stand trial in the case of an accused who wished to set aside a guilty plea claimed to have been made at the time he was unfit. The court, in confirming the "limited cognitive capacity test" set out in *R v Taylor*, gave two reasons for this decision. The

12 362 US 402 (1960) [*Dusky*].

13 Alan R Felthouse, "Competence to Stand Trial Should Require Rational Understanding" (2011) 39:1 *Journal of the American Academy of Psychiatry and the Law* 19.

14 *R v Hureau*, [2014] YJ No 48 (Terr Ct); *R v RCMc*, [2011] SJ No 243 (Prov Ct).

15 [2008] OJ No 2738 (CA) [*MAW*].

first was "consistency." That is, as the Supreme Court of Canada has stated in *R v Whittle*,[16] there should be one standard of mental capacity for decisions at all junctures in the prosecution process. One might respond with the observation that, while the principle in *Whittle* may be sound, perpetuating a standard that is too low is not the best reason to maintain "consistency." The second reason given by the court is that the accused's interest in liberty dictates that they should be permitted to conduct their own defence. To impose a higher standard than the limited cognitive capacity test—one that would require the accused to be rational or to act in their own best interests—would "smack of paternalism." To this, one might draw on the earliest historical origins of the rule and respond that paternalism created and drives the fitness rules *regardless of the standard*, but, more importantly, that the standard should be one that adequately protects the accused. There is no point in having a protection if it is not doing what was intended—preventing an unfair, lopsided trial.

The common law pre-dating Bill C-30, as articulated in the study paper prepared for the Law Reform Commission, begins with the following sentence, "The Criminal Code of Canada provides that a person may not be tried if he is unable to understand the purpose and meaning of the trial or if he is unable to *rationally present his defence* because of some mental disability."[17]

The court in *Taylor* felt that the limited cognitive capacity standard struck "an effective balance" between the objectives of the fitness rules and the right of the accused to choose his own defence and have a trial within a reasonable time.[18] While expediency must be considered in setting the fitness standard, it may be that the "right to choose" is a rather empty right where the accused does not have a rational understanding of the legal predicament; where choice is not rational choice; and where the accused's presenting of a defence cannot be done rationally. Seemingly missing from the *Taylor* court's considerations is the notion that the capacity of mentally ill persons to make choices may be as compromised by the mental disorder, as are other cognitive, perceptual, and emotional processes. The right to choose must be read as

---

16 (1994), 92 CCC (3d) 11 (SCC) [*Whittle*].

17 Criminal Law General Principles, above note 2 at 1 [emphasis added].

18 *Taylor*, above note 2 at para 52.

"rational choice"; otherwise, from a protection perspective, it is a "right" of questionable worth.

Against the concern for expediency is the rationale for the rules in the first place. Principally, as mentioned above, the rules are in place to ensure that an accused who is ill-equipped as a result of mental disorder is not subjected to the prosecution machinery of the state. The rules are to protect the accused. They operate to hold the prosecution in abeyance until the accused is fit to respond. The court in *MAW* found that the cognitive capacity required for a voluntary guilty plea requires "an ability to understand the process and make an active or conscious choice . . . that an accused be capable of making a decision."[19] While we would agree that being *conscious* should indeed be a requirement, we submit that the further (and final) requirement that the *conscious* accused be merely "capable of making a decision" falls short of what the fitness rules were intended to achieve.

In reality, trial judges who attempt to try accused who are not rational recognize this lack of rationality as an impasse and readily find that they are unfit. As well, counsel who attempt to represent accused who are not rational often submit that they are not able to get meaningful instructions. In part, the solution for such problems lies in the "packaging." As in most areas of the law there is often a gulf between rules in theory and rules in practice. Difficulties in practice will be presented as difficulties that comport with the black letter of the law.

There *is* nevertheless a balance to be struck. The fitness rules are to protect the accused but, quite apart from the expediency and "numbers" concerns, they should not constitute an impasse. In this regard, it is noteworthy that the Supreme Court of the United States in *Indiana v Edwards* sets out the American Constitution's "mental competence" standard, which forbids the trial of an individual lacking a rational and factual understanding of the proceedings and sufficient "ability to consult with his lawyer with a *reasonable degree of rational understanding.*"[20]

We will return to the *Edwards* case below in Section B(9), below in this chapter.

---

19 MAW, above note 15 at para 33.

20 554 US 164 at page 12 (2008) [emphasis added].

1) A Return to Rationality?

Recent jurisprudence, particularly the decision in *R v Adam*,[21] has seemingly eroded the narrow perspective that was taken in the *Taylor* case (and was endorsed without fulsome analysis in *MAW* and *Whittle*). As well, two Yukon cases are instructive in this regard. In *R v Blackjack*, Chief Justice Ruddy noted, speaking of the test in *Taylor*, that the caselaw made "evident that the application of the limited cognitive capacity test enunciated in *Taylor* cannot be a simplistic exercise."[22] Chief Justice Ruddy went on to say that "[i]t is not simply a matter of determining whether an accused demonstrates a rudimentary understanding of the legal proceedings. That, in and of itself, is not enough. The level of understanding, while not required to be comprehensive and nuanced, *must be sufficient to enable the accused to participate in his or her own defence in a meaningful way*."[23] One might argue that the term "meaningful" unavoidably imports the requirement that the accused be able to respond to the prosecution "rationally." Curiously, the expression "meaningful way" is lifted from the decision in *Taylor*, which then dismissed "rational understanding" as elevating the test to an unreasonable standard.

Another Yukon-based case, *R v Nehass*, concurred with the view expressed in *R v Blackjack* and emphasized that the test in *Taylor* subsumes "a rational understanding of the fundamental tenets of the process and procedure of the criminal case in which ... [the accused] is involved."[24]

Clearly, the test needs better articulation.

As we have argued elsewhere, requiring an accused to be rational in order to be fit is an essential fitness element recognized in cases pre-dating *Taylor*.[25] Certainly, in the United States, the Supreme Court in *Dusky* held that

> it is not enough ... to find that the defendant [is] oriented to time and place [i.e., "conscious"] and [has] some recollection of events, but ... the test must be whether he has sufficient present ability to consult with his lawyer with a reasonable degree of rational understanding—and

21 [2013] OJ No 222 (SCJ) [*Adam*].

22 [2010] YJ No 120 at para 16 (Terr Ct).

23 *Ibid* [emphasis added].

24 *R v Nehass*, [2014] YJ No 117 at para 71 (Terr Ct).

25 See Schneider & Bloom, above note 11.

whether he has rational as well as a factual understanding of the proceedings against him.[26]

Canadian decisions immediately pre-dating *Taylor*, including *R v Gibbons*,[27] *R v Woltucky*,[28] *R v Hubach*,[29] *R v Roberts*,[30] *Re R v Gorecki (No 1)*,[31] and *R v Trecroce*,[32] like the earlier British case of *R v Pritchard*,[33] all required that accused have a rational understanding of their legal predicament in order to be fit to stand trial. Against these earlier cases, the decision in *Taylor* is an aberration with internal inconsistencies.

Further, the so-called tests to be distinguished—the "limited cognitive capacity test" and the "analytical capacity test" (the latter said to require a "rational understanding" of one's legal predicament)—were standards not known prior to being differentiated and coined in *Taylor*. They are not used in any other jurisdiction. And while the limited cognitive capacity test, confused as it is in *Taylor*, has been formally endorsed, notably in *Whittle* and *MAW*, it should be noted that neither of these decisions focused on a fulsome consideration of the reasons for the fitness rules and the threshold to be met in order to breathe life into the interests of a fair trial. Rather, they decided that "consistency" (at whatever threshold is established) is an overriding important objective.[34]

2) Rationality: What Is It, and Why Do We Want It?

The *Oxford English Dictionary* defines "rationality" in the following way:

1 The quality of being based on or in accordance with reason or logic.

1.1 The quality of being able to think sensibly or logically.

---

26 *Dusky*, above note 12 at 402. Re the term "conscious," see the discussion of *MAW* in Section B, above in this chapter.

27 *R v Gibbons* (1946), 86 CCC 20 (Ont CA).

28 *R v Woltucky* (1952), 103 CCC 43 (Sask CA).

29 *R v Hubach*, [1966] 4 CCC 114 (Alta SCAD).

30 *R v Roberts* (1975), 24 CCC (2d) 539 (BCCA).

31 *Re R v Gorecki (No 1)* (1976), 32 CCC (2d) 129 (Ont CA) [*Gorecki*].

32 *R v Trecroce* (1980), 55 CCC (2d) 202 (Ont CA) [*Trecroce*].

33 *R v Pritchard* (1836), 7 Car & P 303.

34 While Canadian courts have not reconsidered the substance of the fitness test in any depth, the so-called test has been exported to different contexts (e.g., *Italy v Seifert*, [2003] BCJ No 726 (SC)) and other provinces within Canada (e.g., *R c Brigham*, [1992] JQ no 2283 (CA) and many other cases cited elsewhere in this text).

1.2 The quality of being endowed with the capacity to reason.[35]

If our objective with the fitness rules is to ensure a fair trial, then we should ensure that the accused's response to the state will be "based on or in accordance with reason or logic."

3) The Concept of "Best Interests"

It remains unclear to us whether the court in *Taylor* appreciated the nuances inherent in the "best interests" notion it rejected, but we suspect not. Few, if any, courts or legal scholars in Canada have grappled with the issue, although it has received recent attention in New Zealand.[36] In that country, individuals on trial for an offence are expected to contribute to their own defence via liaison with their defence team and to be able to participate meaningfully in the court process. This requirement implicitly imports the notion that the accused be capable of acting in their best interests, to the extent that it is captured by "meaningful participation." Defendants who are unable to participate meaningfully are deemed unfit to stand trial.[37] In Canada, the decisions in *Gorecki* and *Trecroce* deal with the matters of "rational choice" and "best interests" but need to be read quite carefully. They do not clearly stand for the proposition that these factors are not to be considered.

4) Rational Understanding and Meaningful Participation

As the following disparate examples suggest, the caselaw remains uneven with respect to "rational understanding" and "meaningful participation." In *Taylor*, rationality on the part of the accused is not considered to be a factor in determining fitness, nor is the testimonial competence of the accused a condition precedent to the accused being declared fit to stand trial.[38] It is not a prerequisite that the accused be capable of

35 Online: https://en.oxforddictionaries.com/definition/rationality.

36 Warren Brookbanks, "Fitness to Plead—Best Interests Versus Autonomy: Does a Defendant's Paranoia Matter" (2013) 20:1 *Psychiatry, Psychology and Law* 1.

37 Joseph A Sakdalan & Vincent Egan, "Fitness to Stand Trial in New Zealand: Different Factors Associated with Fitness to Stand Trial between Mentally Disordered and Intellectually Disabled Defendants in the New Zealand Criminal Justice System" (2014) 21:5 *Psychiatry, Psychology and Law* 658.

38 See also *R v Iyoho*, [2009] AJ No 950 (Prov Ct).

exercising analytical reasoning in making a choice to accept the advice of counsel or in coming to a decision that best serves their interests.[39] Rather, the accused need only "have sufficient mental fitness to participate in the proceedings in a meaningful way."[40] On the other hand, the court in *R v Jaser* found that "neither *Taylor* nor *Morrissey* [intended that] 'meaningful participation' at trial become the new test for fitness":

> In *R. v. Taylor*, ... Lacourcière J.A. referred to the accused's ability to "participate in the proceedings in a meaningful way" as simply one of the competing policies or values that the Court took into consideration, in adopting the "limited cognitive capacity" test and in rejecting the higher "analytic capacity" test. Similarly, in *R. v. Morrissey*, ... Blair J.A. quoted the full passage from *Taylor* setting out all of the competing policies and values that the Court considered when adopting the "limited cognitive capacity" test, and concluded:
>
>> Meaningful presence and meaningful participation at the trial, therefore, are the touchstones of the inquiry into fitness.
>
> In my view, neither *Taylor* nor *Morrissey* were erecting "meaningful participation" at trial as a new test for fitness.[41]

While it is difficult to say whether the court in *Morrissey* was setting up "meaningful participation" as the proper test for fitness, it is interesting to refer, once again, to excerpts from the above-mentioned study paper, wherein it is observed that "Instructing counsel is tied to the accused's participation at trial and implies the ability to rationally communicate."[42] The point is, regardless of the above-mentioned courts' intentions (and presumably if they'd intended a new test they would have said so), if our objective with the fitness rules is protecting the accused from an unbalanced match at trial, how could it be that we would send the accused into the arena when that individual is not able to meaningfully participate or meaningfully communicate? The point here is similar to that made above with respect to "rational understanding."

Indeed, the distinction between the limited cognitive capacity test and the so-called analytical capacity test was made for the first time

39 *R v Ejigu*, above note 11; *R v Wisniewski*, above note 11.

40 *R v Fortune*, above note 11 at para 42.

41 2015 ONSC 4729 at para 61.

42 Criminal Law General Principles, above note 2 at 9.

by the Ontario Court of Appeal in *Taylor*. What we have, frankly, is an illogical jumble in Canada, where the same court (in *Taylor*) is saying, on the one hand, that "the accused must have sufficient mental fitness to participate in the proceedings in a *meaningful way*" [emphasis added] but, on the other, needn't have a rational understanding of the legal predicament. This is an irreconcilable inconsistency. As Trotter J states in *Adam*, "For an accused person in a criminal trial, meaningful participation can only mean the ability to defend oneself."[43] That, of course, is the mischief to which the rules are directed.

Justice Trotter, in *Adam*, takes a considerably broader view of "meaningful participation" than did *Taylor* and considers it an essential ingredient for a finding of fitness. He takes a view of fitness that, of necessity, must include a modicum of "rationality" in order for the test to comport with the broad intention and spirit of the fitness rules—that is, to protect individuals from the state's prosecution where they are not equipped to respond. We submit that the view taken by Trotter J in *Adam* may be signalling the need for a shift to more formally recognizing what the courts have, in practice, been applying for some time. To dismiss the concern about rationality as "paternalism," or to find that it is unnecessary if it compromises "expediency," is to ignore the objectives inherent in the rules.

The view that rationality and meaningful participation are required is hardly new, as we have seen in the excerpts from the study paper cited above. Moreover, it was emphatically recognized by Professor Freckelton, a highly regarded practitioner and scholar, some time ago. As he stated:

> [W]hile an assessment of fitness must be functional in nature, context-dependent, and pragmatic ... and focus in an informed way upon the capacity of the accused for reasoned evaluation and communication sufficient for the purposes of the case at hand, some fundamentals can be isolated without which an accused cannot properly be said to be fit to stand trial. Chief among these is *cognitive rationality*. [emphasis added][44]

---

43 *Adam*, above note 21 at para 29.

44 Ian Freckelton, "Rationality and Flexibility in Assessment of Fitness to Stand Trial" (1996) 19:1 *International Journal of Law and Psychiatry* 39 at 40.

5) Deconstructing *Taylor*

While it might be true that the common law test (variously articulated) for unfitness to stand trial was less than crystal clear prior to the enactment of Bill C-30 (1992), which produced our first statutory definition of the concept, contained in section 2 of the *Criminal Code* of Canada, a real muddle has arisen in the wake of the *Taylor* decision. *Taylor* is the first and only appellate decision to "fully" consider substantive aspects of the fitness test subsequent to the enactment of section 2 which is set out again below:

> *unfit to stand trial* means unable on account of mental disorder to conduct a defence at any stage of the proceedings before a verdict is rendered or to instruct counsel to do so, and, in particular, unable on account of mental disorder to
> (a) understand the nature or object of the proceedings,
> (b) understand the possible consequences of the proceedings, or
> (c) communicate with counsel

Virtually all commentators maintain that the intention of the section 2 definition was to codify the existing common law, and, indeed, there is no indication that anything other than a codification of the common law was intended. Nevertheless, it is arguable that the statutory definition does not accurately translate the common law.

As mentioned above, the court in *Taylor* was the first, to the authors' knowledge, to specifically hold that a rational understanding of one's legal predicament is *not* a fitness requirement. In that regard, the common law just prior to the enactment of Bill C-30 was reviewed by the Quebec Court of Appeal in *R v Steele*[45] referred to in *Taylor*, as follows:

> An accused is incapable of conducting the defence, within the meaning of s. 615 of the *Criminal Code*, if he or she:
> (a) cannot distinguish between available pleas;
> (b) does not understand the nature or purpose of the proceedings, including the respective roles of the judge, jury and counsel;
> (c) does not understand the personal import of the proceedings;
> (d) is unable to communicate with counsel, *converse with counsel rationally* or make critical decisions on counsel's advice; or

45 (1991), 63 CCC (3d) 149 (Que CA).

(e) is unable to take the stand, if necessary [emphasis added][46]

In contrast, the fundamental test, as articulated in section 2, is whether the accused is "unable on account of mental disorder to conduct a defence . . . or instruct counsel to do so." The subsequent recitals (i.e., section 2(a) through (c)) are to assist in informing that fundamental question rather than separate "tests"; they should be seen as "illustrative" or "*inter alia.*" As Trotter J indicates in *Adam*, "the three arms of the fitness test (in s. 2(a) to (c)) are not free-standing fitness criteria to be mechanically applied; instead, they are tools to assist in determining whether a mentally ill person is able to defend him or herself."[47] They are much like the criteria set out in *R v Steele*. As a matter of practice convention, to assist in the assessment of fitness, other questions have also been adopted, including the following:

- What are the roles of the various people in the courtroom?
- What does the judge do?
- What charges are you facing?
- What are the available pleas?
- What are the consequences of a conviction?
- What is the meaning of an oath?
- Why is it important to tell the truth?
- What is perjury?
- What are the consequences of perjury?
- Do you believe you will receive a fair trial?

This non-exhaustive list of questions is typical of those put to accused in fitness to stand trial ("FTST") assessments. By fleshing out

46 *Ibid* at 181. It should be noted that the criteria re "convers[ing] with counsel rationally" was also one identified as part of the common law in the Law Reform Commission of Canada's report "The Criminal Process and Mental Disorder," Working Paper 14 (Ottawa: Information Canada, 1975) wherein the commission indicated that "Instructing counsel is tied to the accused's participation at trial and implies the ability to *communicate rationally*" (at 36; emphasis added) [LRC]. These five principles are drawn mainly from *Gorecki*, above note 31 at 134–35; *R v McIlvride* (1986), 29 CCC (3d) 348 at 356–57 (CA); *Woltucky*, above note 28 at 46–47; *R v Budic* (1977), 35 CCC (2d) 272 at 278 (Alta SCAD); *R v Wolfson*, [1965] 3 CCC 304 at 314–15 (Alta SCAD); LRC, above in this note at 14.

47 *Adam*, above note 21 at para 29. While phrased variously, fitness has been traditionally seen as a unitary concept that provides that, if an accused's mental state precludes meaningful participation in the trial process, they are deemed unfit to stand trial.

the depth and scope of an accused's understanding of key dimensions of the process, they help examiners and, ultimately, courts in deciding the fundamental question of whether the accused is either able to conduct a defence or instruct counsel to do so.

However, in *Taylor* the three "arms" of the test as set out in section 2 are seen as independent "tests."[48] And while we stated, earlier in this section, that *Taylor* was the first and only appellate decision to "fully" consider the fitness test, that statement is not completely accurate. That is because, before the appeal court, counsel agreed that, with respect to Mr Taylor, the first two criteria were not of concern—that is, he apparently understood (a) the nature or object of the proceedings *and* (b) their possible consequences. The concern was with respect to criteria (c): could Taylor "communicate with counsel"?

What the court in *Taylor* really answers is "the question of the proper test to be applied in determining the accused's ability to communicate with counsel."[49] Justice Lacourcière frames the analysis in the appeal around that particular question, yet, by the end of the decision, the analysis appears to have blurred into a unitary consideration of fitness wherein the court ultimately concludes that it is an error to require "the accused to be capable of making rational decisions beneficial to him in his relationship with counsel."[50]

Rather than providing a fulsome consideration of "fitness to stand trial," then, the decision in *Taylor* amounts to a much more limited consideration of what is required of an accused when communicating with counsel (criterion (c)). The notions of "rationality," the ability to act in one's own "best interests," and "communication with counsel," which come up in earlier caselaw as separate causes for concern, have been conflated into "rational decisions beneficial to . . . [the accused] in his relationship with counsel."

In all other caselaw considering the question of fitness to stand trial subsequent to *Taylor*, this key point has been lost. *Taylor* has been seen as an articulation of a singular fitness test. However, by its own terms of reference, *Taylor* tells us nothing of (a) understanding the nature

48 Again, as seen in *R v Rooney*, [1994] PEIJ No 82 (SCTD) and *R v MacPherson*, [1998] NSJ No 241 (Prov Ct), the enumerated "indicators" of fitness should not be seen as an exhaustive list or as three separate tests.

49 *Taylor*, above note 2 at para 42.

50 *Ibid* at para 57.

or object of the proceedings, or (b) understanding the possible consequences of the proceedings—if indeed these are to be treated as separate "tests," as was clearly the approach in *Taylor*. Perhaps these "understandings" require rationality, but this concept was unnecessary to consider given the issue at hand in the case, and consequently, was not considered. Perhaps, not illogically, understanding "possible consequences" requires that the accused be able to act in their own best interests. For all the talk of the "limited cognitive capacity test," a term coined by the court in *Taylor*, in reality that decision pertains only to the ability to communicate with counsel.

While these considerations certainly have caused considerable confusion to flow in the wake of *Taylor*, it is our view that, as set out in *Adam*, fitness *should* be treated as one fundamental question that may be informed by consideration of *inter alia* one's ability to:

- understand the nature or object of the proceedings,
- understand the possible consequences of the proceedings, or
- communicate with counsel.

What the court needs to know is whether the accused is unable on account of mental disorder to conduct a defence or to instruct counsel to do so.

Keeping in mind the rationale for the fitness rules, in order to conduct a defence or instruct counsel to do so, "the accused must have sufficient mental fitness to participate in the proceedings in a meaningful way."[51] And, as Trotter J has observed, "It cannot seriously be contended that rationality has no role to play in this determination."[52]

In *Taylor*, the court goes on as follows:

> [O]ne must remain cognizant of the rationale for the fitness rules in the first place. In order to ensure that the process of determining guilt is as accurate as possible, that the accused can participate in the proceedings or assist counsel in his/her defence, that the dignity of the trial process is maintained, and that, if necessary, the determination of a fit sentence is made possible, the accused must have sufficient mental fitness to participate in the proceedings in a meaningful way.
>
> . . .

51 *Ibid* at para 50.

52 *Adam*, above note 21 at para 29.

> The "limited cognitive capacity" test strikes an effective balance between the objectives of the fitness rules and the constitutional right of the accused to choose his own defence and to have a trial within a reasonable time.[53]

We agree that the fitness threshold should protect the accused but not constitute an unnecessary impediment to proceeding to trial where, for example, an otherwise unfit accused is "able to conduct a defence" with the assistance of counsel. This scenario is quite different, however, from raw "expediency" as a legitimate competing concern. "Effective balance," referred to by the court in *Taylor*, was never, in our view, intended to create a schism between the threshold for "fitness" and the speed within which a trial should conclude. Such competition would suggest that, as the clock ticks, the standard for fitness should drop. A bad or unfair result does not become better if it is achieved faster. Indeed, it is not clear how these disparate concerns worked their way onto the balance in *Taylor*.

Taylor is the first decision to suggest the pre-existence of a historical debate between two philosophically distinct legal tests for the standard for fitness to stand trial—the limited cognitive capacity and the analytical capacity tests. These two terms and the notion of competing thresholds were unknown prior to *Taylor*, as was the suggestion that the unitary concept of fitness had three discrete tests within it. There are no decisions pre-dating *Taylor* that hold that a rational understanding of one's legal predicament is not a fitness requirement. Moreover, the *Taylor* decision is clearly inconsistent with the American requirement of "rational understanding," as well as earlier Canadian common law, and it would appear to be falling into disfavour among Canadian courts in the past several years.

As Freckelton[54] underscores, cognitive rationality is a fundamental requirement for a finding of "fit to stand trial." Permitting an accused who does not have a rational understanding of their legal predicament to engage in the trial process is unfair and inevitably results in a grossly uneven contest. The state should have no appetite for such an event. That an accused's competency or fitness to stand trial can be watered down by consideration of time lines is illogical and untenable. Conflating

53 *Taylor*, above note 2 at paras 50 and 52.

54 Freckelton, above note 44.

expediency and an accused's right to autonomy in the process does not assist in advancing the argument that compromised accused should be put to trial. This issue was squarely before the court in *R v Xu*:

> While expediency must be considered in setting the fitness standard, it may be the case that the "right to choose" is a rather empty right where the accused does not have a rational understanding of his legal predicament; where choice is not rational choice. The right to choose must be read as "rational choice" otherwise, from a protection perspective, it is a "right" of questionable worth. Against the concern for expediency is the rationale for the rules in the first place. Principally, the rules are in place to ensure that an accused who is ill-equipped as a result of mental disorder is not subject to the prosecution machinery of the state. The rules are to protect the accused. They operate to hold the prosecution in abeyance until the accused is fit to respond.[55]

6) Fluctuating Fitness

The mental state of a mentally ill person, particularly a psychotic individual, is often not static. Fluctuations in mental state (and in the capacities that depend on cognitive, affective, and perceptual intactness) define many serious mental disorders and medical conditions. Serial capacity assessments are fairly common when assessing a patient's capacity to consent to treatment or their testamentary capacity.[56] Although the underlying diagnosis (whether it is schizophrenia, delusional disorder, or some other disorder) is the constant, the symptoms of these and other conditions can vary qualitatively and quantitatively, depending on a number of factors related to both the patient/accused and the environment.

Courts are ever mindful of the presumption of fitness in section 672.22 of the *Criminal Code*: "An accused is presumed fit to stand trial unless the court is satisfied on the balance of probabilities that the accused is unfit to stand trial." Courts may invite an expert to seize the moment, as it were, and provide an opinion that the accused is fit

55 *R v Xu*, above note 7 at para 9.

56 K Shulman et al, "Cognitive Fluctuations and the Lucid Interval in Dementia: Implications for Testamentary Capacity" (2015) 43:3 *Journal of the American Academy of Psychiatry and the Law* 287.

to stand trial, if that is what the clinical evaluation revealed moments earlier. It may be, however, that the accused was not fit to stand trial a short while before the assessment, nor will they predictably be fit to stand trial a short while thereafter. Therefore, obviously, sequential assessments may lead to different conclusions, which might not mean that the experts can't agree. Rather, the accused's clinical condition has varied and, as a result, so has the conclusion.

The definition of "unfit to stand trial" in section 2 of the *Criminal Code*, however, requires that the accused be capable of conducting a defence. To that end, it is reasonable to interpret that fitness to stand trial has a future connotation or contains an element of prospectivity. This is a necessary interpretation in that, typically, the actual trial will be occurring days or weeks in the future. If it cannot be predicted that the accused will maintain fitness to stand trial for the anticipated window of time, and be able to endure and participate in a trial of some complexity, then, arguably, they cannot be said to be fit to stand trial, even if the examiner catches them during a lucid "fit interval."

The problem of fluctuating fitness was recognized in *R v Nehass*.[57] In this case, the accused's beliefs about the roles of certain individuals, entities, and governments fluctuated considerably. There were times when the accused seemed to have a grasp of his legal predicament, and other times when his beliefs "overwhelm[ed] his ability to participate in the criminal law process in a meaningful way."[58] Specifically in respect of his fluctuating mental state, and its impact on fitness, Justice Cozens stated the following:

> While it is no doubt true that Mr. Nehass can for brief periods and at certain times be rationally connected to his involvement in these proceedings, I find that the evidence is overwhelming that he cannot maintain his rational connection for any sustained period of time, and certainly not for anywhere near long enough to participate in the criminal law process in a meaningful way.[59]

The accused was found unfit to stand trial.

---

57 *R v Nehass*, above note 24.

58 *Ibid* at para 75.

59 *Ibid*.

7) Sliding Scales

In Canada, only one "level of fitness" is formally recognized. In practice, however, the "level" required will vary as a function of both time and complexity.

a) The Time Line

One consideration with respect to actual level of fitness is the time line within which a trial is likely to occur and, thus, within which fitness of the accused must be sustained. Of course, an accused who intends to plead guilty and who will be sentenced in short order probably requires a narrower window of predictable fitness to stand trial. Therefore, fitness, while absolute in its threshold capacities, may require more or less robust clinical states depending on how long fitness must be sustained. Therein lies the so-called sliding scale notion, which refers to the stability of fitness (clinical stability) rather than the abilities required.

b) Levels of Fitness

Yet in practice, the "sliding scale" *may* apply to both the level of fitness as well as clinical stability. A complex protracted trial may require considerably greater mental activity/capacity, not only with respect to the sustainability of a stable mental state but also with respect to the cognitive "abilities" of the accused. Arguably, this reality is inextricably part of the test—that is, when one speaks of "inability to conduct a defence," it refers to a *particular accused* and a *particular set of allegations*. So, "level" of fitness will automatically be built into each case. It will take greater *ability* to meaningfully participate in a complex fraud trial, for example, than it will to plead guilty to a minor theft. The same individual's clinical state (abilities) may render them fit with respect to the minor theft but unfit with respect to the complex fraud trial.

This common sense approach has been endorsed by the Ontario Court of Appeal in *Ohenhen (Re)* where, in a discussion regarding the interface of capacity and consent, the court observed: "[A] person may be capable of managing personal care, but not his or her finances. Or, a person may have the capacity to make a will for a simple estate, but not for a complicated one."[60] Similarly, a person may have "partial capacity"

60 *Ohenhen (Re)*, 2018 ONCA 65 at para 80 (heard together with *Kalra*).

that might be bridged with assistance: "[A] person may have the capacity to make decisions regarding certain aspects of a plan, but not all."[61] The court went on to cite *Calvert (Litigation Guardian of) v Calvert*,[62] where that court found that "the petitioner had the capacity to separate and the capacity to divorce, but not the capacity to instruct counsel in connection with the divorce. With the accommodation of a litigation guardian though, she was ultimately able to accomplish her goal."[63]

This recognition of different capacities and gradations of capacity for different tasks is at odds with the Supreme Court of Canada's decision in *Whittle*,[64] and is in need of some resolution. It is appropriate to acknowledge different abilities, both quantitatively and qualitatively, for different domains of capacity.

In England and Wales, a sliding scale with respect to abilities is recognized as the "principle of proportionality," which is becoming more apparent in various civil arenas[65] (see the discussion in Chapter 9, Section A).

8) Context-Specific Fitness

Very much like the notion of a "sliding scale," academics have urged the necessity of assessing fitness to stand trial contextually— that is, an assessment of *this* accused facing *these* charges, confronted with *this* particular sort of evidence, working with *this* particular lawyer.[66] Changes in any one of these variables could change the assessment of fitness or competency. This notion is consistent with the reality that competencies for different tasks require different abilities and are also necessarily bound to the circumstances, contexts, and environments in which they occur. It is trite to observe that we recognize competency to consent to treatment, competency to manage finances, and so on. And,

---

61 *Ibid* at para 84.

62 (1997), 32 OR (3d) 281 (Gen Div).

63 *Ohenhen (Re)*, above note 60 at para 84.

64 *Whittle*, above note 16.

65 Tim Exworthy, "UK Perspective on Competency to Stand Trial" (2006) 34:4 *Journal of the American Academy of Psychiatry and the Law Online* 466.

66 Ronald Roesch et al, "Defining and Assessing Competency to Stand Trial" in Allen K Hess & Irving B Weiner, eds, *Handbook of Forensic Psychology*, 2d ed (New York: John Wiley & Sons, 1999) 327 (Roesch et al).

while there may be some overlap with respect to the abilities required from one competency to the next, they are nevertheless distinct.

Curiously, a recognition that the context of the required decision-making ability will directly affect the competency threshold is not a reality that has been recognized by the Supreme Court of Canada. In *Whittle*,[67] the Court ruled that fitness was the same at whatever juncture the accused was at in the prosecutorial process (an Ontario court reached the same conclusion in *MAW*[68]). Mr Whittle had appealed an earlier decision on the basis that he did not have the requisite mental competency to make a voluntary statement and that the statement (inculpatory) should therefore be excluded. The Court found that

> the accused had the requisite degree of mental competence to make the choices inherent in the confession rule, the right to silence, and the right to counsel. The "operating mind" test, which is an aspect of the confession rule, includes a limited mental component which requires that the accused have sufficient cognitive capacity to understand what he is saying and what is being said. This includes the ability to understand a caution that the evidence can be used against the accused. That same standard applies with respect to the right to silence in determining whether the accused has the mental capacity to make an active choice. *In exercising the right to counsel or waiving the right, the accused must possess the limited cognitive capacity that is required for fitness to stand trial.*[69]

The Court therefore found that one standard for competency applies regardless of the specific ability required, or task to be performed, by the accused.[70]

That different tasks may require different competencies was, as well, not a reality recognized by the Supreme Court of the United States in

67 Above note 16.

68 Above note 15.

69 *Whittle*, above note 16 at headnote [emphasis added].

70 While the Supreme Court of Canada in *Whittle* reviews the "limited cognitive capacity test" articulated in *Taylor*, the question before the Court was whether or not there is "any justification for requiring a higher standard of cognitive capacity in making the choices inherent in the confessions rule, the right to silence and the right to counsel than in respect to fitness to stand trial." The Court did not get into a fulsome review of the fitness standard or review any of the cases preceding *Taylor*. Indeed, the Court has *never* reviewed the fitness standard in a fulsome manner. Arguably, doing so would be very appropriate, given the uncertainty apparent in the recent caselaw.

Godinez v Moran, which followed *Dusky*.[71] The Court indicated therein that competency to plead guilty, to waive counsel, or to stand trial should be considered the same, in that they are all driven by the underlying ability to make "reasoned choice" among alternatives available. However, in dissent, Justice Blackmun found that the ruling of the majority was "contrary to both common sense and longstanding caselaw."[72] He reasoned that competency must be assessed in the context of the particular legal proceedings, and that "competency for one purpose does not necessarily translate to competency for another purpose."[73] He noted that previous Supreme Court cases *had* required competency evaluations to be specifically tailored to the context and purpose of the proceeding.

As Roesch et al point out:

> The problem is not whether or not the standards for various psycholegal competencies are higher, different, or the same, but rather, more fundamentally, whether or not the defendant has been examined with respect to these issues in the first place.[74]

It is quite dangerous to jump, for example, from a finding or presumption of fit to stand trial to a conclusion that the accused had the competency to waive the right to counsel, or make a confession. One would hope that, notwithstanding any presumptions regarding the homogeneity of competencies, the court would delve into the particular abilities at issue.

9) Can Representation Render the "Unfit" Accused "Fit"?

To recap, with the proclamation of Bill C-30 on 4 February 1992, a definition of "unfit to stand trial" was for the first time embedded in the *Criminal Code* of Canada. The provisions are, once again, set out below:

> *unfit to stand trial* means *unable on account of mental disorder to conduct a defence* at any stage of the proceedings before a verdict is rendered *or to instruct counsel to do so*, and, in particular, unable on account of mental disorder to

---

71 *Godinez v Moran*, 509 US 389 (1993); *Dusky v United States*, above note 12.

72 *Godinez v Moran*, above note 71 at 409.

73 *Ibid* at 413.

74 Roesch et al, above note 66 at 329.

(a) understand the nature or object of the proceedings,
(b) understand the possible consequences of the proceedings, or
(c) communicate with counsel[75] [emphases added]

While there has been litigation surrounding the requisite quantity and quality of the underlying mental disorder, and the resulting "inabilities" that might render an accused unfit to stand trial,[76] there has been, up until now, no litigation dealing with how the assessment of an accused's fitness should be contextualized. Should the accused be assessed in the abstract? Or, should they be assessed as they would be if they were equipped with a legal representative and supported at trial?

It is instructive that this issue has been addressed with respect to the assessment of whether a not criminally responsible ("NCR") accused is a "significant threat to the safety of the public" within the meaning of section 672.54 of the *Criminal Code*. Establishing that an accused is a significant threat to the safety of the public is the threshold that must be met for a provincial or territorial review board to maintain jurisdiction over an accused found to have been "not criminally responsible on account of mental disorder." In *Lajoie c Québec (Commission québécoise d'examen)*,[77] the Quebec Court of Appeal concluded that such an assessment must take into consideration the supports and resources that the accused has at their disposal, that they have engaged, and that might reasonably be expected to exist into the future. So, for example, an accused might be found a significant threat to the safety of the public if unsupported but, with appropriate resources and support, might fail to be so found.

Similarly, in the American case of *Indiana v Edwards*,[78] the court held that the accused was competent (fit) to stand trial *so long as he had counsel*. That is, the accused was not competent to represent himself at trial standing alone but, with the assistance of counsel, he met the threshold. In *R v Hureau*[79] the Yukon trial court imported this logic and found that an accused on his own was unfit to stand trial but that if he had counsel he was fit to stand trial and could proceed. That decision was

75 *Criminal Code*, above note 1, s. 2.
76 For example, *Taylor*, above note 2.
77 [1994] JQ no 133 (CA).
78 Above note 20.
79 Above note 14.

appealed[80] and the logic of the trial court rejected. The appeal court responded as follows:

> The *Criminal Code* provides for two possible verdicts on a fitness hearing: either fit to stand trial or unfit to stand trial. The *Code* does not contemplate the verdict pronounced by Judge Lilles that . . . [the accused] is fit to stand trial if he is represented. In making that finding, Judge Lilles exceeded his jurisdiction . . . .
>
> It is important to note that the definition is disjunctive. It uses the word "or." On a plain reading of that definition, it means that a person is unfit to stand trial if that person is unable to conduct a defence on his own, or to instruct counsel to do so. *If either one of those conditions is met, then the person is, by definition, unfit to stand trial.*
>
> In this case, Judge Lilles found as a fact—and that fact is not open to me to interfere with in this proceeding—that this accused, Mr. Hureau, is unable to conduct a defence on his own. He therefore meets the definition of being unfit to stand trial.
>
> That is the end of the analysis. It is unnecessary to consider the second part of the disjunctive definition as to whether he would be able to instruct counsel to do so.[81]

Prior to—and, indeed, subsequent to—the codification of the law regarding fitness in Bill C-30, it had been understood that if the accused is either (1) able to conduct their own defence, *or* (2) able to instruct counsel to do so, they are fit. In contrast, the appellate court in *Hureau* is saying that if accused are *unable to do either* they are *unfit*. Following this stream of logic, if accused *are* able to represent themselves, but, because of mental disorder (e.g., paranoia that causes them to believe prospective lawyers are conspiring with the police to obtain a conviction), they are unable to instruct counsel, then they are unfit. Conversely, if accused *are not* able to represent themselves because of mental disorder (e.g., severe agoraphobia) but *are* able to instruct counsel, then they are, once again, unfit to stand trial. The practical results of the appeal court's decision are illogical and inconsistent with general understanding.

Further, the results of the decision are difficult to reconcile with the objectives of the fitness rules. In essence, the rules regarding fitness are

---

80 *R v Hureau*, 2014 YKSC 48.

81 *Ibid* at paras 3–7 [emphasis added].

to ensure fairness; they are protective. In particular, they are in place to ensure that accused who, because of mental disorder, are unable to defend themselves are not subjected to prosecution. At the same time, they are in place to ensure that if the accused *is* able to "conduct a defence," either on their own or by instructing counsel "to do so," they should be entitled to proceed. It is an axiom of statutory interpretation that courts must read a provision with the purpose and objectives of the entire scheme in mind. Against this cornerstone, we submit that the appeal court's decision in *R v Hureau* misinterprets the intention of the definition of "unfit to stand trial" as set out in section 2.

Of interest with respect to this issue are the findings of the Ontario Court of Appeal in *Ohenhen (Re)*,[82] where the court recognized that capacities come in different shades and that they may be complete or incomplete. Where an accused is capable with respect to only a portion of a task to be performed, the added assistance of counsel (or litigation guardian in a civil context) may fill the gaps sufficiently so that it would be appropriate (fair) to permit the matter to proceed. The spirit of the scheme should be to permit the accused (litigant) to proceed so long as to do so would not create unfairness due to mental disorder.

In fairness to the appeal court in *R v Hureau*, there is ambiguity with the use of the word "or" in the definition contained in the *Criminal Code*. Consequently, the purpose of the legislation must be examined. We submit that, when the purpose of the rules is examined, the answer becomes clear. It would be against the values of our justice system to deprive mentally disordered individuals of a trial where they are unable to defend themselves standing alone but *are* able to instruct counsel to do so. If accused are able to do *either*, they are fit to stand trial.

We submit that the section should be interpreted as follows: "unfit to stand trial" means unable on account of mental disorder to conduct a defence at any stage of the proceedings before a verdict is rendered or *if unable to conduct a defence on one's own* to instruct counsel to do so. In other words, our analysis of the intent of the statutory provision considered in the context of the historical purpose of fitness rules and their jurisprudential antecedents, compels us to the view that "unfit to stand trial" means that, on account of mental disorder, the accused is *neither* able to conduct a defence *nor* able to instruct counsel to do so.

---

82 Above note 60.

The above interpretation of the definition in section 2 is also in keeping with clinical realities. Mental disorder is not a binary proposition: it occurs in gradations, with respect to both "quality" and "quantity." Yet we are forced in the legal world to make binary choices: the accused either is or is not fit to stand trial; the accused either is or is not criminally responsible. The reality, however, is that, just as there are shades of mental disorder, there are shades of unfitness and of criminal responsibility. It is entirely in keeping with this reality that there will be some individuals who are not quite fit but who, with the assistance of counsel, could conduct a defence. It would be fair and appropriate to let such an accused proceed. If the mentally disordered accused is either able to conduct their own defence or to instruct counsel to do so, they are fit to stand trial. The fitness rules have served their purpose for that individual.

Academics have weighed in from slightly different perspectives.[83] Winnick persuasively argued that in some circumstances it may be in the best interests of the defendant to proceed with a trial, even if they are incompetent. Winnick postulated that this could take the form of a provisional trial wherein the support of the defence attorney would serve to ensure protection of the defendant. This would allow the defendant to proceed with their case while maintaining decorum in the courtroom and without violating the defendant's constitutional rights. As well, Bonnie has provided a reformulation of competence to stand trial. Bonnie proposed a distinction between two types of competencies—competence to assist counsel and decisional competence. He argued that defendants found incompetent to assist counsel would be barred from proceeding until they were restored to competence. Defendants found decisionally incompetent, on the other hand, may be able to proceed in certain cases where his or her [*sic*] lawyer is able to present a defence.[84]

---

83 See, for example, BJ Winnick, "Restructuring Competency to Stand Trial" (1985) 32 *UCLA Law Review* 921; BJ Winnick, "Reforming Incompetency to Stand Trial and Plead Guilty: A Restated Proposal and a Response to Professor Bonnie" (1995) 85 *Journal of Criminal Law and Criminology* 571; RJ Bonnie, "The Competence of Criminal Defendants: A Theoretical Reformulation" (1992) 10:3 *Behavioural Sciences and the Law* 291 [Bonnie, "A Theoretical Reformulation"]; RJ Bonnie, "The Competence of Criminal Defendants: Beyond *Dusky* and *Drope*" (1992) 47 *University of Miami Law Review* 539 [Bonnie, "Beyond *Dusky* and *Drope*"].

84 Bonnie, "A Theoretical Reformulation," above note 83; Bonnie, "Beyond *Dusky* and *Drope*," above note 83.

Again, the fitness rules exist to protect the mentally ill accused but *should not constitute an unreasonable barrier* to trial.

In Canada, the notion of the trial proceeding in advance of a determination of fitness has been provided for statutorily in section 672.25 of the *Criminal Code*. The provision allows the process to proceed to the point where there is at least a *prima facie* case for the accused to meet. The advantage, of course, is that an accused's liberty will not be limited where the Crown is not in a position to obtain a finding of guilt.

Ten-Point Review

1) The test for unfitness is based upon "inabilities" due to mental disorder, not upon ignorance.
2) "Mental disorder," defined as "a disease of the mind," is a necessary but not sufficient condition for unfitness.
3) The statutory definition for unfitness includes a timeline only up to the point of a verdict, although courts and most commentators are of the view that an accused must be fit in order to be sentenced.
4) With respect to an accused's ability to "communicate with counsel," the accused must have a rudimentary factual understanding of their legal predicament (*Taylor*).
5) Subsequent to *Taylor*, various courts and commentators have found that an accused must be able to participate in a "meaningful way" and have a "rational understanding" of their legal predicament.
6) An accused need not be able to act in their own best interests.
7) An inability to remember the events in question does not render an accused unfit.
8) Arguably, "fitness" may be a function of the timelines within which the accused must be fit, the complexity of the legal proceedings, and whether or not the accused has counsel to assist in the defence.
9) Arguably, an inherent aspect of the test in section 2 of the *Criminal Code* is a "state" matched to the legal proceedings in respect of which a defence is required; the "state" is, therefore, not absolutely static.
10) Various courts and commentators are of the view that a mentally disordered accused may be able to conduct a defence with the assistance of counsel and, on that basis, may be fit.

CHAPTER 3

When the Issue of Fitness May Arise

The issue of fitness may arise at any point in the proceedings. However, it may not be considered where there is any dispute as to the Crown's ability to demonstrate (*prima facie*) that the accused committed the act or acts alleged in the indictment.[1] Most often, the issue arises at first appearance and is resolved prior to arraignment. Alternatively, the issue may arise during the course of a trial or preliminary hearing, and it may arise on multiple occasions (*per* subsection 672.23(1) of the *Criminal Code*),[2] particularly when an accused has significant fluctuations in his mental state (and fitness). Where the accused disputes the Crown's ability to prove a *prima facie* case, this ability must be proved before commencing a trial of the issue of fitness. This, of course, makes good sense: the state should take no interest in fitness to stand trial if there is no case to meet (i.e., no trial to be held).

In *R v Flowers*, Justice Spies stated that, prior to raising the issue of fitness, the trial judge must be satisfied that

> the Crown is in a position to establish that the accused committed the act alleged or ... that there is some basis to put that accused on trial. The court may postpone the fitness hearing until the end of the Crown's case pursuant to section 672.25 (2)(b) of the *Criminal Code* or even later on motion of the accused. The manifest purpose of that

1 *R v Taylor*, [1992] OJ No 2394 at para 37 (CA).

2 RSC 1985, c C-46.

section is to permit the accused to be discharged at the close of the Crown's case if there is insufficient evidence to put him to a defence.[3]

A. WHEN SHOULD COUNSEL DISCLOSE CONCERNS TO THE COURT?

It may be that counsel has concerns with respect to their client's mental abilities and the adequacy of the instructions they are receiving from them. In general, as long as counsel is not receiving instructions that would cause the court to be misled or lead to an illegal result, those instructions should be followed whether or not counsel views those instructions as "optimal." Counsel may advise their clients as to the relative merits of several courses of action but, ultimately, the decision is that of the accused. Where frankly "bad" decisions on the part of the accused are the product of a mental disorder, counsel must be vigilant. Nevertheless, an accused's disinclination to follow counsel's advice cannot be taken, without more information concerning mental state and/or behaviour, as the basis upon which to order an assessment.[4]

When their client is apparently deteriorating during the trial, is delusional, and/or is responding in a way that does not comport with reality, counsel have an obligation to bring the issue to the attention of the court.[5] In general, as the Ontario Court of Appeal observed in *R v Szostak*,[6] where counsel are of the view that their client may not be fit to stand trial, they have an obligation to bring the matter to the attention of the court.[7] This point was made by the court in *R c Brigham*: "If Mr. Brigham was convicted though unfit, he was in effect not 'present at his trial' . . . . If he was fit, but not called, he was deprived of his right to testify in his own defence."[8] With this the court underscores the importance of counsel raising the issue of fitness noting the peril that could result.

3 *R v Flowers*, [2008] OJ No 4642 at para 7 (SCJ).

4 *R v Michael*, 2015 ONSC 148, where the court followed the reasoning in *R v Steele* (1991), 63 CCC (3d) 149 (Que CA).

5 *R c Brigham*, [1992] JQ no 2283 (CA).

6 [2012] OJ No 3330 (CA).

7 In addition, upon a finding of fitness, counsel may not raise the issue of criminal responsibility without clear instructions.

8 *R c Brigham*, above note 5.

B. THE COURT MAY DIRECT THE ISSUE OF FITNESS TO BE TRIED

Once the question of fitness has been brought to the attention of the court, certain statutory provisions are applicable, *per* the *Criminal Code*:

> **672.23(1)** Where the court has reasonable grounds, at any stage of the proceedings before a verdict is rendered, to believe that the accused is unfit to stand trial, the court may direct, of its own motion or on application of the accused or the prosecutor, that the issue of fitness of the accused be tried.

Section 672.23(1) requires the court to have "reasonable grounds" to believe that the accused is unfit to stand trial. Mere suspicion will not suffice. While the representation of trial counsel may not be sufficient to allow a trial judge to conclude that the accused is unfit to stand trial, counsel's representations to the court may be sufficient evidence to require a more thorough inquiry so as to ensure that there would be no miscarriage of justice.[9] This threshold would be sufficient for the court to find that an assessment was warranted. Medical evidence is not formally required to pass this threshold.

As indicated by the court in *R v McIlvride*:

> If at the opening of the trial an inquiry into the fitness of the accused to stand trial is sought, there will in most cases be put before the judge material supporting the submission that the accused is not fit. There may also be material from the Crown indicating that he is fit, or the Crown may agree that such an inquiry should be conducted. The judge may act on the material placed before him, or may direct that a further assessment of the accused be made. It may, in some cases, be necessary for the judge to hear the evidence of psychiatrists and of other witnesses. The judge's role at this stage is to decide if there is "sufficient reason to doubt" the fitness of the accused. It is for the judge to decide how to proceed in order that there will be before the court sufficient information to resolve the preliminary question.[10]

The first stage of the inquiry is for the judge alone to decide whether there is "sufficient reason to doubt that the accused is, on account of 'insanity' [i.e., "mental disorder"], capable of conducting a defence." The

9 *R v Budic*, [1977] AJ No 516 (SCAD).

10 *R v McIlvride*, [1986] BCJ No 634 at para 34 (CA).

second, "which is pursued only if the first stage is answered affirmatively, is for the jury to determine 'whether the accused is then, on account of insanity, unfit to stand trial.'"[11]

Where there is not "any basis" for the court to consider the issue, an inquiry should not be held, especially if the basis for the defence request was that the accused did not appear to be engaged in their own defence.[12] As seen in *R v BB*, the timing of the request for an assessment of fitness may also assist in determining the motivation and the merit of the request.[13] In that case, the expert opinion was that the accused's lack of engagement was volitional and not the product of a mental disorder. There was no indication that this impasse was due to "inabilities" caused by a mental disorder. On the other hand, where the behaviour of the accused is indicative of a "serious emotional breakdown," an inquiry should be held, commencing with an assessment order.[14]

C. ASSESSMENT ORDERS

Once the issue of fitness is brought to the attention of the court, whether by the accused, the Crown, or the court on its own motion, an inquiry commencing with the ordering of an assessment requires only "reasonable grounds": it does not require expert evidence. Where, notwithstanding counsel's concerns, a client's instructions are to not raise the issue, it may be postponed until there is a case to meet (section 672.25).

As LeSage J stated in *R v Bernardo* with respect to the ordering of an assessment to determine criminal responsibility:

> The court may order an assessment where the court has "reasonable grounds to believe" that evidence obtained by the assessment is necessary to determine the s.16(1) [of the *Criminal Code*] issue. I note that "the section is silent concerning the nature of the foundation to be laid in support of the requisite finding of reasonably grounded belief."[15]

In *R v Sealy*, the court held that

11 *R v McLeod*, [1983] OJ No 81 at para 12 (CA).
12 *R v Bain*, [1994] NSJ No 194 (CA).
13 [2009] OJ No 863 (SCJ).
14 *R v Halfyard*, 2010 NSPC 46.
15 *R v Bernardo*, [1994] OJ No 4382 at para 12 (Gen Div).

> reasonable grounds in the context of s. 672.11 must not be equated with proof beyond a doubt or proof on a balance of probability. Reasonable grounds for an assessment order are not based on a whim, wishful thinking, or mere possibilities. Instead, reasonable grounds in the context of a section 672.11 application are predicated upon "credibly based probability" which dictate that an assessment order is called for.[16]

Behaviour that is simply unusual or even unacceptable in a courtroom does not, by itself, constitute a basis for "reasonable grounds to believe" that an assessment order is necessary.[17] Often, the "reasonable grounds" threshold is attained when a court hears about and/or sees several behaviours that strongly suggest that something is amiss with the accused's mental state and fitness (see the discussion in Chapter 5, Section A). The court is not obligated to direct the jury to try the issue of fitness where there is no evidence called nor any indication from counsel that evidence would be called on the issue.[18] The Ontario Court of Appeal held that, in respect of a second trial, there was no need to conduct a fitness hearing where the issue had been tried seven months earlier and the accused was found to be fit to stand trial. There was no evidence that the accused's mental condition had changed appreciably since the time of the verdict.[19] However, the Alberta Court of Appeal permitted a re-visiting of the fitness issue where there was new evidence that trial counsel may not have been aware of the accused's mistaken perceptions and other factors potentially relevant to the accused's fitness.[20]

An accused's unwillingness to cooperate or collaborate with counsel and a proclivity for disruptive outbursts does not, by itself, render them unfit to stand trial.[21] However, especially when considering a Crown application for an assessment, great care must be taken prior to the granting of such an order. There are great liberty interests at stake.[22] The higher threshold to be met in obtaining assessments in respect of summary matters reflects the reality that a large percentage

---

16 *R v Sealy*, [2010] QJ No 30723 at para 107 (CQ).
17 *R v Sun*, [1999] OJ No 2821 (SCJ).
18 *R v Kolbe*, [1974] AJ No 162 (SCAD).
19 *R v Rockey*, [1999] OJ No 1352 (CA).
20 *R v LSC*, [2003] AJ No 388 (CA).
21 *R v Huruy*, [2015] OJ No 6502 (SCJ).
22 *R v John Doe*, [2011] OJ No 52 (SCJ).

of criminal matters would attract non-custodial dispositions even were the accused to be convicted.[23] While it is presumptive that assessments will be conducted out of custody, the reality is that, where an accused is so compromised as to put her fitness in issue, it may be that an out-of-custody assessment is unrealistic (see Chapter 5 for further discussion). This is especially so when it is recognized that a period of "assessment" is not to be used for the purpose of treatment (section 672.19). As discussed below, for the accused, there may be compelling tactics to forego the matter of judicial interim release until they are in a more stable (fit) condition.

As is apparent from the definition of "unfit to stand trial" contained in section 2 of the *Criminal Code*, and as discussed in Chapter 2, a strict reading of the statutory provisions relates only to unfitness prior to a verdict. Where the issue arises after a verdict is pronounced and prior to sentencing or during the course of sentencing, the statutory provisions would apparently not apply. Nevertheless, it may be that, from a common law or *Charter of Rights* perspective, the prosecution may not be able to proceed. This issue, and the problem created by the definition in section 2, has been raised before Parliamentary committees.

D. POST-VERDICT UNFITNESS

The relevant sections of the *Criminal Code* indicate that the statutory provisions dealing with unfitness to stand trial pertain only up to the point of a verdict. Therefore, if the accused becomes "unfit" after a verdict and prior to sentencing, Part XX.1 of the *Criminal Code* is not available,[24] if the *Code* is to be read strictly. Because most accused are sentenced immediately upon their conviction, this problem only arises from time to time.

One solution, if the accused is being tried by a judge alone, is to set aside the verdict and reopen the "trial," which would then put the court back into business as far as the particulars of the section are concerned.[25] In *R v Proulx*,[26] the court held a fitness hearing after guilty

23 *R v Wride*, [1997] MJ No 508 (QB).

24 For a more thorough discussion of this problem, consult Richard D Schneider, "Fitness to Be Sentenced" (1998) 41 *Criminal Law Quarterly* 261.

25 See, e.g., *R v Lessard*, [1976] OJ No 74 (CA).

26 [2011] SJ No 477 (Prov Ct).

pleas were entered and then used the finding of unfitness to set aside the guilty pleas.

A Standing Committee on Justice has recommended that section 2 of the *Criminal Code* be amended so as to include the sentencing phase of the prosecution. As it stands now, the provisions have been modified (at least for Ontario) with Justice McWatt's decision in *R v GB*.[27] Her Honour, as *Charter* remedy, "read-in" the words "at any stage of the proceedings before a verdict is rendered *or sentence imposed*."[28] This approach is consistent with earlier caselaw and the Law Reform Commission study paper, which, as discussed in Chapter 2, stated the common law as it was understood in 1973.

However, more recently, Code J encountered the same issue in *R v Jaser*.[29] Justice Code found that, while the *Criminal Code* provisions do not extend to the sentencing phase of proceedings, it may be that common law authority exists for such an extension. However, he suggested that no common law rule had ever been formally articulated.[30] Justice Code did not adopt the reasoning of McWatt J with respect to a *Charter* remedy, as no *Charter* issue was raised before him. Although Justice Code seemingly agreed that section 7 of the *Charter* gives a trial judge the power to inquire into an accused's fitness at sentencing, he rejected Justice McWatt's approach in *R v GB* of using section 52 of the *Charter* as a reparative tool that allows reading into section 2 of the *Criminal Code* words that extend the fitness rules to subsume sentencing. Justice Code further raised "conceptual difficulties" and "criminal law policy" in support of his view, including the difficulty that could develop if a sentencing issue arose in a jury trial after verdict, when the jury has already been disbanded. In a similar vein, he questioned whether an accused who did not want the issue of fitness raised in the first place should have sentencing delayed where fitness is raised before sentencing. Finally, Justice Code expressed concern about how convicted but not yet sentenced unfit accused would be managed by provincial Review Boards in light of a current lack of sufficient provisions/amendments in Part XX.1 of the *Criminal Code* to deal with offenders in

27 [2003] OJ No 784 (SCJ).

28 *Ibid* at para. 48 [emphasis added].

29 2015 ONSC 4729.

30 This is debatable. The *Pritchard* decision, below note 39, while British and very old, appears to make it quite clear that fitness at the time of sentencing is imperative.

these circumstances.[31] And, as the case before him evolved, there was no need to arrive at an alternative solution. In Ontario, we have had two Superior Court considerations of the issue without a clear resolution of the matter. Also, of some assistance, and consistent with both Code's decision as well as McWatt J's fundamental finding, the Court of Appeal in *R v Taylor* stated as follows:

> In order to ensure that the process of determining guilt is as accurate as possible, that the accused can participate in the proceedings or assist counsel in his/her defence, that the dignity of the trial process is maintained, and that, if necessary, *the determination of a fit sentence is made possible*, that accused must have sufficient mental fitness to participate in the proceedings in a meaningful way.[32]

This issue of post-verdict fitness is clearly one that would benefit from legislative clarification. Regardless, given the importance and jeopardy inherent in the sentencing process, it would be entirely antithetical to the rationale of the fitness rules to not require a state of fitness at this juncture. We are of the view that, if the existing framework in Part XX.1 cannot manage the issue—and we suggest that it can (see the discussion in Section H, below in this chapter)—then the same legislative brush that corrects the deficiency in section 2 could be used to amend corresponding sections of the *Code* to make a re-jigged scheme work optimally for the purpose it was created. As well, arguably, sentencing an "unfit" accused would provide the accused with a defence if there were to be any breaches of the imposed order, and it would reduce or eliminate the impactfulness of the sentencing process.

The accused in *R v GB* had been convicted of sexual assault. The Crown sought and obtained the permission of the attorney general to bring an application for a declaration that the accused was a dangerous offender pursuant to section 754 of the *Criminal Code*. The accused returned to court at the conclusion of his psychiatric assessment held pursuant to section 756 of the *Criminal Code*. At the outset of the hearing, the psychiatric evidence was to the effect that the accused was unfit to stand trial. Both counsel for the accused and for the Crown invited the court to find that the accused was unfit to stand trial. (As indicated

31 *R v Jaser*, above note 29 at paras 23–25.

32 *R v Taylor*, above note 1 at para 50 [emphasis added].

at the outset of section 753, a dangerous offender application is one that is made following a conviction but before the accused is sentenced.)

E. DOES THE REVIEW BOARD HAVE JURISDICTION OVER UNFIT ACCUSED?

The limited jurisdiction of the Review Board, as set out in section 672.38 of the *Criminal Code*, is to "make or review dispositions concerning any accused in respect of whom a verdict of not criminally responsible by reason of mental disorder or unfit to stand trial is rendered."

As discussed in Chapter 2, with the proclamation of Bill C-30 on 4 February 1992, came the first-ever statutory definition of "unfit to stand trial." The provisions are contained in section 2 of the *Criminal Code* as follows:

> *unfit to stand trial* means unable on account of mental disorder to conduct a defence at any stage of the proceedings *before a verdict is rendered* or to instruct counsel to do so, and, in particular, unable on account of mental disorder to
> (a) understand the nature or object of the proceedings,
> (b) understand the possible consequences of the proceedings, or
> (c) communicate with counsel. [emphasis added]

While prior to the proclamation of Bill C-30 there was no definition of "unfit to stand trial" contained in the *Code*, section 615(1) nevertheless indicated that it was an issue that could be tried "at any time before verdict":

> **615(1)** A court, judge or provincial court judge may, *at any time before verdict*, where it appears that there is sufficient reason to doubt that the accused is, on account of insanity, capable of conducting his defence, direct that an issue be tried whether the accused is then, on account of insanity, unfit to stand his trial. [emphasis added]

As revealed by an examination of the provisions below from Canada's first *Criminal Code* in 1892,[33] the statutory regime has remained essentially the same for the preceding 100 years, up until the proclamation of Bill C-30 in 1992:

---

33 *Criminal Code, 1892*, 55–56 Victoria, c 29.

> **737.** If at any time after the indictment is found, and *before the verdict is given*, it appears to the court that there is sufficient reason to doubt whether the accused is then, on account of insanity, capable of conducting his defence, the court may direct that an issue shall be tried whether the accused is or is not then on account of insanity unfit to take his trial.[34]

The "verdict" is the conclusion of the trial. It is reviewed in *Ralston v Stump*. The court adverts to the dictionary definition of "verdict" in *Webster's Dictionary*: "[T]he definitive answer given by the jury to the court concerning any matter of fact in any cause, civil or criminal, committed to the jury for their deliberation and determination." It further relies upon the decision in *State v Williams* that "the verdict is the definitive answer given by the jury to the court concerning the matters of fact committed to the jury for their deliberation and determination, a process in which not only must deliberation precede determination, but in which so long as the one continues the other has not been reached."[35]

We would submit that, while the court maintains jurisdiction over the accused beyond the verdict (except where the verdict is an acquittal), the verdict in a criminal trial is the determination of guilty, not guilty, or not criminally responsible. Thus, sentencing takes place at the conclusion of a *post-verdict* hearing.

"Unfit to stand trial" is, by statutory definition, limited to the window of time from arraignment up to the point of the verdict: at that point the "trial" has concluded[36]—the jury has been discharged. If that is the case, where the accused's post-verdict clinical condition is such that the accused is incompetent or unfit, they are unfit for some other purpose. Therefore, we submit that consideration of an accused's "fitness" beyond the point of the verdict falls outside of the definition contained in section 2 (as it presently reads) and is therefore outside the jurisdiction of the Review Board. The question remains as to whether unfitness at the sentencing juncture of the prosecution process is a proper concern for the court. If an accused is found to be unfit to be

34 *Ibid* [emphasis added].

35 *Ralston v Stump*, 62 NE 2d 293, 75 Ohio App. 375 at 376–77 (Ohio Ct App 1944), citing *State v Williams*, 89 NJ Law 234, 98 A 416 at 417 (E & A NJ 1916).

36 A trial is that step in an action, prosecution, or other judicial proceeding by which questions of fact are decided: William Allen Jowitt et al, *Jowitt's Dictionary of English Law*, vol 1 (London: Sweet & Maxwell, 1977).

sentenced, not within the meaning of section 2 of the *Code*, what is to be done with them? Surely, this is an untenable situation. However, Justice McWatt's decision in *R v GB*[37] would appear to solve that problem for Ontario.

F. HISTORY

So long as there are no inconsistencies, the fact that Parliament has for the past 100 years formally legislated with respect to "unfitness to stand trial" would not disturb any common law provision dealing with "unfitness" at other junctures that may have existed prior to the legislation or that may have developed since the legislation was enacted. In a decision dealing with an accused's fitness to stand trial, the Ontario Court of Appeal in *Re Regina v Gorecki (No 1)*[38] cited with approval the jury instructions of Anderson B in the 1836 British case of *R v Pritchard*.[39] The jury in *Pritchard* was instructed as follows:

> There are three points to be inquired into:—First, whether the prisoner is mute of malice or not; secondly, whether he can plead to the indictment or not; thirdly, whether he is of sufficient intellect to comprehend the course of proceedings on the trial, so as to make a proper defence—to know that he might challenge any of you to whom he may object—and to comprehend the details of the evidence, which in a case of this nature must constitute a minute investigation.[40]

While the court in *Gorecki* specifically approves of the test for unfitness to stand trial articulated in *Pritchard* (which, as we have seen, has been replaced by the definition contained in section 2 of the *Criminal Code*), the court in *Pritchard* relied upon Justice J Parke's jury instructions in the 1831 case of *R v Dyson*,[41] wherein the justice refers to Lord Hale's *Historia Placitorum Coronae (Pleas of the Crown)* (1736).[42] In *Dyson*, the jury was instructed as follows:

---

37 *R v GB*, above note 27.
38 (1976), 32 CCC (2d) 129 (Ont CA) [*Gorecki*].
39 (1836), 7 Car & P 303 [*Pritchard*].
40 *Ibid* at 304.
41 *R v Dyson* (1831), 7 C & P 305.
42 Sir Matthew Hale, *Historia Placitorum Coronae* (London: E and R Nutt, and R Gosling, 1736).

> If a man in his sound memory commits a capital offence, and before his arraignment he becomes absolutely mad, he ought not by law to be arraigned during such his phrensy, but be remitted to prison until that incapacity be removed. The reason is, because he cannot advisedly plead to the indictment. And if such person after his plea, and before his trial, becomes of non-sane memory, he shall not be tried; *or if after his trial he become of non-sane memory, he shall not receive judgement; or if after judgement he become of non-sane memory, his execution shall be spared;* for, were he of sound memory, he might allege somewhat in stay of judgement or execution.[43]

There is, therefore, a line of authority for the proposition that post-verdict "fitness" was a proper concern for the court at the time of *Pritchard;* as well, it would appear to have been the law of England at the time, and therefore the law of Upper Canada (Ontario) after 1792, when English law was established in the province. Between 17 September 1792 and Confederation in July 1867, the criminal law of Ontario consisted of the criminal law of England,[44] together with any subsequent alterations made by the courts and the legislatures. After Confederation, that mass of law remained in force, with the amending power transferred to the federal government. Thus, the criminal law of England as of September 1792 survives in Ontario unless revoked or altered by the courts, subsequent Acts of the provincial legislature up until 1867, or the federal parliament subsequent to 1867.

1) Post-Confederation Caselaw

The Ontario Court of Appeal in the 1910 decision of *R v Leys* indicated that "[n]o person can be rightly tried, sentenced, or executed while insane."[45] The court relied upon the 1876 British decision in *R v Berry*[46] wherein the court relied upon the above excerpt from Hale's *Pleas of the Crown.*[47] In the *Leys* decision, the accused had been tried, convicted,

43 *R v Dyson*, above note 41 at 307 [emphasis added].

44 *An Act for the further introduction of the CRIMINAL LAW of ENGLAND in this Province, and for the more effectual PUNISHMENT of certain OFFENDERS.* Statutes of Upper-Canada, 1800, 40 Geo III, c 1.

45 (1910), 17 CCC 198 (Ont CA).

46 (1876), 1 QB 447 [*Leys*].

47 Hale, above note 42.

and sentenced while committed to a lunatic asylum. The issue of the accused's fitness had never been canvassed by the trial court. As a result, the Court of Appeal allowed the appeal and discharged the accused (on a *habeas corpus* application) on the basis that the conviction was invalid. The court in *R v Leys* did not have to decide what to do with the accused in that he was already civilly committed. Arguably, there should have been some consideration given to the provisions of section 737 of the *Criminal Code*,[48] which had been in place since 1892. To the best of our ability to determine the issue, the decision in *Leys* has never been distinguished or reversed. We therefore submit that, on the basis of post-Confederation caselaw, the issue of fitness is relevant at the juncture of sentencing.

2) The *Charter of Rights*

Section 7 of the *Canadian Charter of Rights and Freedoms* specifies that

> Everyone has the right to life, liberty and security of the person and the right not to be deprived thereof except in accordance with the principles of fundamental justice.[49]

While there do not appear to be section 7 cases directly dealing with the issue of fitness to be sentenced, the Supreme Court of Canada in *R v Whittle*[50] (see Chapter 2, Section B(8)) makes observations that are of assistance. In determining the admissibility of statements made by a mentally disordered accused, the Court notes that the confession rule, the right to silence, and the right to counsel all have in common the interest that the accused has the right to choose in relation to state action. In particular, the Court considered whether the accused was deprived of his right to choose to make a statement because of his mental disorder. In doing so, the Court considered the *Criminal Code* provisions related to fitness to stand trial and the relevant caselaw. The Court found that the same standard of cognitive capacity necessary to find an accused fit to stand trial should be applied to the determining of whether an accused has sufficient capacity to make choices in the

48 *Criminal Code, 1892*, above note 33.

49 *Canadian Charter of Rights and Freedoms, Part I of the Constitution Act, 1982*, being Schedule B to the *Canada Act* 1982 (UK), 1982, c 11 [*Charter*].

50 (1994), 92 CCC (3d) 11 (SCC).

context of the rights to silence and to counsel, and the confession rule.[51] The Court found that, unless there is some good reason inherent in the right, it makes little sense to differentiate as to the requisite capacity to make that choice, and it endorsed the view that different standards of competency should not be applied for different aspects of criminal proceedings. It indicated:

> The operating mind test, which is an aspect of the confessions rule, includes a limited mental component which requires that the accused have sufficient cognitive capacity to understand what he or she is saying and what is said. This includes the ability to understand a caution that the evidence can be used against the accused.
>
> The same standard applies with respect to the right to silence in determining whether the accused has the mental capacity to make an active choice.
>
> In exercising the right to counsel or waiving the right, the accused must possess the limited cognitive capacity that is required for fitness to stand trial. The accused must be capable of communicating with counsel to instruct counsel, and understand the function of counsel and that he or she can dispense with counsel even if this is not in the accused's best interests. It is not necessary that the accused possess analytic ability. The level of cognitive ability is the same as that required with respect to the confession rule and the right to silence. The accused must have the mental capacity of an operating mind as outlined above.[52]

We submit that such reasoning lends strong additional support to the notion that the same minimal standard of mental capacity (even though one might debate the standard to be applied or whether, from a qualitative rather than a quantitative perspective, different abilities should be canvassed) be present before proceeding with a sentencing hearing (or at *any* other juncture of the prosecution), in that the accused must always be possessed with the ability to "choose."

---

51 The Court notes that, while these three rights originated at common law, the confession rule and the right to silence, as principles of fundamental justice, have acquired constitutional status under section 7 of the *Charter*, and the right to counsel is expressly recognized by section 10(b) of the *Charter*.

52 *R v Whittle*, above note 50 at paras 49–51.

Clearly, very important decisions will typically be made at a sentencing hearing.

G. WHY HAVE STATUTORY PROVISIONS ENDED THE FITNESS CONCERN WITH THE VERDICT?

It is unclear why, from the time of Canada's first *Criminal Code*, statutory provisions governing the trial of the fitness issue and the consequences of a finding of unfitness have consistently provided only for the part of the prosecution to "any time before verdict." As well, the only statutory definition of "fitness" is "fitness to stand trial," which, once again, is limited to the time before the verdict. One possible explanation is that, for the vast majority of criminal prosecutions, liability is resolved by way of a plea bargain; the sentencing is concluded on the day of the verdict or very shortly thereafter, leaving very little opportunity for the clinical condition of the accused to deteriorate from their presumed pre-verdict state of fitness. Therefore, for the vast majority of cases, there is no room in the time line for this issue to arise.

There does not appear to be any reason why an accused who has been found unfit at a point in the prosecution beyond the verdict should be treated any differently than an accused found to be unfit prior to the verdict. This point is particularly relevant because most criminal prosecutions are concluded with a guilty plea (following a "plea bargain" conducted at a pre-trial hearing) and then sentencing. Therefore, for most prosecutions, sentencing is not only the most important aspect of the prosecution, it is the *only* truly substantive part of the prosecution.

Further, to proceed with sentencing in respect of an unfit accused would be to ignore the objective of specific deterrence—an acknowledged principle of sentencing. Specific deterrence is that aspect of sentencing that is designed to bring home to a particular accused the probable consequences of re-offending. Similarly, the general deterrence objective of deterring other "like-minded" accused would appear to be lost if an unfit accused were to be sentenced. Furthermore, a court could not expect an accused who does not have a minimal appreciation of the sentencing process to comply with or be governed by any of the terms the court may impose in its sentence. Finally, an unfit accused who failed to comply with the terms of a sentence imposed while they were unfit would inevitably have a potential defence to any charges laid as a result.

H. DISPOSITION

Assuming that the law does indeed require that an accused be fit prior to the sentencing hearing, the question remains as to what to do with the accused who is found to be unfit at this post-verdict juncture. These concerns, underscored by Justice Code in *R v Jaser*,[53] were touched on in Chapter 2. The definition of "unfit to stand trial" contained in section 2 of the *Criminal Code* combined with the mandate of the Review Board set out in section 672.38 creates a jurisdictional impediment. In this section, we discuss possible solutions.

1) Expand the Scope of Section 672.38

It is submitted that the term "verdict" is not so elastic as to cover post-verdict proceedings up to the point of sentencing. Therefore, one solution would be to apply the remedy of "reading in" to the jurisdiction set out in section 672.38 the words "accused found to be unfit for the purpose of sentencing." Extending the reach of the statute in this way would be consistent with the objectives of Part XX.1 of the *Code*. This was, of course, what was done by Justice McWatt in *R v GB*,[54] as discussed in Section D, above in this chapter.

2) "Undo" the Verdict

Where the trier of fact was a judge sitting alone, it may be possible to vacate a finding of guilt.[55] This would allow for the determination of unfitness to then be moved to within the pre-verdict window and therefore not run afoul of the definition in section 2 of "unfit to stand trial."

Section 672.31 provides that, "Where the verdict on the trial of the issue is that an accused is unfit to stand trial, any plea that has been made shall be set aside and any jury shall be discharged." Arguably, where the determination of unfitness has been made post-verdict, the provision would equally apply. Striking the plea would, of necessity, strike the verdict found upon the plea.

53 Above note 29.

54 *R v GB*, above note 27.

55 *R v Lessard*, [1976] OJ No 74 (CA).

3) Proceed to Assume Jurisdiction

Where the Review Board receives, pursuant to subsection 672.47(1) or (3), a new unfit accused from a court of competent jurisdiction, perhaps it should not look behind the verdict of "unfit to stand trial." Should the Review Board blindly "assume regularity," much the same as it would not second guess a verdict of not criminally responsible. Arguably, the validity of the verdict is a matter that should be left to the Court of Appeal. Perhaps the situation is no different than if the Review Board were to receive an accused found to have been not criminally responsible and was of the view that the verdict was inappropriate. Clearly, the Review Board's view as to the appropriateness of the verdict is unimportant. The distinction between the two verdicts is that, in the case of the unfit accused, fitness must be reassessed by the Review Board at every review. Nevertheless, one solution to the situation would be to "assume regularity" and proceed on the basis that the verdict is valid until set aside by the Court of Appeal. The Review Board's competing interest is that it does not want to be found to have curtailed an accused's liberty where jurisdiction over the accused is questionable. When, as it must, the Review Board reconsiders the accused's fitness, it may come to its own conclusions.

I. GUILTY PLEAS

Clearly, where the accused intends to plead guilty, the fitness rules apply in that the accused must be fit prior to arraignment. In such circumstances, various courts have used the "limited cognitive capacity test" to assess the voluntariness (with reference to a mental disorder) of a guilty plea. The court in *R v MAW* indicated that, if a person is found fit in accordance with the limited cognitive capacity threshold at the time of plea and sentencing, that determination amounts to an acknowledgement that the person's pleas were voluntary.[56] The limited cognitive capacity standard is compatible with the voluntariness test. The standard that is applied when an appellant relies on mental disorder to invalidate a plea because of involuntariness is the same test that

56 *MAW*, [2008] OJ No 2738 (CA).

is used to determine the fitness of an accused to stand trial.[57] (The flaws in this reasoning have been fleshed-out in Chapter 2, Section B(8)).

In determining the voluntariness of a guilty plea, the focus is not on the rationality of the accused in making their choice or whether the guilty plea is in the best interests of the appellant. Rather, the focus is on whether the appellant had the capacity to make an active or conscious choice for reasons the appellant considered appropriate.[58] The standard set out by the limited cognitive capacity test requires only that the court be satisfied that an accused understands the process, can communicate with counsel, and can make an active or conscious choice.[59] As discussed in Chapter 2, whether the accused's choice is wise, rational, or in their best interest forms no part in the consideration of voluntariness. The test of voluntariness requires that the accused understand the nature of the proceedings and its possible consequences, and determines whether or not the accused can communicate with defence counsel and understand advice given.[60]

Again, if there is a gap in the time line between the various elements of entering the plea, admission of the facts, a finding of guilt, conviction, and the actual sentencing hearing, the possibility arises that a clinically fragile accused may decompensate during that window and will be confronted with the same issues raised above (i.e., whether or not satisfaction of the limited cognitive capacity test adequately protects the accused). The courts must be vigilant with the mentally disordered accused, as fitness may come and go and fluctuations may not be outwardly apparent or readily observable.

J. BAIL HEARINGS

Does an accused need to be fit to stand trial in order to have a bail hearing?
Short answer: No.

Does an accused need to be fit to stand trial in order to be released on bail?
Short answer: No.

---

57 *Law Society of Upper Canada v Tollis*, [2011] LSDD No 236.

58 *R v MAW*, above note 56.

59 *Law Society of Upper Canada v Tollis*, above note 57.

60 *Ibid.*

Is mental disorder relevant to judicial interim release?
Short answer: It may be.

For a clear and articulate accounting of the law pertaining to bail (or "judicial interim release"), the reader is referred to Justice Gary Trotter's text entitled *The Law of Bail in Canada*,[61] wherein the history of bail, the current law, and applicable procedure are set out fully and completely. Risking an oversimplified distillation of Justice Trotter's introduction to the topic, it can be said that bail was originally a very *ad hoc* process whereby an accused could be placed into the hands of a surety who would guarantee (through various assurances, undertakings, and "deposits") that the accused, if released, would attend court at a future date to face trial. From those early beginnings,[62] caselaw developed, which was eventually codified and re-codified—a process that has taken us to our current statutory provisions set out in section 515 of the *Criminal Code* of Canada.

Curiously, the interest in bail was originally driven not by concerns for an accused's pre-trial liberty so much as the reality that granting bail was less expensive than incarceration, that pre-trial incarceration was harsh, and that accused were prone to frequent elopement. Now, as well as the *Code* provisions, the right to reasonable bail is guaranteed by section 11(e) of the *Charter*:

> 11 *Any person* charged with an offence has the right
>
> ...
>
> (e) not to be denied reasonable bail without just cause.[63]

In determining whether release is "reasonable," the court will consider three aspects, *per* subsection 515(10) of the *Criminal Code*:

- the primary ground: "to ... ensure attendance in court"[64]
- the secondary ground: "for the protection or safety of the public"[65]
- the tertiary ground: "to maintain confidence in the administration of justice"[66]

---

61 Gary Trotter, *The Law of Bail in Canada* (Scarborough, ON: Carswell, 1992).

62 Justice Trotter, in his review of the literature, indicates that "bail" in a criminal context has been known to us from at least the twelfth or thirteenth century. *Ibid.*

63 Above note 49 [emphasis added].

64 *Criminal Code*, above note 2, s 515(10)(a).

65 *Ibid*, s 515(10)(b).

66 *Ibid*, s 515(10)(c).

In certain more serious circumstances (as enumerated in section 469), the onus of satisfying the court with respect to these grounds is placed upon the accused; otherwise, release is presumptive and detention warranted only where the Crown can demonstrate that reasonable bail is not possible, pursuant to one or more of the grounds not being satisfied. This is, of course, consistent with our fundamental presumption in criminal prosecutions of "innocence." Further, the state has no business detaining an innocent person prior to trial without just cause based upon clear articulable grounds.

While an accused is not "conducting a defence" at a bail hearing and therefore needn't be fit to stand trial in order to have a bail hearing or to be released on bail, that is not to say that mental disorder may not be a relevant concern vis-à-vis one of the three grounds.

1) Psychiatric Aspects of Bail Worthiness

Mentally disordered offenders might experience difficulty obtaining judicial interim release because their mental condition may have implications for both the primary and secondary grounds in subsection 515(10). The bail worthiness of a mentally disordered accused may depend on whether sufficient psychiatric supervision is in place. Psychiatric evaluations with respect to judicial interim release can raise some strategic concerns for defence counsel. The clinician will often find it necessary to review the current allegations against the accused, as they may well have implications for the accused's suitability for release; however, that information may turn out to be inculpatory or otherwise prejudicial. Care should be taken not to include surplusage that is not logically probative of a legitimate bail concern.

a) Primary Ground

Psychiatric evidence may be called by the defence to address the concern that, if released, the accused, as a result of mental disorder, might not attend court when required. Alternatively, the Crown may call psychiatric evidence to show that, because of their mental condition, the accused would not be inclined to attend court. Aside from the general probability of attendance or non-attendance, psychiatric evidence may suggest terms to be included in an order for judicial interim release that would reduce those concerns.

The accused's eligibility on the primary ground may depend upon their understanding of the charge and need to appear in court; whether any cognitive limitation would affect their ability to attend court; whether they have housing and support in the community; and/or their risk for substance abuse or medication non-compliance due to the mental disorder. Some mentally disordered accused are so ill (psychotic) that they cannot process information meaningfully, or are so paranoid that they would do anything to avoid the clutches of the criminal justice system.

b) Secondary Ground

The concern on the secondary ground is whether detention is necessary for the protection of the public, having regard to all the circumstances, including any substantial likelihood that the accused will, if released from custody, commit a criminal offence or interfere with the administration of justice. It is in respect of these concerns that psychiatric evidence is more typically adduced. The accused's current mental disorder and its implications for dangerous behaviour in the community are the key considerations with respect to the secondary ground.

K. BAIL AND FITNESS TO STAND TRIAL

An accused is presumed to be fit to stand trial (section 672.22) and may be released on bail prior to the issue being tried. Even where there are reasonable grounds to believe medical evidence is necessary to determine the issue of fitness (subsection 672.11(a)), a subsequent order for assessment is presumed to take place on an out-of-custody basis (section 672.16). There is no specific provision in Part XX.1 for the ordering of a psychiatric assessment to assist with judicial interim release.[67] As well, there is no necessary requirement that an accused be fit in order to be granted judicial interim release. While, for the most part, an accused who is so compromised as to put fitness in issue may not be amenable to terms of release, where an adequate "plan" can be put in place, judicial interim release is appropriate.

---

67 Trotter, above note 61 at s 5.3(c).

As set out in section 672.16, the provisions from section 515, dealing with judicial interim release generally, have been imported into Part XX.1:

> *Presumption against custody*
>
> **672.16(1)** Subject to subsection (3), an accused shall not be detained in custody under an assessment order of a court unless
>
> (a) the court is satisfied that on the evidence custody is necessary to assess the accused, or that on the evidence of a medical practitioner custody is desirable to assess the accused and the accused consents to custody;
>
> (b) custody of the accused is required in respect of any other matter or by virtue of any other provision of this *Act*; or
>
> (c) the prosecutor, having been given a reasonable opportunity to do so, shows that detention of the accused in custody is justified on either of the grounds set out in subsection 515(10).

The question of whether an accused needs to be fit to stand trial in order to have a bail hearing has been considered, first by the Ontario Superior Court in *R v Southwood*[68] and then by the Quebec Superior Court in *R v Desmarais*.[69] In *R v Southwood*, the court found that there is no statutory or judicial authority that would bar a mentally disordered accused from consideration for judicial interim release. It is a right guaranteed by section 11(e) of the *Charter*. Part XX.1 of the *Criminal Code* contemplates the release on bail of an accused suffering from a mental disorder. It is up to the Crown to show cause why bail should be denied as a result of that person's lack of mental capacity or mental disorder.

In *R v Desmarais*, the Crown argued that "unfit to stand trial," as set out in section 2 of the *Criminal Code*, meant that an accused, if unfit, was precluded from participating "in all criminal proceedings, at every stage, which would include a bail hearing."[70] Further, the Crown argued that the *Code* made no explicit provision for conducting bail hearings in respect of an unfit accused. Upon appeal, the Superior Court did not accept either of these submissions as correct. Section 2 makes no reference to bail hearings being included as a stage of the *trial* proceedings. The definition of "unfit to stand trial" contained in section 2 pertains

---

68 [2003] OJ No 590 (Ct J).

69 *R v Desmarais* (17 November 2016), No 500-36-008237-169 (Que Sup Ct).

70 *Ibid* at para 22.

exclusively to an accused's ability to *conduct a defence* before a verdict is rendered. It may be that the accused is never called upon to conduct a defence. The accused's appearance before the court at the time of the bail hearing is not for the purpose of conducting a defence. Rather, it is limited to a consideration of the three grounds discussed with respect to section 515(10) in Section J, above in this chapter.

Further, section 11(e) of the *Charter* guarantees reasonable bail to *any person* (fit or unfit) without just cause being shown. The accused (fit or unfit) is presumed to be innocent. The fitness rules do not have the effect, nor should they have, of depriving an unfit accused of his fundamental right to reasonable bail. While there is no explicit provision for the unfit accused to have a bail hearing, there is nothing in the *Code* to *prevent* such a hearing.

In a rather remarkable decision, the Court of Appeal for Quebec reversed the decision of the Superior Court in *R v Desmarais* finding, *inter alia*, that (1) a bail hearing is part of the prosecution (i.e., requires a defence), and, alarmingly, (2) that section 11(e) of the *Charter* does not pertain to an unfit accused because "[a]n unfit person is not a person charged with an offence when a verdict confirms he or she is unfit to stand trial."[71] Because of this litigation, the accused was held for an extraordinary length of time while it was argued back and forth. Of course, an unfit accused is just that—an "accused" (i.e., charged with an offence). However, the prosecution of that charge is held in abeyance so long as the accused remains unfit to stand trial. However, the accused is, as a result, no less "accused." Mercifully, this "Kafkaesque procedural nightmare" came to an end with a stay of proceedings granted by the Superior Court.[72]

We would urge an interpretation of the law as articulated in *R v Southwood* and the Quebec Superior Court in *Desmarais* to be more consistent with the spirit of the legislation pertaining to bail and the

---

71 *R v Desmarais* (4 July 2017), No 500-10-006286-163 (Que CA) at para 29.

72 *Desmarais v R*, [2017] QJ No 3864 at para 1 (Sup Ct). Upon the earlier decision from the Court of Appeal in this matter, finding, *inter alia*, that an accused must be fit to stand trial in order to have a bail hearing, the Superior Court granted the accused's application for a stay of proceedings as a result of the "Kafkaesque procedural nightmare" experienced by the accused. The accused, who suffers from a mental disorder, was in custody for over four years without a bail hearing while the matter of his fitness to stand trial was being batted about. Unfortunately, the rather remarkable decision of the Court of Appeal is, as a result, left intact.

admonitions of the Supreme Court in *Winko v British Columbia (Forensic Psychiatric Institute)*[73] to the effect that mental illness is not a basis for perceiving an individual as "dangerous" or less entitled to their liberty.

While not considered in the decisions above, the Supreme Court of Canada's decision in *R v Whittle*[74] warrants further discussion. In that case, the court considered the admissibility of an accused's inculpatory statement at trial. The case involved the accused's mental state at the time he made an inculpatory statement, and the court found that the same standard of cognitive capacity necessary to find an accused fit to stand trial should be applied to the determination of whether an accused has sufficient capacity to make choices in the context of the right to silence, counsel, and the confession rule. The court held that the same standard should be held with respect to cognitive capacity at all junctures of the prosecution process.

A bail hearing is *not*, however, part of the prosecution process *per se*. It is *not* part of the process put in place to either investigate or determine guilt or innocence. So, unlike the process of determining the admissibility of a statement made by a mentally disordered accused at a trial where innocence or guilt are being decided, and in respect of which a statement may be logically probative, a bail hearing is for the purpose of determining whether or to what extent an accused's liberty should be curtailed while the trial process takes place. A bail hearing is best thought of as a process preliminary to or collateral to the proceedings at trial. And while, for example, the results of a bail hearing may ultimately be relevant to the court's final disposition in sentencing (i.e., if convicted, pre-trial custody may be taken into consideration in determining a fit sentence), it is not part of the trial. The matters decided at a bail hearing are not logically probative of an accused's guilt. A bail hearing is not concerned with the "conducting of a defence." Being unfit to stand trial should not be a bar to proceeding with a bail hearing.

There are, however, certain tactical reasons why, on a case-by-case basis, a resolution of the fitness issue might be better resolved prior to the conducting of a bail hearing. If an accused is in such a decompensated state that their fitness to stand trial is in question, it may be that such a condition will be of concern with respect to one of the "grounds"

---

73 [1999] 2 SCR 625 [*Winko*].

74 *R v Whittle*, above note 50.

for bail worthiness. It may be tactically prudent to have the matter of fitness resolved and, if necessary, the accused treated prior to the holding of a bail hearing.

L. CALLING PSYCHIATRIC EVIDENCE

While it is now accepted that mental disorder should not be equated with dangerousness (e.g., *Winko*),[75] there are features of some mental disorders that may render an accused a risk if released. Psychiatric evidence may be called by either party in order to address these issues and the extent to which they should or should not concern the court and/or could be alleviated with appropriate terms of release that could mitigate risk to an assumable level.

M. PSYCHIATRIC ASSESSMENTS: THE *CRIMINAL CODE* AND THE *MENTAL HEALTH ACT* OF ONTARIO

Curiously, section 672.11, which sets out the general provisions with respect to psychiatric assessments in Part XX.1 of the *Criminal Code*, does not provide for psychiatric assessments for the purposes of either judicial interim release or sentencing. Sections 21 and 22 (for out-of-custody and in-custody, respectively) of Ontario's *Mental Health Act*,[76] however, may be used for the purposes of obtaining a psychiatric assessment in that province.[77] In other provinces, civil legislation may be relied upon to fill the gap in section 672.11, where the provisions permit. The Ontario legislation reads as follows:

> *Judge's order for examination*
> 21(1) Where a judge has reason to believe that a person who appears before him or her charged with or convicted of an offence suffers from mental disorder, the judge may order the person to attend a psychiatric facility for examination.

---

75 *Winko*, above note 73.

76 RSO 1990, c M.7.

77 *R v Lenart* (1998), 123 CCC (3d) 353 (Ont CA).

Senior physician's report

(2) Where an examination is made under this section, the senior physician shall report in writing to the judge as to the mental condition of the person.

Judge's order for admission

22(1) Where a judge has reason to believe that a person in custody who appears before him or her charged with an offence suffers from mental disorder, the judge may, by order, remand that person for admission as a patient to a psychiatric facility for a period of not more than two months.

Senior physician's report

(2) Before the expiration of the time mentioned in such order, the senior physician shall report in writing to the judge as to the mental condition of the person.

Note that, where legislation outside of the *Criminal Code* is relied upon to obtain psychiatric assessments, the array of protective provisions attached to section 672.11 (most notably the protected statement provisions in section 672.21) do not apply. It is recommended that the court attach similar conditions as part of any order made outside of the *Criminal Code.*

Ten-Point Review

1) The issue of fitness can arise at any point in the proceedings.
2) The issue of fitness is tested only *after* a *prima facie* case is presented.
3) The issue of fitness is tested *after* the Crown has made its election.
4) An accused must be fit to plead (guilty or not guilty).
5) An accused must (in the authors' view) be fit in order to be sentenced.
6) A bail hearing is not part of the prosecution *per se.*
7) An accused does not need to be fit in order to have a bail hearing.
8) Mental disorder may be relevant in considering the primary or secondary grounds for bail worthiness.
9) An accused does not need to be fit in order to be released on bail.
10) There are no provisions in the *Criminal Code* for the court to make an assessment to assist with bail. Provincial mental health legislation may provide an option to accomplish this.

CHAPTER 4

Psychiatric Aspects of Fitness

It has been common practice for decades for psychiatrists and psychologists to be appointed by courts (and less frequently, to be retained by the parties) to assess accused whose fitness is suspect. That said, mental health expertise to determine fitness is not required by the *Criminal Code*, and, in rare instances, judges will determine the issues without a mental health professional's involvement.

A. MENTAL DISORDER AND FITNESS

1) The Prevalence of Major Mental Disorder

Clinical practice has made clear that psychosis, which occurs most commonly in schizophrenia, is the most frequently found condition leading to a finding of unfitness to stand trial. There is a strong correlation between psychosis, intellectual impairment, and unfitness to stand trial in patients with these conditions.[1]

The point that there is a considerably higher density and severity of psychotic symptoms in accused found unfit, compared to those found fit, was made in a recent study by Lee et al.[2] The authors used the

1 MS Heller et al, "Intelligence, Psychosis and Competency to Stand Trial" (1981) 9 *Bulletin of the American Academy of Psychiatry and the Law* 267.

2 Eugene Lee et al, "Mental Illness and Legal Fitness (Competence) to Stand Trial in New York State: Expert Opinion and Criminal Defendants' Psychiatric Symptoms" (2014) 59:4 *Journal of Forensic Sciences* 1008.

Brief Psychiatric Rating Scale (BPRS),[3] a twenty-four-item scale used in clinical practice and research, to measure the presence and intensity of psychiatric symptoms, and found an inverse relationship between psychotic symptoms (particularly conceptual disorganization, unusual thought content, thought disorder, and hostile suspiciousness) and fitness to stand trial.

Other conditions that are well-represented in populations of unfit accused include delusional disorder, neurocognitive disorders, particularly dementia, and major mood disorders such as mania and psychotic depression.

According to Ogloff and Whittemore,[4] individuals referred for fitness evaluations are most often single, unemployed men living alone, the majority of whom have a previous psychiatric history. Observations on psychiatric wards and forensic units of individuals considered to be unfit indicate that they are more preoccupied, verbally abusive, hostile, assaultive, restless, socially isolated, thought disordered, and bizarre in their affect and behaviour compared to individuals considered fit.[5]

2) The Effect of Symptoms

Table 4.1 provides a broad overview of the relationship between specific symptoms that a mentally disordered individual might experience and the potential impact of the symptom(s) on an area relevant to the individual's fitness to stand trial. Note that any one symptom, if experienced intensely, can impinge upon a number of areas of fitness. The chart's purpose is to suggest the more common relationship between a symptom/limitation and area of deficit with respect to fitness.

---

3 John E Overall & Donald R Gorham, "The Brief Psychiatric Rating Scale" (1962) 10:3 *Psychological Reports* 799.

4 JRP Ogloff & KE Whittemore, "Fitness to Stand Trial and Criminal Responsibility in Canada" in RA Schuller & JRP Ogloff, eds, *Introduction to Psychology and Law: Canadian Perspectives* (Toronto: University of Toronto Press, 2001) 283.

5 Ronald Roesch et al, *The Fitness Interview Test* (Burnaby, BC: Mental Health, Law, and Policy Institute, Simon Fraser Institute, 1998).

TABLE 4.1. EFFECT OF VARIOUS SYMPTOMS ON FITNESS TO STAND TRIAL

Area of Fitness	Conditions/Symptom Complex							
Potentially Compromised	*Hallucinations*	*Delusions*	*Thought Disorder*	*Confusion*	*Depression & Self-Defeating Motivation*	*Mental Retardation (Mild)*	*Mental Retardation (Moderate)*	*Frontal Lobe Syndrome*
Understand Charges	+/-	+/-	++	++	+/-	+/-	++	+/-
Understand Object Proceeding	+/-	+/-	++/-	++	+/-	+/-	++	++/-
Understand Consequences of Conviction	+/-	+/-	++/-	++	+/-	+/-	++	++/-
Understand Roles of Court Officers	+/-	+/-	++/-	++	+/-	+/-	++	++/-
Understand Pleas	+/-	+/-	++	++	+/-	+/-	++	++/-
Understand Strategies	+/-	+/-	++	++	++/-	+/-	++	++/-
Trust Counsel	+/-	+/- *	+/-	+/-	+/-	+/-	+/-	+/-
Relate to Counsel	+/-	+/-	++	++	++/-	++/-	++	++/-
Receive Guidance	+/-	+/-	++	++	+/-	+/-	++/-	++/-
Appraise Evidence	+/-	+/-	++/-	++	+/-	+/-	++/-	++/-
Testify	++/-	++/-	++	++	++/-	+/-	++	++
Act in Self-Preservational Manner	+/-	+/-	+/-	++	++	+/-	++	++
Self-Control	+/-	+/-	+/-	++/-	+/-	+/-	+/-	++/-

* Likely not if the delusions are of a paranoid or grandiose nature.

Hallucinations and delusions (or any other symptoms) do not render someone unfit, *per se*, unless they are implicated in and impinge on one or more of the abilities referred to in section 2 of the *Criminal Code.* Marked lack of insight—that is, a failure to see oneself as suffering from a condition others have diagnosed the individual with—is arguably also a factor to be taken into consideration when determining whether a person is fit or unfit to stand trial. An individual may appear to meet the bare-bones test for fitness to stand trial and yet have a significant limitation in insight that prevents them from recognizing the disease process that may allow for exoneration through a not criminally responsible (NCR) defence.

It would be exceedingly rare for a personality disorder to be the foundational mental disorder underpinning a finding of unfitness.[6] While "personality disorder" meets the section 2 definition of "mental disorder," it will rarely produce the sorts of symptoms necessary to defeat the presumption of fitness. Rarely will a personality disorder result in deficits of the sort relevant to fitness.

B. AMNESIA

At the time of this writing, we are not aware of any cases in Canada, the United States, or Commonwealth countries where amnesia *simpliciter* justified a finding of unfitness to stand trial.[7] There is one anomalous line in *R v Taylor*,[8] apparently endorsed by the court—and not consistent with any other modern decision the writers are aware of—that requires the accused to be capable of recounting the necessary facts of the case. Amnesia could, of course, produce such an incapacity.

Amnesia with respect to the events does not of itself render an accused unfit to stand trial. When it does not represent wilful suppression, apparent memory difficulties are often attributable to substance consumption prior to the act, an inability to register memory because of the marked affective disruption the accused was experiencing at the time of the act, or both. To be fit to stand trial, it is not necessary, *Taylor* notwithstanding, for the accused to be able to remember the events that gave rise to the charges.[9] Moreover, in conducting a defence, an inability to communicate to counsel their own version of the events that have led to the charge is not sufficient to render an accused unfit to stand trial.[10]

In *R v Morrissey*,[11] at the conclusion of the evidence at trial, the defence argued that the accused's inability, due to an amnestic disorder

6 Ian Freckelton, "Fitness to Stand Trial: Learning from the Ezra Pound Saga" (2014) 21:5 *Psychiatry, Psychology, and Law* 625.

7 *R v Eisnor*, 2015 NSCA 64.

8 [1992] OJ No 2394 at para 44 (CA) [*Taylor*], where the "limited cognitive capacity test" that was accepted by the court is described as requiring an inquiry into whether an accused can recount to counsel the necessary facts relating to the offence in such a way that counsel can then properly present a defence.

9 *R v Morrissey*, 2007 ONCA 770; *DRP (Re)*, [2014] ORBD No 2349.

10 *R v Morrissey*, above note 9; *R v Eisnor*, [2013] NSJ No 584 (SC).

11 [2003] OJ No 5960 (SCJ).

(frontal lobe syndrome), to recall the events prior to and at the time he allegedly shot and killed his estranged girlfriend made him unfit to stand trial. The principal concern here was that the accused's memory loss with respect to the critical events and his proneness to confabulation would prevent him from testifying relevantly in his defence. Counsel for the accused argued that the accused's inability to testify in the circumstances, as a result of his brain condition, would result in a breach of his rights to life, liberty, and security of the person, and right to a fair trial, pursuant to sections 7 and 11(d), respectively, of the *Charter of Rights and Freedoms*.[12]

The trial judge concluded that the accused's potential inability to testify as a result of a self-inflicted act (the accused's deficits were the product of a self-inflicted gunshot wound to the head during an attempted suicide), when it was unclear, in any event, whether he would have either been able or would have chosen to testify for his own benefit, did not violate the *Charter of Rights and Freedoms*. The accused's limitations may have provided a sound tactical reason to keep him from testifying, but they did not render his trial unfair. The case also touched on the policy concern that exempting individuals from prosecution on the basis of amnesia would open a floodgate and lead to an untenable result, in that amnesia occurs in 30 to 50 percent of cases of violent crime.[13]

In reviewing the decision of the trial court, the Court of Appeal[14] found no errors and reiterated that, while testimonial competence and fitness to stand trial may overlap, they are different tests. Testimonial competence is not a precondition to a finding of fitness. In particular, amnesia does not, by itself, cause an accused to be unfit to stand trial.[15]

Other jurisdictions have taken similar approaches in considering fitness to stand trial. In *United States v Stevens*,[16] the court concluded that

---

12 Part I of the *Constitution Act, 1982*, being Schedule B to the *Canada Act 1982* (UK), 1982, c 11.

13 Maaike Cima et al, "Claims of Crime: Related Amnesia in Forensic Patients" (2004) 27:3 *International Journal of Law and Psychiatry* 215.

14 *R v Morrissey*, above note 9.

15 Compare *R v Amey*, 2009 NSPC 29 at para 62, where the court found that an inability to remember the events leading to the charge as well as an inability to remember the course of the trial led to a finding of unfitness, as they were important to the ability to give instructions.

16 461 F2d 317 (7th Circ 1972).

amnesia did not bar prosecution of an otherwise competent defendant. In *United States v Andrews*,[17] the US Court of Appeal for the Seventh Circuit considered whether the defendant's amnesia would prevent him and his lawyer from reconstructing the events of the alleged offence and from raising any possible defences to the evidence against him, and it concluded it would not.

What the court did not deal with sufficiently in *R v Morrissey*, however, was the accused's propensity to confabulate. Confabulation, a phenomenon found most commonly in persons with organically based amnesia, involves fabrication of details to fill in memory gaps and might cause the accused to completely mislead the court due to his inability to separate reality from content his mind has conjured up and inserted into his "recollection." This significant problem may bear directly upon the accused's fitness to stand trial.

From a practical perspective, however, the likelihood is fair, if not high, that an accused with significant authentic amnesia will have other cognitive (perceptual and affective) deficits that may in and of themselves render the accused unfit (see *R v Triano*).[18]

It may be that future courts will find that memory loss due to mental disorder rendering one prone to confabulation—an atypical by-product—should be seen as distinguishable from memory loss or amnesia *simpliciter*. In this fairly uncommon scenario, the negative policy argument is neutralized. Second, there is a real possibility that confabulation may not just leave a gap in the evidence but, worse, may distort the evidentiary picture in a way that is most difficult for the trier of fact to detect. One who confabulates cannot separate "real memory" from that which has been subconsciously filled in or created. It is not deliberate or volitional and occurs as a function of a disease process.

C. DEAFNESS AND INABILITY TO SPEAK AS A "MENTAL DISORDER"

In *R v Isaac*,[19] the accused, who was originally from Nigeria, could neither speak nor hear, nor could he sign in any language. The issue was whether Mr Isaac's difficulty amounted to a mental disorder, which, if

17 469 F3d 1113 (7th Circ 2006).
18 [2014] OJ No 2303 (Ct J).
19 [2009] OJ No 5804 at paras 18–28 (Ct J).

that were the case, would allow for an assessment of his fitness. The discourse on point is extracted from the decision made by the court:

> To my mind a central question is as to whether or not being deaf and unable to speak could be viewed as a mental disorder or, as that is defined in s.2, a "disease of the mind."
>
> Mental Disorder:
>
> "Mental disorder" is defined in section 2 of the *Criminal Code* as "disease of the mind." It is a legal concept. "Disease of the mind" has been defined most generally by the Supreme Court of Canada in *Cooper v R.*, [1980] 1 S.C.R. 1149, as follows: "'Disease of the mind' is a legal term embracing any illness, disorder, or abnormal condition that *impairs the human mind and its functioning*'" (emphasis added). As one might expect, "anxiety" (eg. *R v McLeod* (1980), 52 C.C.C. (2d) 193 (B.C.C.A.), "personality disorder" (eg. *Cooper v R.* [1980] 1 S.C.R. 1149), "mental retardation" (eg. *R v Rouse*, [1996] O.J. No. 4688 (Gen. Div.), "*delerium tremens*" (eg. *R v Malcolm* (1989), 50 C.C.C. (3d) 172 (Man. C.A.), "toxic psychosis" (eg. *R v Mailloux* (1985), 25 C.C.C. (3d) 171 (Ont. C.A.), and even "self-induced intoxication" (eg. *R v Hilton* (1972), 34 C.C.C. (2d) 206 (Ont. C.A.), have all been found to be mental disorders (diseases of the mind). These conditions are all ones which *impair the human mind and its functioning.*
>
> Prior to the proclamation of Bill C-30, s.615 of the *Criminal Code* provided as follows for persons who may be "insane at the time of trial":
>
> > 615.(1) A court, judge or provincial court judge may, at any time before a verdict, where it appears that there is sufficient reason to doubt that the accused is, on account of insanity, capable of conducting his defence, direct that an issue be tried whether the accused is then, on account of insanity, unfit to stand his trial.
> >
> > (2) A court, judge or provincial judge may, at any time before verdict or sentence, when of the opinion, supported by the evidence or, where the prosecutor and the accused consent, by the report in writing, of at least one duly qualified medical practitioner, that there is reason to believe that
> >
> > (a) an accused is mentally ill, or
> >
> > (b) the balance of the mind of an accused is disturbed, where the accused is a female person charged with an offence arising out of the death of her newly-born child.

[order that the accused be assessed, etc.]

Being deaf and unable to speak is not a mental illness or a psychiatric disorder, it is a communication disorder. There is no reasonable basis to suspect that Mr. Isaac may be cognitively impaired, or of unsound mind, or that his being deaf and unable to speak has impaired his mind and its functioning. Indeed, the evidence of Dr. MacDougall is that there is no indication of impairment of this kind. At present the formulation is one of a lack of education—a lack of schooling.

The only way to know the limits of Mr. Isaac's ability to learn language given that critical periods for language acquisition have long since passed is to attempt to teach him. This, according to Dr. MacDougall, cannot be accomplished in a jail setting. The probability is that he has the ability to learn to communicate to a standard that would permit him to stand trial. This education might take between 2 and 3 years to accomplish.

Deafness + inability to speak = mental disorder?:

This is not a case where the accused is simply standing mute before the court and there is uncertainty as to whether or not the accused is "mute of malice or not" (as in *Rex v Pritchard*, [1836] 7 Car. & P. 304). Here, Dr. MacDougall and Mr. Isaac's mother have testified that Mr. Isaac is deaf and unable to speak. There is no ambiguity about the basis for his "muteness." An assessment of his mental condition will not elucidate any further the aetiology of his deafness and inability to speak. As well, Dr. MacDougall's uncontroverted opinion is that there is "... no indication of any mental disorder." Although "mental condition" (the term used in s.672.11) is a broader concept than "mental disorder" (see for example: *R v Jones* (1996), 87 C.C.C. (3d) 350 (Ont. C.A.)) it is only the finding of a "mental disorder" which could potentially give rise to a finding of unfitness. While the jurisdictional threshold for the making of an assessment order is quite low it must nevertheless be based upon reasonable grounds.

As indicated at the outset the subject or focus of any court ordered assessment is limited to the "mental condition of the accused." An Assessment Order may only be made where the court has reasonable grounds to believe that an assessment of the accused's *mental condition* is necessary to determine whether the accused is (in this case) unfit to stand trial. As mentioned above, although the *Code* is silent as to what might take the court to the point of "reasonable grounds to believe," it is clear that no particular evidence is necessary. Nevertheless, the basis for the belief must be clear and plainly appear on the record of proceedings. Odd behaviour alleged in the offence has been found to be an insufficient basis (*R v Sun*, [1999] O.J. No. 2821 (Ont. S.C.)); an opinion that the accused may have a viable defence of "not criminally responsible on account of mental disorder" has been found to be an insufficient basis (*R v Muschke*, [1997] B.C.J. No. 2825 (B.C.S.C.)); the mere presence of a mental disorder has been found to be an insufficient basis (*R v Taylor*, [1992] O.J. No.2394 (Ont. C.A.)).

It must also be emphasized that the definition of unfit to stand trial speaks of "inabilities." An accused may not know the nature and object of the proceedings, their possible consequences, or have an ability to communicate with counsel, however, if the accused *has the ability* to understand the nature and object of the proceedings, their potential consequences, and *has the ability* to communicate with counsel, he is not unfit to stand trial. At present we are not able to say whether or not Mr. Isaac will be unable to communicate with counsel sufficiently. This will only be known after a proper educational program has been attempted.

While the fitness rules are in place to protect the accused from a prosecution to which he is unable to respond we should not be attempting to pound square pegs into round holes. The regime enacted in Part XX.1—Mental Disorder is clearly designed to assess, treat, and monitor accused who suffer from mental disorders. I am of the view that parliament did not intend to capture other disabilities with these provisions.

Conclusion:

At this juncture I am of the view that there are no reasonable grounds to order an assessment of Mr. Isaac's mental condition. The only evidence before me is to the effect that Mr. Isaac does not appear to suffer from a mental disorder. Accordingly, the application is dismissed.

(Parenthetically, in any event, the uncontroverted evidence of Dr. MacDougall is that a further assessment of Mr. Isaac would require that he first acquire a language such as A.S.L. This might take a further 2 to 3 years.)[20]

---

20 However, it may be the case that, where the accused's inability to speak is the product of a stroke (which qualifies as a "mental disorder" within the meaning of section 2 of the *Criminal Code*—see *R v Cooper*, [1980] 1 SCR 1149) and will not be improving, the accused may be found unfit to stand trial. *R v Hyslop* (23 February 2006), (Ont SCJ).

While conditions other than those produces by a mental disorder may, on rare occasions, cause an impasse in the trial process, they do not result in a state of unfitness.

D. MENTALLY DISORDERED ACCUSED MISSED BY *TAYLOR*

The *Taylor* decision, in our view, reflects the difficulty courts have in understanding the depth and scope of mental illness and its infiltrative quality, and the extent to which it can interfere with a person's capacity to enlist normal functions of self-preservation. These functions do not depend only on cognitive abilities but on other areas of intrapsychic functioning, such as motivation, insight, affect, and volition. Cases where accused are unfit due to a reason other than cognitive impairment and overt psychosis tend to be relatively subtle. Both counsel and the forensic psychiatric examiner should maintain a high index of suspicion when certain information suggests the possibility or likelihood of a deficit. However, the standard of the limited cognitive capacity test, as suggested by many commentators, is too low, especially with respect to the criteria of instructing counsel,[21] and consequently fails to filter out a number of different types of accused who are probably not fit, and, who, having regard to the purpose and intent of the fitness rules to begin with, should probably not be proceeding to trial. In *R v Adam*,[22] the court noted the observations of commentators that the test may fail to remove from the prosecutorial process a number of different accused who are most likely unfit and should not be proceeding to trial. The shortcomings of the test recognized by the court in *Adam* are the result of that test's primary focus on cognitive functioning, leaving out of consideration elements of mental illness such as judgment, motivation, insight, and the emotional status of the accused.[23]

A test for competency should focus not so much on the individual's exercise of good judgment or ability to make the "right choice" as on

---

21 Richard D Schneider & Hy Bloom, "*R v Taylor*: A Decision Not in the Best Interests of Some Mentally Ill Accused" (1995) 38 *Criminal Law Quarterly* 183; *R v Adam*, [2013] OJ No 222 (SCJ) [*Adam*]; *R v Krivicic*, [2011] OJ No 5005 (CA). As we discussed in Chapter 2, the limited cognitive capacity test emerged from the *Taylor* decision, which was formally limited to a consideration of the accused's ability to communicate with counsel.

22 *Adam*, above note 21.

23 Schneider & Bloom, above note 21.

whether the accused's capacity to judge and choose has not been fettered by mental illness.[24] The inquiry of fitness "demands an assurance that, despite suffering from a mental disorder, the accused person is able to receive a fair trial."[25] Of concern is the ability of the accused to meaningfully participate in the proceedings or assist counsel in conducting a defence.[26] Also required is the ability of the accused to rationally communicate and converse with counsel or to make critical decisions based on counsel's advice,[27] as recognized in the American case of *Dusky v United States*[28] discussed earlier in Chapter 2, Sections B(2) and B(9).

The scenarios described in the balance of this chapter suggest instances in which an accused could meet the limited cognitive capacity test articulated in *Taylor* but still, as a result of defects in judgment, capacity for self-preservation, and a disturbance in affect, be insufficiently capable of meaningful participation to be considered fit. Regardless of the actual diagnosis, marked deficits in insight may be a significant common denominator that inhibits meaningful participation to a degree that an accused could be thought of as unfit.[29] Such deficits (together with reality-based considerations like stigma and self-image) at times serve as the foreground reason why an accused will forfeit and/or not even consider an NCR defence that they may be entitled to and that would undoubtedly result in a better outcome (i.e., better quality of life and less restriction of liberty).[30]

E. THE DEPRESSED PATIENT

A seriously (psychotically) depressed accused's self-castigating mental state may produce a self-destructive posture inconsistent with being able to pursue their best legal interests. For example, a fifty-five-year-old psychotically depressed male kills a family member, believing that

24 *Ibid*; *Adam*, above note 21; *R v Krivicic*, above note 21.

25 *Adam*, above note 21 at para 29; *R v Iverson*, [2014] BCJ No 643 (SC).

26 *R v Fortune*, [2009] OJ No 5135 (SCJ); *R v Krivicic*, above note 21.

27 *R v Jobb*, [2008] SJ No 764 (CA).

28 *Dusky v United States*, 362 US 402 (1960).

29 Andrew D Reisner et al, "Competency to Stand Trial and Defendants Who Lack Insight into Their Mental Illness" (2013) 41 *Journal of the American Academy of Psychiatry and the Law* 85.

30 *Ibid* at 89.

in so doing he is sparing that loved one the worse fate of life in a living hell. His understanding of trial process is intact, but he suffers nihilistic delusions, is guilt ridden and punishment seeking, and is indifferent to his outcome. His willingness to engage in meaningful communication and strategizing that will result in the best disposition of his case is impaired because of marked defects in insight. He *understands* the nature, object, and possible outcome of the proceedings, and can confer with his lawyer in a relatively superficial way, but cannot, due to *impairment*, initiate or respond favourably to any action that might serve to exonerate, mitigate, and so on. A less clinically depressed but self-loathing individual by personality predisposition (i.e., masochistic personality) may similarly fail to disclose information that could exonerate or mitigate.[31]

F. THE INTELLECTUALLY LIMITED AND SUGGESTIBLE ACCUSED

Intellectually limited persons often try to conceal their deficits. In addition, they are known to be much more vulnerable to suggestion than the rest of the population.[32] Intellectually limited accused who, for whatever reason, have come to *falsely* believe that they are culpable for an act are more than likely incapable of appreciating the legal predicament itself. The issue here is not choice but capacity.[33]

G. THE PARANOID ACCUSED

Paranoid accused are likely to view criminal prosecution as an extension of a conspiracy against them and, as such, a perversion of justice. Paranoid delusions are not synonymous with unfitness. Paranoid accused often have well-preserved cognitive abilities. Their perspective on the world, however, is unique and skewed. Pervasive paranoia detracts from the "implicit assumption (that the accused's) primary

---

31 Kenneth L Appelbaum, "Criminal Defendants Who Desire Punishment" (1990) 18 *Bulletin of the American Academy of Psychiatry and the Law* 385.

32 Bryan Tully & David Cahill, *Police Interviewing of the Mentally Handicapped: An Experimental Study* (London: Police Foundation, 1984).

33 ICH Clare & GH Gudjonsson, "Interrogative Suggestibility, Confabulation, and Acquiescence in People with Mild Learning Disabilities (Mental Handicap): Implications for Reliability During Police Interrogations" (1993) 32:3 *British Journal of Clinical Psychology* 295.

goal is to be acquitted."[34] For example, an intelligent middle-aged woman charged with mischief and harassment understood "the mechanical elements of court process," the charges against her (which she believed to have been conjured up), and the supposed benefit of having a lawyer. Believing that her lawyer was not to be trusted, she chose to forfeit representation, much the way Taylor did. She was found unfit to stand trial. Her rejection of the benefit of legal representation was the decision of a person suffering from active mental illness that was impinging on her *ability* to decide. The paranoia was so pervasive that she was "unable ... to conduct [her] defence."[35]

H. THE MANIC ACCUSED

Grandiosity is often a central finding in mania. Grandiose patients may have preserved cognitive functioning, so that they would easily be able to recite the basics of the trial process. Such accused may, however, have a distorted view of the trial process and their role in it. The accused may believe that they are above the trial process, may see it as little more than a contrived source of amusement, or may wish to use the trial as a vehicle for disseminating their delusional views. For example, a forty-year-old manic man demonstrated a good understanding of the trial process. He believed, however, that he was a powerful god-like being, and that he therefore could not be tried by an ordinary person or persons. Criteria (a) and (b) of the *Criminal Code* definition of "unfit to stand trial" require only that he *understand* the trial process and the possible consequences of a conviction (as opposed to *appreciating* them), and he was able to meet that threshold. He could certainly communicate with counsel (criterion (c)), if he chose to, but his mental illness *prevented* him from taking advantage of legal representation.

* * * * *

In summary, there are many common clinical conditions that produce symptomatology sufficiently impactful that the accused will not

---

34 Robert D Miller et al, "Evaluation of Competency to Stand Trial in Defendants Who Do Not Want To Be Defended Against the Crimes Charged" (1987) 15:4 *American Academy of Psychiatry and the Law Online* 371.

35 *Criminal Code*, RSC 1985, c C-46, s 2.

receive a fair trial, yet these conditions will not be detected with the limited cognitive capacity test.

Ten-Point Review

1) Accused found to be unfit to stand trial are so found predominantly as a result of psychosis.
2) The most common diagnostic category among those deemed unfit is schizophrenia.
3) Intellectual deficit or organic disorders may also give rise to unfitness.
4) Mental disorder is a necessary but not sufficient condition with respect to a finding of unfitness.
5) An inability to remember the events leading to the charge before the court does not, by itself, lead to a finding of unfitness.
6) Being deaf and unable to speak does not, by itself, lead to a finding of unfitness.
7) There are several diagnostic categories that may produce conditions that would be missed by the limited cognitive capacity test yet would render the accused unfit to stand trial, from a fairness perspective.
8) From a fairness perspective, it is central that an accused's capacity to judge and choose has not been compromised by a mental disorder.
9) An ability to rationally communicate with counsel has been seen by some courts to be an essential ability.
10) Meaningful participation in the trial process requires a modicum of rationality.

CHAPTER 5

Assessing Fitness to Stand Trial

The evaluation of an accused person's fitness, or competency, to stand trial is one of the most fundamental psycholegal tasks that bring psychiatrists or psychologists into contact with the criminal courts. The assessment of fitness is a critical part of forensic psychiatry or psychology in the criminal setting, and the finding of such an assessment is clearly a matter of significance for the accused. From the court's perspective, assessment is an issue that will often require input from an "expert," although, strictly speaking, expert involvement is not required.

An evaluation of fitness to stand trial involves assessing the accused's functional abilities, behaviour, and capacities in relation to the charges being faced and the accused's overall legal predicament.[1] The elements of fitness include not only specific aspects of knowledge (i.e., the accused's ability to understand their legal situation and the trial process as well as their ability to communicate with counsel) but also the individual's beliefs, capacity to weigh variables, and affective state, as they relate to being fit to stand trial.

The approach to assessing fitness to stand trial is similar to the general principles used in the clinical approach to evaluating all competencies: individuals are competent for a particular task or with respect to a matter if they understand the nature of the matter at issue and the implications of acquiescing to or engaging in the task or function, or of foregoing it.

1 T Grisso, *Evaluating Competencies: Forensic Assessments and Instruments* (New York: Plenum, 1986) at 69.

An accused must have the intellectual/cognitive, psychological, and emotional wherewithal to participate in a criminal trial (and, as we've argued in Chapter 2, Section 4, to participate "meaningfully"), although varying degrees of these capacities will be called into play, depending on the complexity and duration of the criminal charges. The rules for fitness to stand trial protect both the accused and the criminal justice system by ensuring fairness through presence of mind and meaningful participation of the accused and the integrity and dignity of the criminal justice system, respectively. Although the fitness rules ultimately evolved out of a need to protect an accused from being subjected to criminal process unfairly (that is, when they were not well enough to respond to it), one should not forget the potentially onerous implications of a finding of unfitness. This is particularly so having regard to the presumption of innocence that should favour every accused. A finding of unfitness, particularly for an unwell accused who is refractory to treatment, could result in months, or potentially years, of deprivation of their liberty. In Canada, it may also result in the making of a treatment order, which compels the accused to submit to treatment with or without consent or capacity, for the limited purposes of rendering them fit.

This chapter will first provide the reader with an understanding of the statutory mechanism for bringing about a psychiatric assessment of an accused's fitness and the parameters within which it takes place. The chapter will then review the clinical considerations involved in conducting a fitness assessment and reporting its results. Third, we consider specific legal considerations in dealing with unfit accused—for example, the biennial need to establish a *prima facie* case, fluctuating fitness, and the consequences of a finding of unfitness. Reports in fitness cases is the fourth and concluding area of focus in this chapter.

A. EVIDENCE SUGGESTING UNFITNESS

Both the parties and the court are invested in ensuring that an unfit accused is not subject to criminal prosecution. Because of this shared concern, and a diminished climate of adversariness in respect of fitness concerns, the standard of "reasonable grounds" for a court to order an assessment (pursuant to section 672.11(a) of the *Criminal Code*[2]) is generally not too difficult to establish.

---

2 RSC 1985, c C-46.

Notwithstanding the generally less adversarial atmosphere of fitness matters, defence counsel must be vigilant about potential signs of unfitness in a client and must challenge opinions that an accused is fit if their experience with or appraisal of their client is at odds with that individual's history in court thus far and/or the clinical records. This issue has yet to emerge full-force in Canada, but American caselaw reflects numerous cases in which a lawyer's "failure to investigate *bona fide* signs of incompetence (i.e., unfitness) constitutes ineffective assistance of counsel and grounds for reversal of a criminal conviction."[3]

Signs that an accused is mentally unwell and could have difficulty managing the legal process may have been observed on arrest or once the accused is in custody at the police station or detention centre. Similarly, first observations of something amiss with the accused may have been noted by court staff and flagged for duty counsel, the prosecutor, or the judge. Some of the more commonly seen behaviours in accused that may raise concerns about fitness include the following:

- uncontrollable behaviour
- ranting/raving
- disjointed, vague, eccentric, and/or incomprehensible communications
- marked suspiciousness (e.g., looking about room, furtive glances, fearfulness)
- markedly dishevelled appearance
- markedly inappropriate affect (e.g., expressing anger or laughing for no apparent reason)
- expressing strange ideas
- lack of meaningful responses
- talking to self
- unresponsiveness or muteness
- withdrawal
- a high level of distraction or distractibility

The mere fact of a past psychiatric history or display of some problematic behaviour is generally insufficient for requiring an assessment, although it is clearly up to the judge to decide what factors or observed

3 See the discussion in Douglas Mossman et al, "AAPL Practice Guideline for Forensic Psychiatric Evaluation of Competence to Stand Trial" (2007) 35:4 *Journal of the American Academy of Psychiatry and the Law Supplement* S3 at S13.

behaviours support the decision to order an assessment. Table 5.1 provides some guidelines with respect to behaviours that might suggest the need for an assessment and those that would not necessarily support that need.

TABLE 5.1. REASONS TO ORDER A FITNESS ASSESSMENT

Evidence Supporting the Need for Assessment	Evidence Not Supporting the Need for Assessment
• specific information seen or heard indicating that the accused does not understand and/or cannot participate in court process • evidence of hallucinations and delusions impacting on the accused's understanding or ability to participate • evidence of significantly disordered thought • confusion • evidence of difficulty processing information • inability to concentrate • apathy or withdrawal • muteness • marked disruptive behaviour together with evidence of abnormal affect, perception, thought processes, and/or delusions • information about or evidence of marked impairment of mood (significant depression or elation) • evidence that the accused is suicidal	• accused has a psychiatric history, although there is no clear evidence of active mental illness at present • accused or counsel asks that the accused go to hospital • accused is homeless • desire to understand how and why the accused became a habitual criminal • accused is angry and loud (with no evidence or history of mental disorder or compromised understanding of the process) • accused's family conveys that the accused should be in hospital and not jail • accused is unkempt, dishevelled, and/or malodorous • allegations or evidence that the accused's behaviour at the relevant time was bizarre • accused interrupts the proceedings (with no evidence or history of mental disorder or compromised understanding of the process) • accused is seen muttering to self

B. ASSESSMENTS

Judges can order an assessment of an accused's fitness to stand trial where they have reasonable grounds to believe that psychiatric evidence is necessary to determine that issue.

1) Initiating the Assessment Process

According to the *Criminal Code*, an assessment order can be made at any stage of the proceedings (section 672.11) by the court upon its own motion or upon that of the accused or the Crown where there are reasonable grounds to believe that evidence regarding fitness is necessary. Where the Crown is making the application in respect of a summary conviction matter, subsection 672.12(2) of the *Code* specifies certain limitations. Undoubtedly, this is because the assessment process can be a tremendous incursion upon the liberty of the accused and therefore should be permitted only in the most obvious of cases. Many summary conviction matters may not justify such an incursion.

2) What Is Meant by "Assessment" and Who Can Carry It Out

According to section 672.1(1) of the *Criminal Code*, "assessment" means:

> ... an assessment by a medical practitioner or any other person who has been designated by the Attorney General as being qualified to conduct an assessment of the mental condition of the accused under an assessment order made under section 672.11 or 672.121, and any incidental observation or examination of the accused;

Note that an amendment to the definition of "assessment"[4] allows the attorney general to designate a non-medical practitioner as qualified to conduct an assessment of an accused for the purposes set out in subsections 672.11(a)–(e). (This ability presumably would apply most often in instances or geographical locations where medical practitioners familiar with the task of assessment are unavailable or scarce.)

While the above provisions pertain to the making of a court-ordered assessment, any witness who is able to give relevant information may be called at the actual trial of the issue of fitness. Key experts at such proceedings are typically psychiatrists and psychologists. Experts may be retained independently by either or both the Crown and the defence where the trial of the issue of fitness is particularly contentious.

The circumstances that allow a court to order a psychiatric assessment are specifically set out in section 672.11(a) of the *Criminal Code*:

4 *Criminal Code*, above note 2, s 672.1(1).

> **672.11** A court having jurisdiction over an accused in respect of an offence may order an assessment of the mental condition of the accused, if it has reasonable grounds to believe that such evidence is necessary to determine
> (a) whether the accused is unfit to stand trial;
> (b) whether the accused was, at the time of the commission of the alleged offence, suffering from a mental disorder so as to be exempt from criminal responsibility by virtue of subsection 16(1);
> (c) whether the balance of the mind of the accused was disturbed at the time of commission of the alleged offence, where the accused is a female person charged with an offence arising out of the death of her newly-born child;
> (d) the appropriate disposition to be made, where a verdict of not criminally responsible on account of mental disorder or unfit to stand trial has been rendered in respect of the accused;
> (d.1) whether a finding that the accused is a high-risk accused should be revoked under subsection 672.84(3); or
> (e) whether an order should be made under section 672.851 for a stay of proceedings, where a verdict of unfit to stand trial has been rendered against the accused.

A sample form for an assessment order is in Appendix B.

3) Where Fitness Assessments Should Be Conducted

As Roesch and Golding argued decades ago, the assessment of fitness to stand trial should generally not require an "inpatient" hospital remand.[5] More often than not, assessments of fitness to stand trial do not require fulsome "psychiatric assessments" that include lengthy medical histories and ancillary information not directly related to the question of the accused's fitness to stand trial. These assessments can be highly focused and circumscribed and can be conducted on an outpatient basis, at remand centres, or, especially with the emergence of mental health courts, at the courthouse.[6] This exercise can be facilitated and expedited

---

5 Ronald Roesch & Stephen L Golding, *Competency to Stand Trial* (Urbana: University of Illinois Press, 1980).

6 At the Mental Health Court in Toronto, which opened in 1998, a significant part of the work is the quick determination of fitness queries. The court is staffed by forensic psychiatrists who perform "stand down" assessments. These typically

with any number of "screening devices," described in Sections C(4) and (8) below, that have been developed over the past few decades.

a) In-Custody Fitness Evaluations

Section 672.16 of the *Criminal Code* presumes that an accused will be assessed out of custody. This occurs infrequently, however, as the preponderance of fitness evaluees are almost invariably too psychiatrically unwell for release. Once the court has reasonable grounds to question an accused's fitness for trial, it can remand the accused to the custody of a forensic facility (i.e., a hospital) for a period not exceeding five days in order to have their fitness evaluated. Where the accused and prosecutor agree, this period can be extended to thirty days (section 672.14) or, in compelling circumstances, for up to sixty days (section 672.15).

When an accused is in custody, there is greater opportunity to do a more comprehensive multidisciplinary assessment than is generally the case when the accused is in the community. These more intensive assessments allow for observation by various assessment team members when the accused may not be as guarded or defensive as they might be in a one-time out-of-custody clinical interview.

As with all issues in criminal prosecution, strategy is an important consideration. Some defence counsel may wish to carefully consider and discuss with their clients the merits and pitfalls of unnecessarily acquiescing to an inpatient assessment when an out-of-custody assessment is within reach. Although an inpatient assessment provides a richer understanding of the accused's psychiatric issues and limitations, and may afford the accused an opportunity for fuller stabilization, there are several risks, including the following:

If the accused's condition has deteriorated to the point that assessors were concerned about that individual's well-being, this could compel the assessors to pursue treating the accused involuntarily, by obtaining substitute consent, if the accused were found incapable and was not inclined to take medication.

The potential exists that, within the relatively high scrutiny of an inpatient assessment unit, the accused could reveal some information, or say something contrary to their interests, to persons and in

---

obviate the necessity for an inpatient assessment. The assessments are performed within hours of the accused's arrest (or the next day). Where there are grounds to believe the accused is unfit, the issue is tried at the court the same day.

circumstances that do not provide the accused with the protections contemplated by section 672.21 of the *Criminal Code* (i.e. protected statements).

In the past, it was more common for fitness assessments to be carried out at jails or in the holding cells of courthouses. This may still be the case in some jurisdictions, although these environments are generally noisy, stressful, and, at times, lacking in privacy. Because environmental factors are known to enhance or diminish capacity, mental health courts often provide suitable offices where fitness assessments can be conducted by psychiatrists.

b) Out-of-Custody Fitness Evaluations

Because fitness can usually be determined through a brief assessment, many clinicians and others argue that inpatient assessments (especially "in-hospital" assessments) are costly and ultimately unnecessary to decide a fitness issue.[7] If the accused is able to have an out-of-custody evaluation, the defence lawyer may ask the judge to designate a particular clinician or facility for the evaluation (section 672.13(1)(a)). Most communities, even larger cities, generally have only one psychiatric facility where a fitness assessment could be carried out on an out-of-custody accused. If the parties do not select a particular clinician (who usually will have been approached beforehand), then only the facility or "forensic service" of the facility will be named in the assessment order.

In Part XX.1 of the *Criminal Code*, the court is not entitled to order that the accused be assessed at any hospital. It is limited to those hospitals that have been "designated" by the provincial/territorial Minister of Health.

> "hospital" means a place in a province that is designated by the Minister of Health for the province for the custody, treatment or assessment of an accused in respect of whom an assessment order, a disposition or a placement decision is made[8]

It is both cost effective and more expeditious to deal with the question of fitness in a way other than through lengthy inpatient assessments, which typically generate unnecessarily bulky reports with much

---

7 Patricia A Zapf & Ronald Roesch, "A Comparison of the MacCAT-CA and the FIT for Making Determinations of Competency to Stand Trial" (2001) 24:1 *International Journal of Law and Psychiatry* 81.

8 *Criminal Code*, above note 2, s 672.1(1).

surplusage and potentially protracted incursions upon the accused's liberty.

4) Duration of Assessments

Mindful of the extent to which assessments may infringe the liberty of a presumptively innocent person, the *Criminal Code* sets fairly tight temporal parameters for the conducting of assessments. In this regard, the *Code* states that:

> **672.14(2)** No assessment order to determine whether the accused is unfit to stand trial shall be in force for more than five days, excluding holidays and the time required for the accused to travel to and from the place where the assessment is to be made, unless the accused and the prosecutor agree to a longer period not exceeding thirty days.
>
> *Exception for compelling circumstances*
>
> (3) Despite subsections (1) and (2), a court or Review Board may make an assessment order that remains in force for sixty days if the court or Review Board is satisfied that compelling circumstances exist that warrant it.
>
> *Extension*
>
> **672.15(1)** Subject to subsection (2), a court or Review Board may extend an assessment order, of its own motion or on the application of the accused or the prosecutor made during or at the end of the period during which the order is in force, for any further period that is required, in its opinion, to complete the assessment of the accused.
>
> *Maximum duration of extensions*
>
> (2) No extension of an assessment order shall exceed thirty days, and the period of the initial order together with all extensions shall not exceed sixty days.

While assessment orders are operative, all other hearings and applications are put on hold. For example, *per* section 672.17, no order for the release or detention of an accused shall be made while an assessment order is in force:

> During the period that an assessment order made by a court in respect of an accused charged with an offence is in force, no order for the

interim release or detention of the accused may be made by virtue of Part XVI or section 679 in respect of that offence or an included offence.

C. CLINICAL CONSIDERATIONS

1) Mental Disorder

As discussed in the preceding chapters, mental disorder and lack of fitness to stand trial are not synonymous. The reference to "mental disorder" in section 2 of the *Criminal Code* reflects back to the term "disease of the mind," which is a legal term and not a medical one. "Disease of the mind" has been defined by the Supreme Court of Canada in *R v Cooper* as "any illness, disorder, or abnormal condition which impairs the human mind and its functioning."[9] Consequently, fitness problems can be the result of a number of conditions that impair cognitive functioning (e.g., problems related to memory, attention/concentration, judgment), perception (e.g., hallucinations), thought content (e.g., delusions), thought processes (e.g., lack of clarity of thought and comprehension), affect (e.g., inability to regulate emotions), and/or behaviour (e.g., lack of impulse control).

2) Psychopathology Encountered in Assessments

a) Characteristic Clinical Presentations

As was discussed in Chapter 4, clinical practice and the literature in the field make it clear that forms of psychotic disorders, particularly schizophrenia, are the most common mental disorders or conditions underpinning an initial concern, and, subsequently, a finding that the accused is unfit to stand trial.[10] A US study found a strong correlation between either psychosis or mental retardation (now "intellectual disability") and subsequent findings of unfitness to stand trial in patients with those conditions.[11]

---

9 *R v Cooper*, [1980] 1 SCR 1149 at 1159.

10 AE Daniel et al, "Factors Correlated with Psychiatric Recommendations of Incompetency and Insanity" (1984) 12:4 *Journal of Psychiatry and Law* 527; Ronald Roesch et al, "Evaluating Fitness to Stand Trial: A Comparative Analysis of Fit and Unfit Defendants" (1981) 4:1–2 *International Journal of Law and Psychiatry* 145.

11 MS Heller et al, "Intelligence, Psychosis, and Competency to Stand Trial" (1981) 9:4 *Bulletin of the American Academy of Psychiatry and the Law* 267.

Other conditions that are well represented in populations of people who were unfit to stand trial include mania, psychotic depression, and disorders associated with cognitive functioning (particularly intellectual disability and major neurocognitive disorder (formally dementia).[12] Neuropsychiatric conditions (e.g., Huntington's disease) are relatively uncommon foundational conditions for a finding of unfitness, and yet there are a number of accused with Huntington's who have been declared unfit and are subject to the jurisdiction of provincial review boards.[13]

Fetal alcoholic spectrum disorders (FASD), a range of congenital conditions arising from prenatal exposure to alcohol, are over-represented in the criminal justice arena, particularly in the area of youth criminal justice.[14] Of the various hallmark diagnostic features of FASD (including sentinel facial features, limitations in language and communication, behavioural problems, and impulse control), which in the *Diagnostic and Statistical Manual of Mental Disorders* of the American Psychiatric Association (DSM-5) is diagnosed as "Other Specified Neurodevelopmental Disorder: Neurodevelopmental Disorder Associated with Prenatal Alcohol Exposure (ND-PAE),"[15] cognitive limitations (related to learning, memory, executive functioning, intelligence, and attention) feature prominently and may impact fitness to stand trial.[16] Brown et al summarize the various cognitive limitations in FASD/ND-PAE accused that have implications for their fitness, as follows:

---

12 Robert A Nicholson & Karen E Kugler, "Competent and Incompetent Criminal Defendants: A Quantitative Review of Comparative Research" (1991) 109:3 *Psychology Bulletin* 355.

13 Huntington's disease is an inherited disease (autosomal dominant) leading to progressive degeneration of certain parts of the brain, and associated with physical, cognitive, emotional, and behavioural dyscontrol. On Huntington's as a basis for unfitness to stand trial, see, for example, *Harrison (Re)*, [2012] ORBD No 1344; *Whittaker-Johnson (Re)*, [2003] ORBD No 1483, and the discussion in Ian Freckelton, "Huntington's Disease and Fitness to Stand Trial" (2016) 24 *Psychiatry, Psychology and Law* 1.

14 Kent Roach & Andrea Bailey, "The Relevance of Fetal Alcohol Spectrum Disorder in Canadian Criminal Law from Investigation to Sentencing" (2009) 42 *University of British Columbia Law Review* 1.

15 American Psychiatric Association, *Diagnostic and Statistical Manual of Mental Disorders*, 5th ed (Washington, DC: American PsychiatricPublishing, 2013) [DSM-5].

16 Karina R Gagnier et al, "A Need for Closer Examination of FASD by the Criminal Justice System: Has the Call Been Answered?" (2011) 18:3 *Journal of Population Therapeutics and Clinical Pharmacology* 426; JM Brown et al "Fetal Alcohol Spectrum Disorders (FASD) and Competency to Stand Trial (CST): Suggestions for a 'Best Practices' Approach to Forensic Evaluation" (2017) 52 *International Journal of Law and Psychiatry* 19.

- *Intellectual deficits* could impact understanding of the process, appreciation of one's place in it, decision making, and communication with counsel.
- *Deficient attentional control* could impinge on psychological abilities related to fitness. Notably, in this regard, attention deficit hyperactivity disorder (ADHD) is the most frequent comorbid condition among people with FASD and may affect an accused's ability to follow the proceedings and communicate with counsel in a meaningful way.
- *Memory and learning* problems, common in FASD, may prevent such accused from learning and remembering important legal information.
- *Shortcomings in executive functioning* could affect an accused's ability to weigh options, foresee consequences, integrate past experiences with present learning, and fetter impulses.
- *Deficits in communication skills* (language, comprehension, verbal reasoning, and social communication) are often a function of cognitive impairment and/or active psychotic symptoms associated with FASD. With respect to the issue of fitness, these can compromise the accused's ability to communicate with counsel.[17]
- *Suggestibility* could impinge on an accused's ability to participate meaningfully in the proceedings, as the accused's testimony may mislead the court if accepted (as is the case with confabulation) and cause an unjust result. FASD patients can be childlike and passive,[18] particularly in their dealings with those in authority.[19] Concerns about suggestibility should increase in the face of an FASD accused who also has significant cognitive deficits.[20]

3) Uncooperative Accused and Mutism

Lack of cooperation is a fairly common feature in the assessment of mentally ill accused. Limited cooperation can take many forms, including

17 See, for example, Nicholson & Kugler, above note 12 at 363.

18 Sadie Westrup, "Fetal Alcohol Spectrum Disorders: As Prevalent as Autism?" (2013) 29:3 *Educational Psychology in Practice* 309.

19 Natalie N Brown et al, "Suggestibility and Fetal Alcohol Spectrum Disorders: I'll Tell You Anything You Want to Hear" (2011) 39:1 *Journal of Psychiatry and Law* 39.

20 Jerrod Brown et al, "Deleterious Effects of Fetal Alcohol Spectrum Disorder on Competency to Stand Trial" (2016) 1 *Journal of Special Populations* 1.

muteness (wilful or psychotic), disinclination to give clear and/or full answers due to thought disorder and/or a psychotic process, negativistic behaviour, anger and belligerence, evasiveness, and facetiousness.

Deciding whether an accused is purposefully or psychotically mute—"mute of malice" or "mute by visitation"—has a long history in the common law.[21] Mutism can occur in a wide range of psychiatric conditions, including depression, schizophrenia, anxiety disorders (especially in children), organic states, and hysteria (or as a purely physical condition, as in the *R v Isaac* case discussed in Chapter 4).[22] Paranoid patients may be wary of speaking to assessors, whom they may perceive to be part of the system that has "done them wrong" or is "out to get them."[23]

Assessors faced with an uncooperative accused who cannot or will not answer the usual fitness-related questions may feel at a loss regarding what to say in a report and in court. Options may include suggesting re-evaluation on another day or remanding the accused to a forensic psychiatric assessment facility for a longer (five- to thirty-day) assessment. An assessor may also interpret a lack of cooperation, particularly muteness, as strong, but obviously refutable, evidence that the accused is unfit.

Lack of cooperation should be treated as an abnormal finding until evidence to the contrary is provided. At the same time, muteness purportedly on the basis of a psychiatric condition is uncommon these days. Its presence should, therefore elevate the clinician's index of suspicion about the possibility of malingering,[24] a theory best disposed of through scrupulous and detailed assessment.

4) Malingered Unfitness

Malingered unfitness is relatively uncommon—in the US context, it occurs in about 10 percent of fitness evaluations[25]—but the phenomenon

21 Nigel Walker, "*Butler v the CLRC* and Others" [1981] *The Criminal Law Review* 596; AE Daniel & Phillip J Resnick, "Mutism, Malingering, and Competency to Stand Trial" (1987) 15:3 *Bulletin of the American Academy of Psychiatry and the Law* 301.

22 *R v Isaac*, [2009] OJ No 5804 (Ct J).

23 CM Haw & CC Cordess, "Mutism and the Problem of the Mute Defendant" (1988) 28:2 *Medicine, Science and the Law* 157.

24 Daniel & Resnick, above note 21 at 308.

25 Shayna Gothard et al, "Feigning Incompetence to Stand Trial: An Investigation of the Georgia Court Competency Test" (1995) 19:4 *Law and Human Behavior* 363 at 368.

is known to all forensic clinicians. Its uncommonness may be because, in most contexts, it is of no strategic advantage. Being found unfit does not make a prosecution "go away" and may in fact result in protracted limitations on one's liberty. Nevertheless, malingered unfitness does occur.

In *R v Sabourin* (2006),[26] the accused, who pled guilty to tax evasion and fraud, argued that he was unfit to be sentenced. Sabourin, it was demonstrated, had feigned a dementing illness based on inconclusive evidence of a heritable cerebrovascular ischemic condition and on likely artifactual but (at first blush) seemingly impressive intracranial opacities that could be seen on an MRI. The accused went as far as being admitted to a facility for patients with dementia and attending Alzheimer's Society meetings. His answers to the usual fitness-related questions were for the most part absurd and, in any event, out of keeping with the condition he purported to suffer from. A careful investigative approach uncovered numerous inconsistencies and fabrications as well as abilities that did not accord with his condition. He was found to be malingering unfitness in order to avoid incarceration.

Although malingering must be hypothesized and ruled out (or ruled in) in every psycholegal assessment, extra care and a high index of suspicion are in order where circumstances suggest that it is squarely on the table. Apart from accessing collateral information (documents about and individuals who have known the accused), special forensic context tests can be very helpful. The Structured Interview of Reported Symptoms (SIRS 1992)[27] and the Miller Forensic Assessment of Symptoms Test (M-FAST 2005)[28] are commonly used instruments to test for the presence of feigned psychiatric illness and impairment, whereas the Test of Memory Malingering (TOMM)[29] assists in evaluating malingered cognitive impairment. Unusual circumstances, special conditions, uncommon claims, and concerns about malingering should prompt clinicians to pursue consultation with a psychologist.

26 *Sabourin (Re)*, 2006 CanLII 63721 (Ont SCJ).

27 Richard Rogers, "Structured Interview of Reported Symptoms" in Irving B Weiner & W Edward Craighead, eds, *Corsini Encyclopedia of Psychology* (Odessa, FL: Psychological Assessment Resources, 2010) at 1–2.

28 Holly A Miller, "The Miller Forensic Assessment of Symptoms Test (M-FAST) Test Generalizability and Utility across Race Literacy, and Clinical Opinion" (2005) 32:6 *Criminal Justice and Behavior* 591.

29 Tom N Tombaugh, *Test of Memory Malingering: TOMM* (Toronto: MHS, 1996).

5) Amnesia

Amnesia is a vexing problem in the criminal arena. It is claimed quite frequently by accused — in 25 to 75 percent of cases, depending on the severity of the charges (claims of amnesia increase with the severity of the charge faced).[30]

Many violent (non-predatory) offences are committed in highly charged emotional states. These states can impact the storage and retrieval of memory, as can alcohol and drugs, which are also a frequent feature in violent crime. Moreover, there is high co-occurrence between serious mental disorder and substance use.[31] These intersecting considerations of mental illness, substance abuse, violent crime, and amnesia can be, and often are, of linchpin significance in forensic assessments of fitness (and criminal responsibility).[32]

As discussed in Chapter 4, amnesia with respect to the events giving rise to criminal allegations does not, of itself, render an accused unfit to stand trial. Memory impairment for the critical events is a common finding in violent crime.[33] When "memory difficulties" are not actually the result of wilful suppression, they are often attributable to substance use prior to the act, the inability to create and retrieve memory because of the marked affective disruption the accused experienced at the time of the act, or both. Dissociation, psychosis, or organic factors can also be implicated.[34] Interestingly, but perhaps not unexpectedly, accused with psychotic disorders are much less likely to claim amnesia than accused with other diagnoses, particularly substance abusers.[35]

30 Maaike Cima et al, "Claims of Crime-Related Amnesia in Forensic Patients" (2004) 27 *International Journal of Law and Psychiatry* 215; Daniel Schacter, "Amnesia and Violent Crime; How Much Do We Really Know?" (1986) 41 *American Psychologist* 286; G Swihart, J Yuille, & S Porter, "The Rule of State-Dependent Memory in 'Red-Outs'" (1999) 22:3–4 *International Journal of Law and Psychiatry* 199.

31 Elizabeth Reisinger Walker & Benjamin G Druss, "Cumulative Burden of Comorbid Mental Disorders, Substance Use Disorders, Chronic Medical Conditions, and Poverty on Health Among Adults in the USA" (2017) 22:6 *Psychology, Health and Medicine* 727.

32 RG Stout & RS Farooque, "Claims of Amnesia for Criminal Offenses: Psychopathology, Substance Abuse, and Malingering" (2008) 53:5 *Journal of Forensic Sciences* 1218.

33 Dominique Bourget & Laurie Whitehurst, "Amnesia and Crime" (2007) 35:4 *Journal of the American Academy of Psychiatry and the Law Online* 469.

34 See *ibid* for a review of amnesia and crime.

35 Stout & Farooque, above note 32.

American courts have consistently refused to equate amnesia with unfitness.[36] The leading US case in the area, *Wilson v United States* (1968),[37] set out six factors to assist courts in determining whether an accused claiming amnesia was fit:

- the impact of amnesia on the accused's ability to consult with and assist their lawyer;
- the effect of the amnesia on the defendant's ability to testify, should they choose to do so;
- the extent to which the evidence—including evidence specific to the alleged offence or any potential alibi evidence—can be reconstructed using extrinsic information;
- the extent to which governmental agencies or individuals (e.g., law enforcement and prosecution) contributed to the reconstruction of events;
- the strength of the prosecution's case, and whether the accused could establish a defence or alibi is they were not amnestic; and
- any other factors relevant to the question of whether the defendant's trial was fair.[38]

6) The Clinical Assessment

The evaluation of an accused's fitness to stand trial may combine a brief general psychiatric assessment (to establish the nature of the mental disorder) with a series of specific questions designed to access the accused's understanding of their legal predicament and its potential outcomes, the trial process, and ability to relate to counsel.

It is incumbent on the evaluator to establish that the accused

- understands the charges
- understands the object of the proceedings (i.e., what is at issue)
- understands the possible consequences of a conviction
- understands the roles of the judge, prosecutor, defence counsel, witnesses, experts, and so on

36 Ronald Roesch, Patricia A Zapf, & Stephen D Hart, *Forensic Psychology and Law* (Hoboken, NJ: John Wiley & Sons, 2009).

37 *Wilson v United States*, 391 F 2d 460 (DC Cir 1968).

38 *Ibid* at 463–64.

- understands the pleas available to a person facing charges
- understands the purpose of taking an oath and is aware that there are consequences for perjury
- understands the role of a jury and has the ability to exercise a choice with respect to a jury trial
- has the ability to evaluate available legal strategy and defences
- has the ability to understand potentially available psychiatric defences and make a choice in that regard
- has the ability to provide their lawyer with an intelligible version of the events and engage in a meaningful dialogue with that lawyer in order to answer questions relevant to their defence
- has the capacity to work with counsel to appraise the evidence and challenge witnesses
- has the capacity to disclose relevant information
- has the capacity to testify, if necessary

While an expert psychiatrist always needs to satisfy themself that an accused has a sufficient understanding of their charges, it may be unclear how much detail need be gone into. That will depend on the accused and the circumstances.

Notwithstanding the protected statements provisions in section 672.21 of the *Criminal Code* and the evaluator's cautions to the accused about lack of confidentiality provided at the outset of the assessment, evaluators should be careful about posing questions or developing a line of questioning that put accused in the position of providing potentially inculpatory information about the events in question. Evaluees referred for fitness assessments have presumptively been identified as having mental health problems, and hence may be perceptually and/or cognitively compromised. In the event that an accused embarks on a potentially self-damaging discussion, it would be reasonable for the evaluator to intervene and re-caution the accused on point.

Even with the above approach, if the evaluator receives inculpatory information, they could be faced with the decision of whether and how much to include in the report (beyond indicating that the accused was aware of their charges). In instances like this, the evaluator might choose to leave the problematic detail out but flag in the report that information of this kind was received, and then look to the parties and/or the court for guidance.

As a general rule, information received in the context of a fitness (or any) assessment should only be included in a report to the extent that it is necessary to support the opinions.

A fitness evaluation would also seek to establish if abnormalities in the accused's mental state could interfere with their ability to participate in their defence. Examples of such abnormalities include the following:

- self-defeating motivation (e.g., a psychotic depression), which may drive the accused to seek punishment and to not seek a defence
- cognitive impairment (e.g., Alzheimer's disease), which may prevent the accused from being able to follow the proceedings
- a thought disorder (e.g., schizophrenia), which may prevent the accused from processing information in a logical and coherent manner
- psychosis and a high level of agitation (e.g., schizophrenia, mania, organic psychosis), which may prevent the accused from being able to control behaviours and impulses well enough to manage being in court

As Mossman points out (and as is the case for all things in respect of which an individual may or may not be capable), "most actual competence to stand trial evaluees are neither completely lacking in, nor perfectly endowed with, competence-related capacities and qualities."[39] He invites examiners to keep in mind the dimensional nature of fitness-related attributes and skills including intelligence, rationality, cooperation, and so on.

7) Focus Required in a Forensic Evaluation

As a cautionary note, the clinician/assessor/expert must not lose sight of the unusual circumstances of the forensic arena within which they are operating. First of all, the "client" is not the "patient" or "accused" being assessed, but rather the court that ordered the assessment, or the lawyer who retained the expert for the purposes of their client's defence. This situation, which is unlike most other areas of practice,

39 Douglas Mossman, "Conceptualizing and Characterizing Accuracy in Assessments of Competence to Stand Trial" (2008) 36 *Journal of the American Academy of Psychiatry and the Law* 340 at 340.

is significant in that, when the court orders an assessment to assist with the determination of, for example, fitness to stand trial, opinions regarding other issues are generally not admissible, as they are not logically probative of the issue in dispute. Courts may receive opinion evidence only in very limited circumstances in respect of very specific issues when it is *necessary* to do so. So, while in typical practice a psychiatrist may often provide a robust, wide-ranging, and complete psychiatric report to a referral source, that is not what is required in a court-ordered assessment. Clinicians must contain their report so that it is responsive only to the question(s) of the court. Background and context should be provided only to the extent that it is necessary in order to understand the ultimate opinion provided. At times, the expert not only reports on the question of fitness but overshoots the mark by providing opinions about certifiability, dangerousness, and criminal responsibility, which not only goes beyond the Court's Order or counsel's retainer but may provide confounding and obfuscating information. This scenario presents problems, as the other opinions, provided gratuitously, may not just be surplusage and unhelpful, but could be highly prejudicial to the accused. In the forensic arena, clinicians must suppress their reflex to tell all that they have discovered.

8) Fitness Evaluation Tools

Grisso[40] (2003) has consistently extolled the virtues of using forensic assessment instruments (FAIs) to determine an accused's fitness. FAIs create a common language for communicating results in terms that lend themselves to scientific investigation, and, perhaps most importantly, they assist examiners in ensuring that assessments capture clinical information specifically germane to the legal criteria for the matter at hand.[41]

Numerous fitness evaluation instruments are available. Most have been studied and found to have good psychometric properties (i.e., they reliably measure what they purport to measure). One of the earliest tools developed was the Fitness Interview Test, which was originally written in 1984 to assess fitness to stand trial in Canada based on

40 Grisso, above note 1.

41 Ames Robey, "Criteria for Competency to Stand Trial" (1965) 122 *American Journal of Psychiatry* 616.

the *Criminal Code* of Canada.[42] The test was revised in 1998 and is now known as the Fitness Interview Test Revised (FIT-R).[43] The revised version was designed specifically to assess competence to stand trial in the United States,[44] based on the Federal Standard for Competencies in the *United States Code*.[45] Some tests have been designed to follow the standard within a particular jurisdiction: for example, the Evaluation of Competency to Stand Trial—Revised (ECST-R)[46] accords with the *Dusky* test used in the United States for competency to stand trial.

The MacArthur Competence Assessment Tool—Criminal Adjudication (MacCAT-CA)[47] is a twenty-two-item test that assesses three domains:

1) the evaluee's *understanding* of basic information about the legal process;
2) their ability to *reason* what information, drawn from a vignette read to the accused at the outset of the assessment, would be important to tell the lawyer; and
3) their ability to *appreciate* their own legal predicament.

Pinals et al[48] have expressed some concerns about the MacCAT-CA's limits, particularly its inability to tap into the complexities of an accused's case. In addition, that test does not address concerns about either amnesia (if raised) or malingering.

The Interdisciplinary Fitness Interview (the IFI and IFI-Revised)[49] probes thirty-one relatively specific psycholegal abilities related to

---

42 R Roesch, CD Webster, & D Eaves, *The Fitness Interview Test: A Method for Examining Fitness to Stand Trial*, Research Report of the Centre of Criminology, University of Toronto (Toronto: Centre of Criminology, 1984).

43 Zapf & Roesch, above note 7.

44 Jodi L Viljoen, Gina M Vincent, & Ronald Roesch, "Assessing Adolescent Defendants' Adjudicative Competence: Interrater Reliability and Factor Structure of the Fitness Interview Test–Revised" (2006) 33:4 *Criminal Justice and Behavior* 467.

45 18 USC § 4241.

46 Richard Rogers, Chad E Tillbrook, & Kenneth W Sewell, *Evaluation of Competency to Stand Trial—Revised (ECST-R)* (Odessa, FL: Psychological Assessment Resources, 2004).

47 SK Hoge et al, *The MacArthur Competence Assessment Tool—Criminal Adjudication* (Odessa, FL: Psychological Assessment Resources, 1999).

48 Debra A Pinals et al, "Practical Application of the MacArthur Competence Assessment Tool—Criminal Adjudication (MacCAT-CA) in a Public Sector Forensic Setting" (2006) 34 *Journal of the American Academy of Psychiatry and the Law* 179.

49 IFI: Stephen L Golding et al, "Assessment and Conceptualization of Competency to Stand Trial: Preliminary Data on the Interdisciplinary Fitness Interview" (1984) 8:3–4 *Law and Human Behavior* 321. IFI-Revised: Stephen L Golding, *Interdisciplinary*

competence to stand trial. The IFI was designed to compel consideration of both mental status and legal items. It contemplates scoring on a scale ranging from "no or minimal incapacity" to "substantial incapacity." The designers of the instrument suggest that, ideally, it should be scored by a lawyer and mental health professional who are jointly conducting the interviews.

The Georgia Court Competency Test (GCCT),[50] which assesses foundational (basic) fitness more so than decisional competency, has undergone a number of revisions by different groups. It was originally developed to screen out accused who are clearly competent. The twenty-one-item screening tool has shown high levels of validity and reliability.[51] The three domains the GCCT looks at are courtroom layout (i.e., visual knowledge of the physical court environment), general legal knowledge, and specific legal knowledge.

Other tests include the Competency Assessment Instrument (CAI),[52] which uses a thirteen-item semi-structured interview format, with items scored on a 5-point scale, and the Competency Screening Test (CST),[53] which uses a twenty-two-item sentence-completion format to screen out clearly competent accused, thereby avoiding costly and lengthy assessments.

Fitness tests have been developed for special populations, including accused with intellectual limitations. The Competence Assessment for Standing Trial for Defendants with Mental Retardation (CAST-MR)[54] is a fifty-item questionnaire, administered orally to an accused, that is based on the US *Dusky* standard. It is recommended as just one component of a wider assessment of intellectual disability in an accused.

Fitness Interview — Revised (Salt Lake City: University of Utah, Department of Psychology, 1993).

50 RW Wildman et al, *The Georgia Competency Test: An Attempt to Develop a Rapid Quantitative Measure of Fitness for Trial* (Milledgeville, GA: Forensic Services Decision, Central State Hospital, 1978) [unpublished].

51 Robert A Nicholson et al, "A Comparison of Instruments for Assessing Competency to Stand Trial" (1988) 12:3 *Law and Human Behavior* 313.

52 AL McGarry & WJ Curran, *Competency to Stand Trial and Mental Illness* (Rockville, MD: National Institute of Mental Health, 1973).

53 Paul D Lipsiff et al, "Competency for Trial: A Screening Instrument" (1971) 128:1 *American Journal of Psychiatry* 105.

54 Caroline T Everington, "The Competency Assessment for Standing Trial for Defendants with Mental Retardation (CAST-MR): A Validation Study" (1990) 17:2 *Criminal Justice and Behavior* 147.

Siegert and Weiss[55] have recently underscored the value of using such a tool when evaluating accused with intellectual deficits, a group that often learns to mask deficits through adaptation, as seen in a number of developmental conditions.

Evaluation of Competency to Stand Trial—Revised (ECST-R),[56] a tool designed to assess adults facing criminal charges, including accused who have an IQ in the 60–69 range, has eighteen items organized on three scales to address a defendant's factual and rational understanding of the trial process in accordance with the *Dusky* standard. The uniqueness of the tool lies in its inclusion of twenty-eight additional scaled items to screen for malingered psychosis and cognitive impairment.[57]

D. LEGAL CONSIDERATIONS

1) The *Prima Facie* Case

As discussed in Chapter 2, Section 9, and Chapter 3, the fitness issue will not be litigated until the Crown has established a *prima facie* case—that is, until the Crown is in a position to show that the accused committed the alleged acts. A trial judge can therefore delay dealing with the fitness issue until the Crown has established that there is sufficient evidence as to the accused's culpability that a defence/response is required. A *prima facie* case can be brought out in evidence, or, alternatively, the accused may waive their right in that regard—for example, when it seems clear to the defence that the facts will be proven and there is nothing to be gained by putting the Crown to that task.

After a *prima facie* case has been established and the accused has been found unfit to stand trial, section 672.33(1) of the *Criminal Code* requires the court to hold an inquiry within two years of the verdict of unfit, and every two years thereafter, into whether a *prima facie* case continues to exist. Again, the onus to establish a *prima facie* case is on the

55 Mark Siegert & Kenneth J Weiss, "Who Is an Expert? Competency Evaluations in the Mental Retardation and Borderline Intelligence" (2007) 35 *Journal of the American Academy of Psychiatry and the Law* 346.

56 R Rogers & CE Tillbrook, *Evaluation of Competency to Stand Trial—Revised (ECST-R)* (Denton, TX: University of North Texas, 1998) [unpublished].

57 R Rogers et al, "The Detection of Feigned Mental Disorders on Specific Competency Measures" (2002) 14:2 *Psychological Assessment* 177.

Crown. As noted by Roach, "[t]hese safeguards are designed to ensure that a factually innocent accused is not subject to detention in the same manner as an accused who committed the criminal act."[58]

The requirement that the Crown establish a *prima facie* case in the first instance, and then every two years post-verdict, perhaps helps to offset the Crown's right to raise the fitness issue (as can the court, on its own accord), thereby creating a scenario in which a yet-to-be-tried but unfit accused remains subject to the jurisdiction of both the Review Board and the court. If the accused remains unfit and continues to represent a significant threat, and if a *prima facie* case is repeatedly established, an accused could be detained indefinitely (either in hospital, if required, or in the community, subject to conditions and restrictions).

2) Fluctuating Fitness

As discussed in Chapter 2, Section B(6), oscillating fitness presents a particular challenge to the legal process and to clinicians attempting to assess and characterize an accused's fitness. Fluctuations in mental state (and the capacities that depend on cognitive, affective, and perceptual intactness) are a characteristic of many serious mental disorders and medical conditions. The mental state of a mentally ill accused, particularly a psychotic individual, is often not static and may fluctuate on an hour-to-hour (if not minute-to-minute) basis. Serial capacity assessments are commonly conducted by consultation-liaison psychiatrists whose frequent role in hospital is to evaluate capacity to consent to treatment in medically unstable patients with fluctuating mental abilities.[59]

What, then, can be said of an individual whose mental state has been fluctuating in tandem with their fitness to stand trial? Anecdotally, this occurs with some regularity in many mentally ill accused and can be a vexing problem for both the parties and the court. The underlying condition — for example, delusional disorder — may remain constant, but variations in the intensity with which the accused harbours the beliefs and concomitant affective disturbance (and impact on behaviour) can result in impairment of capacities needed for fitness. The unfortunate

58 Kent Roach, *Criminal Law*, 7th ed (Toronto: Irwin Law, 2018) at 314.

59 Mary Alice O'Dowd et al, "A Noncompliant Patient with Fluctuating Capacity" (1998) 20:5 *General Hospital Psychiatry* 317.

net effect for an accused who is found fit one day and unfit another, on a recurring basis, is to end up in the "no-man's land of law and psychiatry,"[60] in which pre-trial detention is prolonged and treatment potentially delayed—a result that is anathema to the spirit of the fitness rules, which is to ensure fairness and protection.

Courts, ever mindful of the presumption of fitness contained in section 672.22 of the *Criminal Code*, expect an expert to seize the moment, as it were, and provide an opinion that the accused is fit to stand trial, if that is what the clinical evaluation revealed at the time of the evaluation. Yet it may be that the accused was not fit to stand trial a short while before the assessment, nor will they predictably be fit to stand trial a short while after. It may be that the accused's fitness on the exact occasion of the assessment was fairly circumscribed to that brief temporal envelope. If the clinician believes this to be the case, this view must be communicated to the court.

As well, clinicians must remember that they are called to court because of their expertise with respect to mental illness, not the law. Nonetheless, fitness is a legal concept, and thus to opine on questions of fitness is to opine on the law. The question of fitness might be informed by evidence from an expert as to how an accused is presently functioning; but determining whether or not an accused is fit to stand trial is an "ultimate issue" decision to be made by the court. In the past, there were strictly enforced rules with respect to an expert offering opinions on such an ultimate issue. In recent years, these proscriptions have been relaxed considerably, but the principles remain the same.

As discussed in Chapter 2, Section A(3), the definition of "unfit to stand trial" in section 2 of the *Criminal Code of Canada*, requires that the accused be capable of "conduct[ing] a defence."[61] To that end, it is reasonable to interpret fitness to stand trial as having a prospective dimension. For accused subject to fluctuating fitness, it cannot be predicted that they will maintain fitness to stand trial for the foreseeable future, even after a pronouncement of fitness has been made. If it cannot be said that the accused can endure and participate in a trial of some complexity, then, arguably, they cannot be said to be fit to stand trial even if the examiner catches them in a fit or lucid interval.

---

60 Duncan Maccourt & Alan A Stone, "Caught in Limbo Between Law and Psychiatry" (2005) 22 *Psychiatric Times* 1.

61 *Criminal Code*, above note 2, s 2.

True fitness arguably requires (or should require) a degree of durability to the accused's mental state such that they will be able to engage meaningfully up to and throughout the legal proceeding. The corollary to this is that fitness is not an absolute or fixed value, but one on a sliding scale, tied to the duration and complexity of the legal proceeding with which the accused is confronted.[62] Clinicians familiar with the long list of areas in which an individual may or may not be competent (e.g., testamentary and contractual capacity, competence to consent to treatment, and so on) appreciate that there are many permutations and combinations of factors related both to the evaluee and the environment that enhance or diminish capacity for the given task.

Regarding assessments of fitness to stand trial, it is at least worth thinking about the physical environment of the assessment, the comfort level of the evaluee, and the skill of the examiner, to name but a few variables. As regards an accused's ability to communicate with counsel, the lawyer's experience (particularly with mentally ill clients) is rarely talked about but is clearly relevant to the discussion. The complexity and seriousness of the charge(s) and the level of court that tries the accused are also key considerations relevant to the question of fitness. Buchanan[63] notes that it is intuitive to be more careful in avoiding mistakes when the stakes are higher. An accused, for example, contending with a relatively minor charge, for which they intend to plead guilty and be sentenced in short order, probably requires a narrower window of predictable fitness to stand trial than would be the case if they were facing a more serious charge or charges and more complex/protracted proceedings. Perhaps the question for an evaluator should not be "Is the accused fit?" (the answer for which, in any case, lies with the judge, not the clinician), but rather, "How much fitness is present, is it fitness of the sort required, and what is its shelf-life?"[64]

Although the phenomenon of fluctuating fitness is (clinically) common, and an issue for courts and Review Board panels, it has, curiously, received little to no attention from legal or psychiatric writers or the

62 Alec Buchanan, "Competency to Stand Trial and the Seriousness of the Charge" (2006) 34:4 *Journal of the American Academy of Psychiatry and the Law* 458.

63 *Ibid.*

64 David B Bekelman & Joseph A Carresse, "A Practical 3-Step Model for Managing Treatment Refusal" (2006) 55:5 *Journal of Family Practice* 403.

courts. Mossman's[65] highly detailed article on the practice guideline of the American Academy of Psychiatry and the Law for fitness to stand trial does not even refer to the clinically relevant phenomenon of fluctuating fitness, let alone recognize the legal (and practical) difficulty it can create.

The issue has been recognized, however, in the US case of *Johnson v State* (2001),[66] in which the appellate division of the Nevada Supreme Court considered an accused's right to represent himself. Because of oscillations in the intensity of his delusions, his "competency" to stand trial was considered by the experts to be more "fluid than static ... [H]e may be more competent on one day than another."[67] The anticipated stress of the trial (on a murder charge) was such that the accused would need to be examined daily "to determine if [he was] competent on that particular day."[68] Because of the accused's "tenuous condition ... there was a substantial likelihood that the fluctuating intensity of his delusional belief system would have eventually led either to his inability to abide by 'rules of procedure and courtroom protocol,' or to a complete loss of his mental competency to proceed."[69] The court's focus in *Johnson v State* was explicitly forward-looking with respect to responding to evidence that the longevity of the accused's mental stability was highly questionable.[70]

In *R v Volpini*,[71] the accused, who had been found unfit to stand trial on a number of assault and threatening charges, was assessed by the expert as meeting the criteria for fitness set out in *R v Taylor*.[72] Nevertheless, the expert considered the accused as unfit due to his fluctuating fitness and irritability, which the expert believed would prevent him from managing in court. Consequently, the expert opined that his "bottom-line" opinion was that the accused was unfit, notwithstanding meeting the *Taylor* criteria. A 3:2 majority of the Review Board concluded that the accused was unfit "in the immediate foreseeable future"; the minority, while conceding that fitness was marginal, did not appear

65 Mossman, above note 39.
66 *Johnson v State*, 117 Nev 153 (2001)
67 *Ibid* at 155.
68 *Ibid.*
69 *Ibid.*
70 *Ibid.*
71 *Volpini (Re)*, [2005] ORBD No 1494.
72 *R v Taylor*, [1992] OJ No 2394 (CA).

as concerned about the fluctuations in the accused's mental state and fitness, and was prepared to accept a snapshot of the accused's fitness, however tenuous, as sufficient evidence of his fitness.

In *Re: HH*,[73] a case of a precariously fit psychotic adolescent female charged with assault, the British Columbia Review Board adopted an approach taken by many courts and Review Board panels. After concluding that the accused had a "perhaps slightly better than rudimentary understanding of the court process, its consequences and an ability to instruct counsel," it made a "keep fit" order (pursuant to section 672.49(1)) to detain the accused in hospital in order to preserve fitness in a marginally fit but fragile accused.[74] This common practice, albeit beneficial to the accused, sidesteps the problem of fluctuating fitness, which, we would suggest, may actually amount to non-fitness.

3) Consequences of a Finding of Unfitness

A finding of unfitness means that, while the accused remains vulnerable to prosecution, proceeding on the charges is deferred until a finding of fitness. In such cases, the court retains jurisdiction over the accused until the final disposition of the charges. As noted in Section D(1), above in this chapter, the court is obliged by section 672.33(1) of the *Criminal Code* to revisit the issue of "prosecutability" (that is, the ability to establish a *prima facie* case) every two years until such time as the accused is fit to stand trial.

The implications of a finding of unfitness are serious for the accused and for the judicial system as a whole, as matters remain unresolved as long as the accused remains unfit to stand trial. Justice Lacourcière in the *Taylor* decision makes it clear that the timely resolution of pending criminal charges is also an important consideration for the application of the fitness rules:

> [O]ne must consider that principles of fundamental justice require that a trial come to a final determination without undue delay. The adoption of too high a threshold for fitness will result in an increased number of cases in which the accused will be found unfit to stand trial even

73 *HH (Re)*, [2007] BCRBD No 21.

74 *Ibid* at para 15.

> though the accused is capable of understanding the process and anxious for it to come to completion.[75]

The desirability of speed and efficiency, we contend, should not discount the requisite abilities that an accused must possess in order to be fit to stand trial.

In practical terms, accused are kept under a provincial or territorial Review Board's jurisdiction (reporting to, or in, a hospital or other care facility) only until their fitness to stand trial returns. This return to fitness is ordinarily accomplished through stabilization with medication, resolving medical and/or substance use issues that have negatively affected the accused's mental state (and cognitive capacities), and education.

Following a finding that the accused is unfit, the court must hold a "disposition hearing" to determine where the accused would best be placed, if requested by either party (*Criminal Code* section 672.45(1)). Upon the hearing, the court may make a disposition "if it is satisfied that it can readily do so and that a disposition should be made without delay" (section 672.45(2)). If the court does not hold a hearing and make a disposition, the Review Board must hold a disposition hearing and issue a disposition within forty-five days (section 672.47(1)). If a disposition is not made by the court, the accused will more than likely be remanded to a designated psychiatric hospital pending a first appearance before the Review Board. The provision for this remand is contained in section 672.46. Where the court does make a disposition, it is reviewed by the Review Board within ninety days (subsection 672.47(3)).

E. REPORTS

While assessments are ordered routinely by the courts, "reports"—that is, written reports—are not always required. However, the court has the ability to order that a written report be provided:

> **672.2(1)** An assessment order may require the person who makes the assessment to submit in writing an assessment report on the mental condition of the accused.

75 *R v Taylor* above note 72 at para 50.

Where a report is ordered, it shall be filed with the court, as directed (section 672.2(2)):

> An assessment report shall be filed with the court or Review Board that ordered it, within the period fixed by the court or Review Board, as the case may be.

Copies shall be provided to the prosecutor, the accused, and counsel for the accused:

> **672.2(4)** Subject to subsection 672.51(3), copies of any report filed with a court or Review Board under subsection (2) shall be provided without delay to the prosecutor, the accused and any counsel representing the accused.

1) The Written Report in a Fitness Evaluation

While we routinely see very complete and comprehensive reports tendered as exhibits, especially where they are produced by a "designated facility" (a "hospital," as defined in section 672.1(1)), a completely satisfactory report may be produced in a much more compressed manner. The issue of fitness to stand trial is typically an important but relatively straightforward matter that does not require an extensive report. From the perspective of the court, defence counsel, and prosecution, if the immediate psycholegal question is properly addressed, a complete report may be brief, perhaps only a page or two in length. Or it may be provided to the court orally, as is often done in a mental health court. Often, the "extra" material provided (i.e., the accused's mental health history) is not specifically relevant to the legal issues, although it may be necessary for the practitioner to include such material to meet professional standards and/or abide by guidelines of the psychiatric facility they may be affiliated with.

As is the case with all forensic psychiatric assessments, reports are the typical vehicle for conveying the clinician's observations, diagnostic impressions, and psycholegal opinions. Importantly, and notwithstanding the subject matter of the report (e.g., whether it addresses criminal responsibility, fitness, risk, rehabilitation for sentencing, and so on), the critical, if not defining, task for the clinician is to support their conclusions with the necessary data and ensure that the body of the report shows the long division supporting those conclusions. Basic to the assessment report is defining symptoms and psychopathology—observed in and/or described by collateral interviews and records—and establishing a diagnosis. Almost all accused should have a diagnosis that is consistent with disorders listed in the DSM-5.[76]

Major mental disorder—the most common reason for unfitness—causes symptoms, but symptoms (or a diagnosis alone) are insufficient to support a finding of unfitness. Whether the symptoms involve perpetual disturbances, abnormal beliefs, disordered thought, affective instability, behavioural dysregulation, confusion, or cognitive impairment, the report must demonstrate their effect on the capacities and understanding needed to be fit to stand trial.[77]

The report must demonstrate that all areas relevant to fitness have been addressed. Whether the information has been obtained through clinical assessment and/or any of the tools listed in Section C(8) of this chapter is not particularly important; what is important is a methodical approach that ensures that the necessary information has been considered. The report will need to demonstrate that special diagnostic considerations and challenges in the assessment process have been addressed (e.g., with respect to atypical diagnoses, intellectual deficits, malingering, and lack of cooperation). Scott[78] underscores the importance of considering others' observations that are inconsistent with the presence of extreme mental illness, as an accused may be attempting to portray such a state in order to avoid criminal prosecution.

The following list provides elements of a typical fitness-to-stand-trial report:

1) *Identifying information:*
   - name
   - date of birth
   - charges
   - date(s) of interview
   - referral source and reason for referral

76 DSM-5, above note 15.

77 Steven K Hoge, "Competence to Stand Trial: An Overview" (2016) 58:6 *Indian Journal of Psychiatry* 187.

78 CL Scott, "Competency to Stand Trial and the Insanity Defense" in RI Simon & LH Gold, eds, *Textbook of Forensic Psychiatry*, 2d ed (Washington, DC: American Psychiatric Publishing, 2010).

- qualifications of examiner
- preliminary cautions reviewed with accused (for example, as to limits in confidentiality)
- focused clinical assessment
  - ▹ history of illness
  - ▹ recent and current circumstances
  - ▹ educational level attained
  - ▹ brief social history
  - ▹ mental status examination

2) *Information reviewed:*
   - police documents and witness statements
   - health care records from detention centre
   - medical and psychiatric records
3) *Focused review of fitness evaluation:*
   - understanding of charges and consequences of conviction
   - knowledge of role of courtroom personnel
   - knowledge of trial procedure, pleas, and purpose of oath
   - ability to communicate with and respond to counsel
   - ability to challenge witnesses
   - ability to testify
4) *Opinions and conclusions:*
   - diagnosis
   - opinion re malingering
   - concerns about reliability of accused's history (from clinician's perspective)
   - concerns about safety (suicidal or violent)
   - fitness to stand trial (from a "psychiatric perspective")
   - treatment—restoration of fitness to stand trial
   - availability for court
   - Providing opinions about an accused's fitness to stand trial is, needless to say, a highly imperfect science.[79] Moreover, while convention has blurred the distinction, the question is really not one for the mental health expert.

As Mossman et al point out, there is no gold standard for establishing an accused's fitness.[80] Ultimately, experts should concede the risk

79 Buchanan, above note 62.

80 Mossman et al, above note 3.

of false positives (a fit accused is found unfit) and false negatives (unfit accused are missed and prosecuted). Consequently Mossman et al suggest that experts provide opinions about competence as graded levels of confidence to avoid restricting themselves to binary (competent or not) opinions.[81]

Ten-Point Review

1) Assessment orders must be made upon "reasonable grounds."
2) Applications for orders may come from any party or may be made by the court upon its own motion.
3) The accused's "inabilities" must be based upon a mental disorder. A mental disorder is a necessary but, on its own, insufficient reason for a finding of unfitness.
4) Assessments are presumptively done on an out-of-custody basis.
5) The most common mental disorders underlying unfitness are psychoses and intellectual deficit.
6) Amnesia is, by itself, not a basis for unfitness.
7) There are many specific psychopathology/intellectual limitation–based tools to assist in the determination of fitness to stand trial.
8) The issue of fitness to stand trial will not be tried until the Crown has established a *prima facie* case.
9) Upon a verdict of unfit to stand trial, the Crown may bring an application for a treatment order.
10) Where the accused remains unfit to stand trial they will be traversed to the jurisdiction of the Review Board, which will assess the accused not less than annually, as mentioned in Chapter 3. Within every two years of the finding of unfit to stand trial the Crown must demonstrate that it remains able to prove a *prima facie* case.

81 *Ibid.*

CHAPTER 6

Trial of the Issue of Fitness

A. JURISDICTION TO TRY THE ISSUE OF FITNESS

In order for the court to have jurisdiction to try the issue of fitness, "reasonable grounds," as set out in subsection 672.23(1) of the *Criminal Code*[1] (see Chapter 3), are required to believe that the accused is unfit to stand trial.[2] Such grounds are most often supported by medical or psychological evidence obtained as a result of an assessment order, although this is not strictly necessary. Without more information, evidence that the accused "may be mentally ill" is insufficient to provide the court with reasonable grounds to believe that the accused may be unfit to stand trial.[3] Under subsection 672.22, all accused are presumed to be fit to stand trial until the contrary is proven on a "balance of probabilities" (i.e., more likely than not). Similarly, a verdict of unfit is displaced upon a balance of probabilities.

In cases where an accused has previously been found unfit to stand trial, the court may "retry" the issue of fitness. In these circumstances, a determination of fitness by a Review Board (a quasi-judicial administrative tribunal) may provide the court with reasonable grounds to retry the issue, although a determination by the Review Board is not a prerequisite for such a retrial.[4] A retrial may be initiated by the court on its own or on application by a party. In either case, the presumption at this juncture is that the accused remains unfit.

B. COUNSEL FOR THE ACCUSED REQUIRED

Where the court has reasonable grounds to believe that an accused may be unfit to stand trial (grounds most often supported by an assessment) and the accused is not represented by counsel, the court shall order that the accused be represented by counsel (subsection 672.24(1)). Counsel must be appointed prior to the making of an assessment order. As the British Columbia Court of Appeal found in *R v Verma*, it could not be concluded "that the [trial court's] failure to order the appellant's representation by counsel at the assessment stage of the proceedings and failure to address the fitness issue with counsel present after an assessment was ordered were inevitably harmless and resulted in no prejudice to the appellant."[5]

The threshold for ordering an assessment is not "reasonable grounds to believe that the accused is unfit to stand trial" (as in section 672.24(1)) but rather "reasonable grounds to believe that evidence is necessary to *determine* whether the accused is unfit" (section 672.11 [emphasis added]). Nevertheless, the accused is quite vulnerable at this stage of the process. Fairness dictates that an accused who is so unwell as to cause the court this concern should clearly have the assistance of counsel. It is arguable whether, strictly speaking, the provisions of section 672.24 pertain at this juncture; however, it would be most prudent and consistent with the court's objective in ensuring fairness that counsel be appointed at this early stage. There may be compelling arguments to be made that would be greatly assisted by counsel. Once the assessment has been ordered, the process for which the accused should have had counsel present may all be a *fait accompli*. We submit that, in accordance with the Yukon Territory decision in *R v Waranuk*,[6] to the extent that there is ambiguity, erring on the side of appointing counsel is most appropriate.

Where counsel is appointed pursuant to these provisions and the accused is not covered by legal aid and is unable to pay, counsel's fees will be paid by the provincial or territorial attorney general. However, in *Canada (Attorney General) v Savard*, an interesting decision from Yukon, the Court of Appeal found that, with respect to the mandatory appointment of counsel for unfit accused pursuant to the provisions

---

5 *R v Verma*, [2011] BCJ No 165 at para 25 (CA); see also *R v Waranuk*, [2008] YJ No 48 (SC).

6 *R v Waranuk*, *ibid*.

of section 672.24(1), the court, notwithstanding the provisions of section 672.24(2), does not have the authority to order the attorney general of Canada to pay counsel who represents an accused as a result of an order made under this section.[7] Justice Rowles indicated that:

> This case does not require us to decide what *Charter* remedy may be available to an accused should an order made under s. 672.24 go unanswered, but I make these observations. In order to meet the standard of procedural fairness required by the *Charter*, an accused who is or may be unfit to stand trial must be represented by counsel. An order made under s. 672.24 is consistent with achieving that constitutional standard. If an order made under s. 672.24 is not met, the court may decline to take any further step in the proceedings until the accused is represented. But that would not be a satisfactory *Charter* remedy should the accused remain in custody and be unable, without the assistance of counsel, to proceed with a fitness hearing or a judicial interim release hearing. That leaves the alternative of the court granting a temporary stay of proceedings and releasing the accused from custody.[8]

1) Difficulties for Counsel

Where counsel is retained by someone other than the accused — usually a concerned family member — it must be remembered that the client is the accused. Counsel will often encounter situations where family members are offering advice and instructions that sound more rational than those obtained from the accused/client. Counsel will nevertheless be obligated to take instructions from their client so long as the instructions are not unethical or illegal and would not mislead the court in any way.

Unfortunately, family members may welcome, or even encourage, the laying of a criminal charge in order that a process may unfold that will access assessment and treatment opportunities that had been difficult to obtain in the civil mental health care system. While this (generally) well-intended effort to route the accused into the forensic stream could have the effect of improving the accused's clinical well-being, there may be a self-serving agenda at play. Family members

---

7 *Canada (Attorney General) v Savard*, [1996] YJ No 4 (CA).

8 *Ibid* at para 114.

may have been the accused's victim on multiple occasions and/or may have become demoralized and frustrated by repeated unsuccessful attempts at securing predictable and sustained treatment for the accused through the revolving doors of the criminal justice system (e.g., brief stays in jail) or the civil mental health system. Moreover, the accused may have resisted such opportunities. Despite such considerations, counsel is bound to follow the client's instructions.

2) *Amicus Curiae*

The appointment of *amicus*—that is, counsel appointed to assist the court—while potentially of great assistance to the court, does not satisfy the statutory requirement that counsel *for the accused* be appointed. While the breadth of the traditional role of *amicus* has been expanding of late,[9] it is not a substitute for counsel for the accused.[10] Young or inexperienced counsel often find stepping into the role of appointed counsel for a psychotic accused who is unfit (or in respect of whom fitness is in question) and/or who is not willing to speak with counsel a challenge, to say the least. Yet it is a role that can be assumed, with some care and delicacy.

C. THE ACCUSED'S PRESENCE AT THE TRIAL

With very few extraordinary exceptions, the accused is to be present in court during the entirety of their trial, *per* section 650 of the *Criminal Code.*

> **650(1)** Subject to subsections (1.1) to (2) and section 650.01, an accused, other than an organization, shall be present in court during the whole of his or her trial.
>
> *Video links*
>
> (1.1) Where the court so orders, and where the prosecutor and the accused so agree, the accused may appear by counsel or by closed-circuit television or any other means that allow the court and the accused to engage in simultaneous visual and oral communication, for any part of the trial other than a part in which the evidence of a witness is taken.

9 See, for example, *R v Imona-Russell*, 2011 ONCA 303.
10 *Ontario v Criminal Lawyers' Association of Ontario*, [2013] 3 SCR 3.

Video links

(1.2) Where the court so orders, an accused who is confined in prison may appear by closed-circuit television or any other means that allow the court and the accused to engage in simultaneous visual and oral communication, for any part of the trial other than a part in which the evidence of a witness is taken, if the accused is given the opportunity to communicate privately with counsel, in a case in which the accused is represented by counsel.

Exceptions

(2) The court may

(a) cause the accused to be removed and to be kept out of court, where he misconducts himself by interrupting the proceedings so that to continue the proceedings in his presence would not be feasible;
(b) permit the accused to be out of court during the whole or any part of his trial on such conditions as the court considers proper; or
(c) *cause the accused to be removed and to be kept out of court during the trial of an issue as to whether the accused is unfit to stand trial, where it is satisfied that failure to do so might have an adverse effect on the mental condition of the accused.*

To make defence

(3) An accused is entitled, after the close of the case for the prosecution, to make full answer and defence personally or by counsel.[11]

Section 650(2)(c) is the comparable provision to section 672.5(10)(b)(ii) in Part XX.1 of the *Criminal Code*, which deals with disposition hearings in respect of unfit accused. These sections are designed to keep accused away from proceedings that could prove psychologically injurious to them.

672.5(10) The court or the chairperson of the Review Board may

(a) permit the accused to be absent during the whole or any part of the hearing on such conditions as the court or chairperson considers proper; or
(b) cause the accused to be removed and barred from re-entry for the whole or any part of the hearing
    (i) where the accused interrupts the hearing so that to continue in the presence of the accused would not be feasible,

11 *Criminal Code*, above note 1, s 650(1) [emphasis added].

(ii) on being satisfied that failure to do so would likely endanger the life or safety of another person or would seriously impair the treatment or recovery of the accused, or

(iii) in order to hear, in the absence of the accused, evidence, oral or written submissions, or the cross-examination of any witness concerning whether grounds exist for removing the accused pursuant to subparagraph (ii).

It is submitted that these provisions should be used only in the most compelling cases and should be based on evidence establishing "reasonable grounds." Where the provisions are invoked, an accused nevertheless remains present "through counsel." While we have located no reported cases on this point, in the authors' experience accused have been removed from Review Board hearings very rarely. The circumstances in such instances almost invariably involve behaviour by an accused that precludes the hearing from proceeding and where it is clear the accused could neither benefit from nor contribute to the hearing.[12]

D. FITNESS IN RESPECT OF WHAT CHARGE(S)?

In *R v Hogan*,[13] the court conducted one fitness hearing and, at its conclusion, found that the accused was fit to stand trial in respect of charges on two different informations. Although exceptions exist, and the parties may consent to it, applying an omnibus in respect of fitness to face multiple charges of varying complexity is not generally a sound procedure. Where there are to be separate trials, there must be separate considerations of fitness. The substance of the trials, their complexity, the role the accused must play, and the timing of the matters might all be quite different, such that the accused at a particular point in time is fit in respect of one matter but unfit in respect of another.[14]

---

12 It has been held that to hold a hearing in the accused's absence, where the accused can neither benefit from nor contribute to the hearing, is an error. See *Evers v British Columbia (Adult Forensic Psychiatric Services)*, [2009] BCJ No 2450 (CA).

13 *R v Hogan*, [1985] BCJ No 195 (Co Ct).

14 Such a view is related to the discussion in Chapter 2, Section B(7) about fitness being on a sliding scale.

E. WHO TRIES THE ISSUE OF FITNESS?

The responsibility for trying the issue of fitness falls to the trier of fact: either a judge, when sitting alone, or a jury (section 672.26). In summary procedure matters, the issue will be tried by a provincial or territorial judge. In an indictable matter, the accused's election will determine who will be the trier of fact and thus who will try the matter of the accused's fitness. These provisions are set out in the *Criminal Code* as follows:

> **672.26** Where an accused is tried or is to be tried before a court composed of a judge and jury,
> (a) if the judge directs that the issue of fitness of the accused be tried before the accused is given in charge to a jury for trial on the indictment, a jury composed of the number of jurors required in respect of the indictment in the province where the trial is to be held shall be sworn to try that issue and, with the consent of the accused, the issues to be tried on the indictment; and
> (b) if the judge directs that the issue of fitness of the accused be tried after the accused has been given in charge to a jury for trial on the indictment, the jury shall be sworn to try that issue in addition to the issues in respect of which it is already sworn.

When the issue of fitness arises, as it often does, prior to the selection of a jury (as trier of fact at the trial), the issue of fitness will be tried by a jury, which may be discharged upon the conclusion of the trial of the issue of fitness. This approach makes considerable practical sense, especially where the verdict reached is one of unfit to stand trial and it might be weeks, months, or even years before a jury would be recalled for the trial. Where, however, the matter of fitness is disposed of quickly, and the trial is to proceed, the same jury that tried the matter of fitness may, with the accused's consent, proceed to hear the trial proper.[15] Where the accused had earlier obtained a verdict of unfit to stand trial and had made a previous election to be tried by a judge and jury, and the issue of fitness is to be retried, the issue of fitness will be tried by a judge and jury.[16] At the retrial of the issue of fitness, the presumption is that the accused remains unfit to stand trial, and this presumption must

15 See *R v Semenovitch*, [2010] AJ No 1285 (QB).

16 *R v Pietrangelo*, [2003] OJ No 2035 (CA).

be displaced on a balance of probabilities.[17] The court must find that there are reasonable grounds to doubt the accused's fitness to stand trial before the matter is put to a jury, and counsel will be able to put the same questions to prospective jurors trying the issue of fitness as they would to prospective jurors in respect of the trial proper.[18]

At least one court has held that the jury conducting the trial of the issue of fitness should be apprised of the nature of the allegations.[19] There are cogent arguments to both sides of this issue. On the one hand, it could be argued that serious/repugnant allegations would cast the accused in a very unfavourable light and that it is unnecessary for the jury to hear the particulars of the allegations. On the other hand, it could be argued that the criterion of "unable on account of mental disorder to conduct a defence" must be referable to a particular set of allegations. Whether the accused is unable to conduct a defence will, in part, be a function of the sort of offence (and trial proceeding) the accused is confronting.

F. WHEN IS THE ISSUE OF FITNESS TRIED?

The issue of fitness to stand trial may not be tried until the prosecution has made its election (if applicable) as to mode of trial:

> **672.25(1)** The court shall postpone directing the trial of the issue of fitness of an accused in proceedings for an offence for which the accused may be prosecuted by indictment or that is punishable on summary conviction, until the prosecutor has elected to proceed by way of indictment or summary conviction.

More generally, as mentioned in Chapter 2, a trial of the issue may be deferred. The issue of fitness to stand trial may arise at any point in the prosecution but is most often an issue recognized at the outset of the proceedings.[20] The issue of fitness to stand trial may arise on more than one occasion during the same prosecution, as occurs when mental state and fitness fluctuate. Often such accused are clinically frail

17 *R v Song*, [2008] AJ No 746 (CA).

18 *R v HSR*, [1994] OJ No 1131 (Gen Div).

19 *R v Brideau*, [2015] NBJ No 59 (QB).

20 But the issue may also be relevant at the time of sentencing (i.e. post-verdict). See *R v GB*, [2003] OJ No 784 (SCJ) and the discussion in Chapter 3, Section D.

and move back and forth across the fitness threshold. In that fitness to stand trial is always referable to the accused's *current* mental abilities, it is not a determination in respect of which *res judicata* is logically applicable. And, where the accused has been found to be fit but is nonetheless clearly unwell, the court must be vigilant, as fluctuations in their condition may cause the accused to decompensate to the point where the issue must be revisited[21] as the clinical condition changes.

1) Postponing the Trial of the Issue

The trial of the issue may be postponed, where it arises at a preliminary inquiry before the close of the prosecution's case, until a time that is not later than the time the accused is called on to answer the charge (subsection 672.25(2)(a)); or, at a trial, to a time not later than the opening of the case for the defence; or, upon application of the accused, until any later time directed by the court (section 672.25(2)(b)).[22] And, as mentioned earlier (see, e.g., the discussion at the beginning of Chapter 3), where the accused is disputing the Crown's case, a trial of the issue of fitness should not occur until the Crown has shown a *prima facie* case. Where the Crown is put to the test and cannot demonstrate a *prima facie* case, the accused is acquitted, and, obviously, the issue of fitness disappears.

a) Demonstrating a *Prima Facie* Case

As the court sets out in *R v Le*:

> [W]here an accused disputes the Crown's ability to prove a *prima facie* case, a fitness hearing should not take place until the Crown demonstrates that it is in a position to show a *prima facie* case. To my mind this requirement may be satisfied by something less than a full evidentiary hearing. It would be impractical and inappropriate to require that the Crown engage in two preliminary inquiries. In fact, if that were the requirement it would not be possible to hold a fitness hearing prior to a committal for trial. At this juncture a more informal showing of

---

21 See, for example, *R v Miller*, [2011] BCJ No 1801 (SC). While the accused may be presently fit to stand trial but nevertheless quite unwell, the issue of fitness to stand trial may, during the course of the proceedings, be revisited as required.

22 See also *R v Le*, [2004] OJ No 3374 (Ct J).

> the nature of the Crown's case is appropriate. It is possible to mold a procedure to fit the situation or position where the accused currently sits in the proceedings. At this juncture, prior to a bail hearing and prior to arraignment the requirement that the Crown show that it is in a position to prove a *prima facie* case could be satisfied, for example, by having the Officer in Charge testify as to the witnesses and sorts of evidence it intends to call.[23]

2) *Charter* Applications by Unfit Accused

In the case of *R v Flowers*,[24] Justice Spies held that the court had jurisdiction to hear an application for a stay of proceedings of an unfit accused on the basis of unreasonable delay and consequent violation of the accused's *Charter* rights as set out in section 11(b).[25] The court imported the same logic as contained in section 672.25 of the *Criminal Code*, in that, if a *Charter* violation could be established and, as a result, the charge should be stayed, it would be inappropriate to have the accused languish as unfit. Here, the court went on to hear the application, notwithstanding the accused's unfitness:

> In this case, section 672.25(2)(b) does not apply *per se* because I must proceed on the basis that Mr. Flowers is unfit to stand trial at this time. In my view, however, the principal purpose of this section still applies. If the section 11(b) application is argued and I determine that these proceedings should be stayed because Mr. Flowers› section 11(b) rights have been infringed, then why should he be held due to mental health issues? The fact that the Crown can prove its case is not the point here if there has been unreasonable delay. If there has, the Crown should not be permitted to proceed with the case at all as there would be no basis to put Mr. Flowers on trial.[26]

Where there is a failure to prove a *prima facie* case or where some other process occurs, as in *Flowers*, that brings the prosecution to an end, the accused is acquitted and the issue of fitness is not tried:

---

23 *Ibid* at para 15.

24 *R v Flowers*, [2008] OJ No 4642 (SCJ).

25 *Canadian Charter of Rights and Freedoms*, Part I of the *Constitution Act, 1982*, being Schedule B to the *Canada Act 1982* (UK), 1982, c 11.

26 *R v Flowers*, above note 24 at para 8.

672.3 Where the court has postponed directing the trial of the issue of fitness of an accused pursuant to subsection 672.25(2) and the accused is discharged or acquitted before the issue is tried, it shall not be tried.

G. BURDEN OF PROOF

In a trial on the issue of fitness, the burden of proof must be met by the party asserting the accused's unfitness (subsection 672.23(2)). The presumption of fitness is displaced on a "balance of probabilities." Similarly, under the same section, where a party subsequently asserts that the accused has become fit to stand trial, that party has the burden of proof. As is the case with criminal responsibility, "an accused is presumed fit to stand trial unless the court is satisfied on the balance of probabilities that the accused is unfit to stand trial."[27]

H. A VERDICT OF UNFIT TO STAND TRIAL

Upon a verdict of unfit to stand trial, one of three things happens:

1) the Crown brings an application for a treatment disposition (or, as it is more commonly referred to in the courts, a treatment order),
2) the court holds an initial disposition hearing, or
3) the accused is remanded to the Review Board for an initial disposition hearing.

1) Treatment Dispositions

Where a verdict of unfit to stand trial is rendered and the court has not made a disposition under section 672.54 in respect of an accused, the court may, on application by the prosecutor, direct, by order, that treatment of the accused be carried out for a specified period not exceeding sixty days, subject to such conditions as the court considers appropriate. The application for treatment may be brought only by the prosecutor (section 672.58). Where the accused is not detained in custody, the court may direct that the accused submit to that treatment by the person or at the hospital specified.

27 *Criminal Code*, above note 1, s 672.22.

Note that it has not been formally decided when the clock starts ticking on such an order, although most would agree that the sixty-day window starts at the moment the order is made rather than at the time the accused eventually arrives at the hospital. Treatment may be ordered in or out of custody and subject to any other terms the court considers appropriate. The start date may be set by the court to begin at a future date (section 672.63).

In order to effect treatment orders, judges do not have jurisdiction pursuant to the provisions of section 532(2)(a) to vacate an accused's bail on their own motion without cause being shown, regardless of the accused's history of failing to attend court as directed.[28] However, section 672.58 provides as follows:

> Where a verdict of unfit to stand trial is rendered and the court has not made a disposition under section 672.54 in respect of an accused, the court may, on application by the prosecutor, by order, direct that treatment of the accused be carried out for a specified period not exceeding sixty days, *subject to such conditions as the court considers appropriate and, where the accused is not detained in custody, direct that the accused submit to that treatment by the person or at the hospital specified.* [emphasis added]

Arguably, the accused could be ordered (as part of the treatment order) to submit to inpatient treatment for the purpose of effecting the treatment order, thus leaving the order for judicial interim release in place. Upon the conclusion of the treatment order, the bail order would remain in place. It is commonly thought that "treatment," which typically involves the involuntary injection or ingestion of psychotropic medications, is safely done only with the patient/accused in a hospital so that they may be monitored and any side effects attended to.

2) Criteria for a Treatment Disposition

Section 672.59 sets out the criteria a court must be satisfied exist, on the basis of expert testimony, before a disposition can be made to administer treatment to an accused in order to make the accused fit to stand trial. The criteria set out below must be satisfied by the *testimony* of a medical practitioner:

28 *R v Jackson*, [2016] OJ No 4780 (SCJ).

1) The accused must have been found unfit to stand trial.
2) The proposed treatment will likely render the accused fit within sixty days.
3) Without treatment, the accused will likely remain unfit.
4) Risk of harm is not disproportionate to anticipated benefits.
5) The treatment proposed is the least restrictive and least intrusive treatment option.
6) The proposed treatment facility or practitioner has consented to receive the accused.[29]

In the interest of procedural fairness, the *Criminal Code* provides the accused with the right to be notified in writing in advance of an application by the Crown and the right to challenge the application for a treatment disposition (section 672.6).

3) Monitoring as Part of "Treatment"

One case has held that necessary monitoring of the accused's medical condition may be an ancillary part of a treatment order. The following is taken from the findings of the Ontario Court of Justice in the case of *R v Xu*:

> Ms. Xu has been found unfit to stand trial within the meaning of s.2 of the *Criminal Code.* Upon that verdict the Crown brought an application for a Treatment Order pursuant to the provisions of s. 672.58 of the *Criminal Code.* She suffers from an intractable psychotic disorder which has not been responsive to mainstream anti-psychotic medications.
>
> [2] With the testimony of Dr. DeFreitas the statutory criteria set out in s.672.59 have been generally met. However, the treatment specified by Dr. DeFreitas includes "'Clozapine' or other anti-psychotic medications." Clozapine is a new "2nd Tier" psychoactive drug typically prescribed where the older generation mainstream drugs have failed to have any effect. The prescription of Clozapine requires careful weekly blood monitoring in order to avoid severe suppression of white blood cell function.
>
> [3] The argument of counsel for Ms. Xu is that the court has no authority to Order blood monitoring, only "treatment." And, because

29 The first five criteria are from section 672.59(2); the sixth is from section 672.62.

blood monitoring is required with the prescription of Clozapine it cannot be a specified "treatment."

[4] Steadmans's Medical Dictionary defines "treatment" as: "the medical or surgical management of a patient." The Canadian Oxford Dictionary defines "treatment" as: "the application of medical care or attention to a patient." Treatment is not limited to the prescription of a particular drug but, of necessity, includes any necessary ancillary monitoring and care. Whether the required monitoring consists of close behavioural observation, psychological testing, or the analysis of blood, it is all encompassed within the envelope of what is meant by "treatment." Treatment is a multi-dimensional intervention not limited to the prescription of the most appropriate drug.

[5] Therefore, for the sake of clarity, the Order should read: "Clozapine or other anti-psychotic drugs including any necessary monitoring which may consist of blood analysis."[30]

4) Consent of the Hospital to Treat the Accused

No court shall make a disposition under section 672.58 without the consent of (1) the person in charge of the hospital where the accused is to be treated; or (2) the person to whom responsibility for the treatment of the accused is assigned by the court.

Note even, where the statutory criteria set out in section 672.59 have been met, discretion remains with the judge as to whether the order should be made. Further, while the statutory provisions require as a condition precedent the consent of the hospital prior to the making of the treatment order, the Supreme Court of Canada in *R v Conception*[31] held that, notwithstanding this provision, the court *may* make a treatment order without the hospital's consent in exceptional circumstances:

> While we think the circumstances under which this inquiry is appropriate will be rare, the *Charter* assures that judges and not the person in charge of the hospital where the accused is to be treated will have the last word in terms of the disposition order where the accused's *Charter* rights would otherwise be compromised.[32]

30 *R v Xu (No 2)*, (20 April 2007), File No 0710000305 (Ont Ct J) at paras 1–5.

31 *R v Conception*, [2014] 3 SCR 82.

32 *Ibid* at para 43.

In an appropriate case, a judge proposing to make a treatment disposition may consider whether a hospital's refusal to consent will offend the accused's section 7 *Charter* rights. If so persuaded, the judge is entitled to consider whether ordering an immediate admission would be an appropriate and just remedy for that breach. The circumstances in which such an order may be made should be rare.

Legal considerations and prerogatives, while fundamental, do not end the discussion of institutional consent. Courts and their personnel often establish enduring professional relationships with clinicians and hospitals specializing in matters of this kind. Reservations about administrative considerations like bed space, or clinical considerations like the appropriateness of a particular patient for a specific hospital milieu, need to be, and generally are, taken seriously and factored into the court's decision.

5) The Exclusion of Certain Treatments

Even where the criteria in section 672.59 are met and the court has prepared a treatment order for the circumscribed purpose of rendering the accused fit to stand trial, certain invasive interventions/treatments are excluded from consideration:

> **672.61(1)** The court shall not direct, and no disposition made under section 672.58 shall include, the performance of psychosurgery or electro-convulsive therapy or any other prohibited treatment that is prescribed.
>
> *Definitions*
>
> (2) In this section,
>
> *electro-convulsive therapy* means a procedure for the treatment of certain mental disorders that induces, by electrical stimulation of the brain, a series of generalized convulsions . . . ;
>
> *psychosurgery* means any procedure that by direct or indirect access to the brain removes, destroys or interrupts the continuity of histologically normal brain tissue, or inserts indwelling electrodes for pulsed electrical stimulation for the purpose of altering behaviour or treating psychiatric illness, but does not include neurological procedures used

to diagnose or treat intractable physical pain, organic brain conditions, or epilepsy, where any of those conditions is clearly demonstrable.

6) Hearing the Application for a Treatment Disposition

Prior to a hearing of the Crown's application for a treatment disposition, (1) the accused must have counsel, and (2) the accused must have received written notice as soon as practicable.

Blacklock J, in *R v Worrie*,[33] insisted that the accused be brought to court for the purpose of the hearing of an application for a treatment order where the charges were very serious and a number of preconditions (see Section H(2), above in this chapter) had been dispensed with "on consent." The court noted the serious consequences of the order sought and, quite appropriately, refused to dispense with any procedural or evidentiary requirements.

Where a treatment order is made, the case is returnable to court, and the Review Board is not notified. At the conclusion of the treatment order, the case is retried — or, if no party is asserting the accused's fitness, the provisions of section 672.45 for a disposition hearing and following pertain. The court may hold a disposition hearing and may make a disposition, although this is rarely done. Typically, the matter is remanded to the Review Board where an "initial" disposition hearing will be set (section 672.47(1)).

7) The Court's Discretion in Granting a Treatment Disposition

A treatment disposition is arguably one of the most invasive orders in respect of medical care that any court can make. The powers of the court pursuant to the provisions of Part XX.1 of the *Criminal Code* permit the ordering of involuntary treatment that can be physically forced on an unwilling accused. The order supersedes any notions of treatment capacity, consent, or the involvement of substitute decision-makers.

Assuming the criteria set out in section 672.59 have been met, the court *may*, on application, make such an order. The making of the order is not mandatory, and the court may decline to make an order, even where the criteria are met. Perhaps the most compelling circumstance

33 *R v Worrie* (11 September 2015), Court File No Brampton 15-47-42 (Ont Ct J).

supporting a decision not to make an order is where the accused is in custody and no hospital bed is available. (Recall that the hospital's consent is a precondition for a treatment order.) It may be that, as against several weeks waiting in a jail (while presumed to be innocent), an immediate order to the Review Board, which does not require hospital consent, is a preferable course of action.

In *R v Walker*,[34] the court at first instance declined to make an order, even though the criteria had been met. The court appeared to be injecting a notion of "proportionality" into the mix, in that the accused had no criminal record, she was facing relatively minor charges, and she had instructed her counsel that she would refuse treatment pursuant to the court's order and that she would prefer to be subject to the provincial civil mental health regime. Her counsel argued—incorrectly, given section 672.72—that, with a treatment order, there was no right of appeal, whereas, under the civil system, an appeal could be made and the client would have "rights." Upon review at Superior Court, it was held that the trial court had placed too much emphasis on the unfit (and civilly "incapable") accused's "instructions" to counsel, and that these instructions had, in any event, been misunderstood by the trial judge. Ms Walker wasn't receptive to treatment anywhere, whether through the civil or criminal justice system. As well, the court found that to accede to the trial court's line of logic (that the accused's (seemingly) preferred avenue of treatment should be abided by) would be to eviscerate the purpose of the provision.[35]

As a practical matter, we note that, where treatment orders are made, the accused is typically rendered "fit" within thirty days.[36] If, on the other hand, the accused is simply sent to the Review Board as "unfit," it typically takes six months or more employing various provisions of the civil mental health system before the accused is rendered fit.

34 *R v Walker*, [2016] OJ No 2082 (SCJ).

35 *Ibid* at para 40.

36 We would typically make an order for the maximum of sixty days but bring the accused back to court at thirty days to see how they were progressing. It is known that, if psychotropic medications are going to work, they will typically have exerted their effect within three to four weeks. If the accused appeared to be fit at the interim date, the issue would be retried and, if a finding of fitness were made, the remainder of the treatment order would be aborted.

I. PRESERVING FITNESS: "KEEP-FIT ORDERS"

Even upon a verdict of fit to stand trial, the court may still have concerns about the accused maintaining their fitness. Section 672.29 provides a mechanism for placing fit accused who are in custody into a hospital when the court has reasonable grounds to believe that the accused would become unfit to stand trial if released:

> **672.29** Where an accused is detained in custody on delivery of a verdict that the accused is fit to stand trial, the court may order the accused to be detained in a hospital until the completion of the trial, if the court has reasonable grounds to believe that the accused would become unfit to stand trial if released.

It is not open to the hospital to return the accused to a detention centre while subject to an order pursuant to the provisions of section 672.29.[37] It should be noted that this provision speaks only to accused who are detained in custody; it does not apply to a situation where the unstable accused is *not* in custody (e.g., an accused who is out on bail).

In *R v Reid*,[38] the court overlooked the strict wording of section 672.29, which refers to jurisdiction arising at a specific juncture in the proceedings—that is, "on delivery of a verdict that the accused is fit to stand trial"—to find that such an order can be made to preserve fitness even upon the conclusion of an assessment that the accused was fit to stand trial. It is clear here that the court looked behind the particular wording of the section to find that the intended well-being of an accused that is core to section 672.29 should not be limited only to accused found fit on a verdict.

Ten-Point Review

1) A trial of the issue of fitness to stand trial requires reasonable grounds to believe that the accused may be unfit.
2) Where the accused's fitness to stand trial is in issue, counsel must be assigned to the accused; *amicus curiae* is not a substitute.

---

37 *R v Kurd*, [2005] OJ No 2794 (SCJ).

38 *R v Reid*, [2013] BCJ No 2679 (SC).

3) Save exceptional circumstances, the accused must be present at a trial of the issue of fitness.
4) Fitness to stand trial pertains to a specific charge or charges on a specific information/indictment. If there are multiple charges, consideration needs to be given to the accused's fitness for each.
5) Fitness is determined by the trier of fact.
6) Fitness to stand trial may arise at any stage of the proceedings and may be postponed until there is a case to meet.
7) Even where the statutory criteria are met, the making of a treatment order is discretionary.
8) While the hospital's consent is presumptively required prior to the making of a treatment order, it is within the court's discretion to make the order where the accused's *Charter* rights might otherwise be violated.
9) "Treatment" includes any necessary monitoring of the accused.
10) "Keep-fit" orders may be made where there is a verdict of fit but the accused might otherwise become unfit.

CHAPTER 7

Upon a Verdict of Unfit

In the 1700s in Britain, an accused found to be insane upon arraignment was taken to prison (or sometimes sent home to be supervised by family) pending a return to sanity and resumption of the trial. Refinement and formalization of the aftermath of a verdict of unfit to stand trial came with the proclamation of the *Criminal Lunatics Act* of 1800,[1] which provided that:

> If any person indicted for any offence shall be insane, and shall upon arraignment be found to be by a jury lawfully empaneled for that purpose, so that such person cannot be tried on indictment ... it shall be lawful for the Court ... to direct such finding to be recorded, and thereupon to order such person to be kept in strict custody until his Majesty's pleasure shall be known.

The *Criminal Lunatics Act* was included along with the other criminal statutes in a draft criminal code that Britain never adopted but that Canada seized upon as its first *Criminal Code* in 1892. Individuals obtaining a verdict of unfit to stand trial could be detained indefinitely (typically in a hospital), with no review required. These provisions remained essentially unchanged until the proclamation of Bill C-30 in 1992.

As discussed in Chapter 1, Section B, much of the content of Bill C-30 is now contained in Part XX.1 of the *Criminal Code* of Canada.[2] The lieutenant governor (in lieu of the monarch) is no longer part of the process. Determinations with respect to fitness to stand trial have been

1 *Criminal Lunatics Act, 1800* (UK), 39 & 40 Geo 3, c 94.

2 *Criminal Code*, RSC 1985, c C-46.

put in the hands of quasi-judicial administrative tribunals known as Review Boards, which have been created for every province and territory. The decisions of the boards are known as dispositions.

Where an accused remains unfit to stand trial and a treatment order has not been made by the courts (see the discussion in Chapter 6, Section H), or has been made but has failed to result in a finding of fitness, a disposition must be made, either by the court or, more typically, by the Review Board. The trial in respect of which the accused was found to be unfit is held in abeyance until either:

- the accused becomes fit;
- the Crown fails to demonstrate a *prima facie* case (*per* section 672.33 of the *Criminal Code*); or
- the proceedings are stayed pursuant to the provisions of section 672.851 of the *Criminal Code.*

A. CUSTODY OF THE ACCUSED

1) *Status Quo* Presumed

Subject to the court's order, if the court does not make a disposition, any order for the release or detention of the accused shall remain operative until a disposition by the Review Board is made. However, the court may, upon application, vary any order for release or detention, or order that the accused be remanded to hospital pending a disposition hearing by the Review Board (section 672.46). (Parliament did not create a form for an order of this sort; however, the form reproduced in Appendix F is commonly used for this purpose.)

B. DISPOSITIONS

1) Assessment Orders to Assist with Disposition

Where the court is considering holding a disposition hearing, it may order an assessment to assist in the making of an appropriate disposition where it has reasonable grounds to believe that such evidence is necessary (section 672.11(d)). In other, albeit rare, circumstances, where the court renders a verdict of unfit to stand trial and the accused is either out of custody or in jail, it is preferable that an assessment order be made by the court pursuant to section 672.11(d) to ensure that disposition information will be available at the time the Review Board conducts its initial hearing. Where the accused, in these latter circumstances, will not be in hospital prior to the initial hearing before the Review Board, an assessment order directed to the designated hospital in the appropriate catchment area should be made. The assessment report will be returnable to court and, from there, can be forwarded to the Review Board.

2) Who Makes the Disposition?

Upon the verdict of unfit to stand trial (and assuming either that the court has not made a treatment order or that such an order has been made but has failed to result in a finding of fitness), the trial court *may* of its own motion, and *must* upon a request of either of the parties, hold a disposition hearing. Upon holding a disposition hearing, the court *shall* make a disposition if (1) it is satisfied that it can readily do so, *and* (2) a disposition should be made without delay (section 672.45). If the court does not make a disposition, the matter is remanded to the Review Board, which must within forty-five days hold a hearing and make a disposition (section 672.47).

In practice, courts rarely make the initial disposition. There are several reasons for this reluctance. First, typically not be enough relevant "disposition information" is before the court. The evidence leading to the verdict of unfit to stand trial most often does not address the issues to be decided in the making of a disposition. By the time that information is gathered, the matter might just as easily be remanded to the Review Board. Second, most courts deal with unfit accused very infrequently. Thus, they are disinclined to wade into the unfamiliar fray of a disposition hearing unless there are compelling circumstances to do so. Third, when courts are in unfamiliar territory, they tend to make rather conservative dispositions. For this reason, the accused, in particular, might rather have the matter heard by the Review Board, which has greater experience in such matters.

Nonetheless, there may be circumstances where the court would be inclined to make a disposition:

1) The verdict might have been anticipated and the appropriate disposition information is before the court at the time of the verdict.

2) There is a "joint submission" with respect to a disposition.
3) The circumstances are obvious and compelling. Such circumstances could include the following:
   - The accused is profoundly unwell and violent, and it is clear that, at least initially, detention in a secure setting is appropriate.
   - The accused was on judicial interim release at the time of the verdict and is doing well in the care of their family. It is not expected that the terms of a disposition should differ substantially from the judicial interim release order.

Once the initial disposition has been made, the accused's disposition is reviewed by the Review Board not less than every twelve months thereafter.

3) Matters to Consider

For every unfit accused, at every review, the first matter to be considered is whether the accused remains unfit to stand trial. The Review Board's jurisdiction is maintained only so long as the accused remains unfit to stand trial. If the Review Board determines that the unfit accused is fit, the matter *must* be returned to court for the issue of fitness to be retried. If the Review Board is of the view that the accused remains unfit, it will make a new disposition.

4) If the Review Board Determines That the Accused Is Fit

If the Review Board determines that the accused is fit to stand trial, the accused is ordered back to court for the issue of fitness to be formally tried. However, the Review Board maintains jurisdiction, and any disposition remains operative until such time as the court formally determines that the accused is fit. The board's advice to the court that the accused is fit may or may not be endorsed by the court. The accused's condition may have changed between the time of the board's assessment and the retrial of the issue by the court.

If the accused is determined to be fit by the Review Board at a disposition review (and is therefore subject to a disposition pursuant to the provisions of section 672.54), the disposition remains operative so long as the initial verdict of unfit remains formally undisturbed. Where the issue is retried and the court is of the view (the Review Board's determination notwithstanding) that the accused remains unfit, this is not a *new* verdict of unfit. Rather it is a situation where the previously arrived at verdict of unfit has not been displaced on a balance of probabilities.

In these circumstances, it is not mandatory that the existing disposition be reviewed, as it otherwise would be (section 672.83). Where there is a determination by the Review Board at an initial hearing that the accused is fit, the board shall order the accused back to court, but the board may, where there are reasonable grounds to believe that the accused would otherwise become unfit, order the accused to be detained in hospital pending a retrial of the issue before the court (section 672.49). In *Evers v British Columbia*[3] the court held that these provisions of section 672.49 pertain only to initial hearings of the Review Board (section 672.47). Accused, other than those at an initial hearing, maintain their disposition, which remains undisturbed by the Review Board's determination of fitness.

5) If the Review Board Determines That the Accused Is Unfit

Assuming the Review Board is of the view that the accused remains unfit, and therefore a disposition must be either made or reviewed, there are certain factors that need to be taken into consideration.

> **672.54** When a court or Review Board makes a disposition under subsection 672.45(2) or section 672.47, subsection 672.64(3) or 672.83 or section 672.84, it shall, taking into account the safety of the public, which is the paramount consideration, the mental condition of the accused, the reintegration of the accused into society and the other needs of the accused, make one of the following dispositions that is necessary and appropriate in the circumstances:
>
> (a) by order, direct that the accused be discharged subject to such conditions as the court or Review Board considers appropriate; or
>
> (b) by order, direct that the accused be detained in custody in a hospital, subject to such conditions as the court or Review Board considers appropriate.

A "discharge" under Part XX.1 should not be confused with the same terminology in the sentencing provisions of the *Criminal Code.*

3 *Evers v British Columbia (Adult Forensic Psychiatric Services)*, [2009] BCJ No 2450 (CA).

Accordingly, probation is never part of such an order. "Treatment" shall not be a part of any disposition under section 672.54 unless the accused consents, and the court considers such a condition to be "reasonable and necessary" in the interests of the accused (subsection 672.55(1)).[4]

Hearings before the Review Board are typically rather informal, relative to proceedings in a court. The rules of evidence are more relaxed, and the hearing is more akin to a sentencing hearing:

> **672.5(2)** The hearing may be conducted in as informal a manner as is appropriate in the circumstances.

It is mandatory that the unfit accused have counsel for such a hearing (subsection 672.5(8)).

a) Items in the Record of the Proceedings

The court or Review Board shall state its reasons for making a disposition in the record of the proceedings and shall provide every party with a copy of the disposition and those reasons. Where the court makes a disposition, it shall send a transcript of the hearing, as well as all disposition information and other exhibits to the Review Board:

> **672.52(2)** If a court holds a disposition hearing under subsection 672.45(1), whether or not it makes a disposition, it shall send without delay to the Review Board that has jurisdiction in respect of the matter, in original or copied form, a transcript of the hearing, any other document or information related to the hearing, and all exhibits filed with it, if the transcript, document, information or exhibits are in its possession.

C. *PRIMA FACIE* CASE REVIEWS

As discussed in Chapter 6, Section F(1)(a), within every two years of a verdict of unfit to stand trial, the court *shall* hold an inquiry to determine whether the prosecution is able to show a *prima facie* case (section 672.33).[5] (The court *may* revisit the issue upon application at any other time.) This is, as discussed above, to ensure that an accused is not being held as unfit in respect of a charge or charges that the Crown is not in

4 See *Ohenhen (Re)*, 2018 ONCA 65 regarding the "consent" required in this context.

5 This obligation arises once a year for youth, pursuant to the *Youth Criminal Justice Act*, SC 2002, c 1, s 141(10).

a position to prove. Where the Crown is unable to meet this obligation, the accused is acquitted.

While there is to be a demonstration of a *prima facie* case within every two years of a verdict of unfit to stand trial, the timeline may be extended by the court:

> **672.33(1.1)** Despite subsection (1), the court may extend the period for holding an inquiry where it is satisfied on the basis of an application by the prosecutor or the accused that the extension is necessary for the proper administration of justice.

While it is reasonably clear that modest departures from the expected timelines will not result in a loss of jurisdiction,[6] the Crown should ensure that these matters are managed in a timely manner. When considering whether the timeline has been exceeded such that loss of jurisdiction may result, the court will likely consider any prejudice to the accused caused by the delay, which will, in part, be a function of the length of delay, versus the public's interest in disposing of the case on the merits. Such considerations will be informed, by *inter alia*, the seriousness of the allegations.

When and under what circumstances the court may order an inquiry as to the existence of a *prima facie* case are set out in the *Criminal Code* as follows:

> **672.33(2)** On application of the accused, the court may order an inquiry under this section to be held at any time if it is satisfied, on the basis of the application and any written material submitted by the accused, that there is reason to doubt that there is a *prima facie* case against the accused.
>
> *Burden of proof*
>
> (3) At an inquiry under this section, the burden of proof that sufficient evidence can be adduced to put the accused on trial is on the prosecutor.
>
> *Admissible evidence at an inquiry*
>
> (4) In an inquiry under this section, the court shall admit as evidence
>
> (a) any affidavit containing evidence that would be admissible if given by the person making the affidavit as a witness in court; or

6 See, for example, *R v Karimian-Kakolaki*, [2016] OJ No 3015 (Ct J); *R v Faraz*, [2006] OJ No 5612 (Ct J); *R v Talbot*, [1996] OJ No 5323 (Ct J); *R v Isbister*, [2005] AJ No 265 (Prov Ct); *R v Scurvey*, 2002 YKTC 48.

(b) any certified copy of the oral testimony given at a previous inquiry or hearing held before a court in respect of the offence with which the accused is charged.

Conduct of inquiry

(5) The court may determine the manner in which an inquiry under this section is conducted and may follow the practices and procedures in respect of a preliminary inquiry under Part XVIII where it concludes that the interests of justice so require.

In a similar manner, the accused is entitled to cross-examine witnesses or affiants tendered by the Crown in order to establish the Crown's *prima facie* case.[7]

The result of a failure to make out a *prima facie* case is set out in the *Code.*

Where prima facie *case not made*

(6) Where, on the completion of an inquiry under this section, the court is satisfied that sufficient evidence cannot be adduced to put the accused on trial, the court shall acquit the accused.[8]

D. IF THE ACCUSED IS PERMANENTLY UNFIT

With the proclamation of Bill C-10 on 19 May 2005, a number of changes were made to Part XX.1 of the *Criminal Code* (and other legislation). The most significant aspect of the Bill pertains to the court's ability to stay proceedings in respect of a permanently unfit accused. The court is now permitted to hold an inquiry and order a judicial stay of proceedings for an accused found to be unfit to stand trial if the accused is not likely to ever become fit to stand trial and does not constitute a significant threat to the safety of the public, and if a stay is in the interests of the proper administration of justice.

1) Background

Prior to the proclamation of Bill C-10, an unfit accused would remain subject to the jurisdiction of the Review Board indefinitely, so long as that individual remained unfit to stand trial (unless, as required by

7 *R v Pawlivsky*, [1998] AJ No 1092 (QB).

8 *Criminal Code*, above note 2, s 672.33(6).

section 672.33, the Crown failed to show a *prima facie* case within every two years post-verdict). In such cases, jurisdiction over the accused was not based on their dangerousness, unlike in cases where an accused is found to be not criminally responsible (NCR). Where, for example, the "mental disorder" mediating the unfitness was intellectual disability, brain injury, or some other intractable condition, the accused could, in theory (and, at times, in practice), remain subject to the jurisdiction of the Review Board forever. This situation was frustrating both for the accused and the Review Board, which had no ability to discharge the accused as it might were the accused deemed NCR. Prior to Bill C-10, stays, where entered, were the result of the Crown exercising its discretion on an *ad hoc* basis.

2) Specific Changes to the *Criminal Code*

a) Assessment Orders

The first significant change permits the court to order an assessment of the unfit accused to determine whether a stay should be entered:

> **672.11** A court having jurisdiction over an accused in respect of an offence may order an assessment of the mental condition of the accused, if it has reasonable grounds to believe that such evidence is necessary to determine
>
> . . .
>
> (e) whether an order should be made under section 672.851 for a stay of proceedings, where a verdict of unfit to stand trial has been rendered against the accused.

b) The Review Board May Order an Assessment

The Review Board may also order an assessment for the purpose of making a recommendation for a stay to the court:

> **672.121** The Review Board that has jurisdiction over an accused found not criminally responsible on account of mental disorder or unfit to stand trial may order an assessment of the mental condition of the accused of its own motion or on application of the prosecutor or the accused, if it has reasonable grounds to believe that such evidence is necessary to
>
> (a) make a recommendation to the court under subsection 672.851(1).

Forms related to such assessments orders can be found in the appendices. Appendix B contains an amended Form 48 for the courts; Appendix C contains a new form, Form 48.1, which has been created for the Review Board.

c) Stays

Upon receiving a recommendation for such a stay from the Review Board, or upon its own motion, the court may hold an inquiry to determine whether a stay of proceedings should be ordered. If the court decides to hold an inquiry, it shall order an assessment of the accused. At the conclusion of an inquiry, the court may order a stay of proceedings if it is satisfied, *on the basis of clear information,* that the accused (1) remains unfit, (2) is not likely to ever become fit, and (3) does not pose a significant threat to the safety of the public, and that a stay is in the interests of the proper administration of justice.

Factors to be considered by the court in deciding whether a stay of proceedings is in the interests of the proper administration of justice include, among others:

1) the nature and seriousness of the alleged offence;
2) the salutary and deleterious effects of the order for a stay of proceedings, including any effect on public confidence in the administration of justice;
3) the time elapsed since the commission of the alleged offence; and
4) whether a *prima facie* case has been proven under section 672.33.

i) Evidentiary Burden

In *R v Kearly,*[9] the court decided that a stay of proceedings inquiry pursuant to the provisions of section 672.851 would, as much as possible, be carried out in the same manner as a disposition hearing pursuant to the provisions of section 672.54 and that, to a large extent, the Supreme Court of Canada's rulings in *Winko v British Columbia (Forensic Psychiatric Institute)*[10] were applicable. Those key provisions arc as follows:[11]

9 *R v Kearly,* [2005] OJ No 5394 (Ct J). See also *R v Pollard,* [2007] OJ No 615 (Ct J); *R v Wong,* [2006] BCJ No 1539 (Prov Ct).

10 *Winko v. British Columbia (Forensic Psychiatric Institute),* [1999] 2 SCR 625 at 628–29 [*Winko*].

11 *R v Kearly,* above note 9 at para 13.

1) there is no presumption that the mentally disordered accused poses a significant threat to the safety of the public,
2) the accused is never in a position of having to disprove dangerousness—the accused is therefore relieved of any legal or evidentiary burden—the accused need do nothing (unless, of course, dangerousness is otherwise established),
3) this tactical incentive to adduce evidence is not properly described as a shifting of the legal or evidentiary burden to the accused,
4) if the court or Review Board is unable to conclude that the accused constitutes a significant threat to the safety of the public, he or she must be absolutely discharged,
5) jurisdiction over the accused cannot be maintained where there is doubt regarding dangerousness; continued jurisdiction requires an affirmative finding of significant threat,
6) the threat posed must be more than speculative in nature; it must be supported by the evidence,
7) the threat must also be "significant," both in the sense that there must be a real risk of physical or psychological harm occurring to individuals in the community and in the sense that this potential harm be serious. A minuscule risk of a grave harm will not suffice. Similarly, a high risk of trivial harm will not meet the threshold,
8) the conduct or activity creating the harm must be criminal in nature,
9) finally, it is up to the court or Review Board to ensure that it has sufficient information in order to make the determination.

A reading of the Supreme Court's decision in *R. v. Demers*[12] makes it quite clear that, to the extent possible, a permanently unfit accused who does not constitute a significant threat to the safety of the public should be treated the same as an NCR accused who does not pose a significant threat to the safety of the public. Of course, the NCR accused has obtained a final verdict on the merits after a trial, whereas the permanently unfit accused has not been tried (or the trial may not have concluded). The permanently unfit accused is still presumed to be innocent, whereas there has been a finding of guilt in respect of the NCR accused.

Provisions related to the holding of hearings are set out in the *Criminal Code* as follows:

12 *R v Demers* (2004), 185 CCC (3d) 257 (SCC).

Notice

672.851(2) If the Review Board makes a recommendation to the court to hold an inquiry, the Review Board shall provide notice to the accused, the prosecutor and any party who, in the opinion of the Review Board, has a substantial interest in protecting the interests of the accused.

Inquiry

(3) As soon as practicable after receiving the recommendation referred to in subsection (1), the court may hold an inquiry to determine whether a stay of proceedings should be ordered.

Court may act on own motion

(4) A court may, of its own motion, conduct an inquiry to determine whether a stay of proceedings should be ordered if the court is of the opinion, on the basis of any relevant information, that

(a) the accused remains unfit to stand trial and is not likely to ever become fit to stand trial; and

(b) the accused does not pose a significant threat to the safety of the public.

...

Proper administration of justice

(8) In order to determine whether a stay of proceedings is in the interests of the proper administration of justice, the court shall consider any submissions of the prosecutor, the accused and all other parties and the following factors:

(a) the nature and seriousness of the alleged offence;

(b) the salutary and deleterious effects of the order for a stay of proceedings, including any effect on public confidence in the administration of justice;

(c) the time that has elapsed since the commission of the alleged offence and whether an inquiry has been held under section 672.33 to decide whether sufficient evidence can be adduced to put the accused on trial; and,

(d) any other factor that the court considers relevant.

Effect of stay

(9) If a stay of proceedings is ordered by the court, any disposition made in respect of the accused ceases to have effect. If a stay of proceedings is not ordered, the finding of unfit to stand trial and any

> disposition made in respect of the accused remain in force, until the Review Board holds a disposition hearing and makes a disposition in respect of the accused under section 672.83.

The new legislation includes at least one serious inconsistency. Subsection 672.851(5) clearly contains a mandatory requirement that the court holding an inquiry order an "assessment" of the accused. Subsection 672.11(e), on the other hand, is clear that such an assessment may be ordered only where the court has "reasonable grounds to believe that such evidence is necessary." Where the court receives a recommendation for a stay from the Review Board, it will inevitably have the benefit of the board's record, which will typically include an assessment report focused on the same issue. In such a case, it may be that the court is left without "reasonable grounds" to order yet another assessment, subsection 672.851(5) notwithstanding. In any event, the court need not order an assessment "report." It may be that the process can be greatly abbreviated, with an "oral report" or confirmation of a previously performed assessment.

The court's holding of an inquiry in response to the Review Board's "recommendation" would appear to be discretionary, given the use of the word "may" in subsection 672.851(4). However, it is not at all clear why the court would decline to hold such an inquiry where a recommendation was made or, after it had initiated the process, on its own motion.

3) Clinical Considerations

From a practical perspective, the issue of permanent unfitness in accused who are otherwise not a significant threat to the safety of the public is likely to arise infrequently. Only a small percentage of chronically unfit accused fall into this category. Most unfit accused who come under the Review Board's jurisdiction are rendered fit through treatment and/or education (where needed) and returned to court. The lapse of time is one key factor in establishing the permanent nature of an accused's unfitness, even apart from the condition causing them to be unfit.

In the authors' experience, clinicians and hospitals are attuned to this issue of the permanently unfit and the remedies that may be obtained, and they will raise it (as will defence counsel and Crown counsel) at a chronically unfit accused's annual hearing.

Permanently unfit accused are, generally speaking, more likely to suffer from intractable or deteriorating congenital or acquired conditions associated with intellectual limitations that have either prevented them from acquiring the "understandings" relevant to fitness in the first instance, from acquiring these understandings through deliberate efforts to educate them, or from retaining information relevant to this capacity, as a result of marked memory deficits. The following is a list of conditions more likely to be associated with permanent unfitness.

- *Congenital conditions*
  - intellectual developmental disorder (formerly called mental retardation)
  - severe fetal alcohol spectrum disorder (FASD)
  - congenital metabolic disorders associated with significant intellectual limitations

- *Acquired conditions*
  - autism spectrum disorder
  - brain injury
  - major neurocognitive disorder (e.g., Alzheimer-type & other dementias, cerebrovascular disease (i.e. stroke))
  - Huntington's disease
  - substance-induced neurocognitive disorders

- *Functional mental disorders*
  - severe chronic schizophrenia

Figure 7.1 provides a broad schematic representation of the general timelines associated with either promoting or restoring fitness based on the nature and degree of the mental disorder in question.

Clinicians and hospitals that address routine fitness considerations at initial hearings of unfit accused (*per* sections 672.47(1) and 672.48(1)) or annual hearings of such accused (*per* sections 672.81(1) and 672.48(1)) ordinarily provide opinions based on "here and now" assessments of the accused's fitness, as well as the dispositional considerations listed in section 672.54 (see Section B(5), above in this chapter).

Clinicians who assess an accused with respect to that individual's eligibility for a recommendation for a stay pursuant to section 672.851 will need to go beyond providing an opinion concerning the accused's present fitness to stand trial and forecast whether the accused is ever

FIGURE 7.1. PSYCHOPATHOLOGY-BASED ILLUSTRATIVE TIMELINE FOR BECOMING FIT

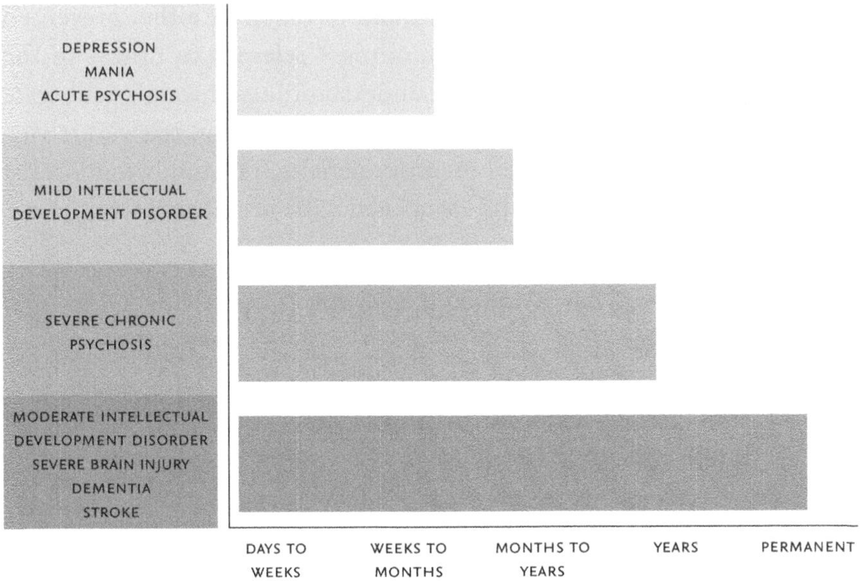

likely to become fit to stand trial. Then, if it is the clinician's opinion that the accused is permanently unfit, the clinician must further address whether the accused represents a significant threat to the safety of the public, as one would in assessing an NCR accused.[13]

From a practical perspective, many unfit accused suffer from deteriorating conditions that incrementally limit their physical and cognitive abilities to engage the public and may lead them to act out violently. With respect to whether an accused is permanently unfit, the court and Review Board having jurisdiction over the accused will want the expert to address the following issues:

- Is the accused's diagnosis consistent with a condition frequently associated with permanent unfitness?
- How long has it been since the accused was found unfit to stand trial in the first instance?
- What has the accused's course in hospital been?
- What clinical parameters have or have not improved?

13 See *Winko*, above note 10.

- How often has the treatment team attempted to address the accused's fitness to stand trial, and what is the most recent assessment of this kind?
- What efforts have been made to educate the accused with respect to the charges and other areas inherent in being fit to stand trial?
- What specific deficits are responsible for the permanent unfitness (e.g., inability to acquire new information, communication problems, extreme apathy, confusion, memory problems, severe unremitting psychotic symptoms)?
- Are there any therapies or interventions on the horizon likely to positively impact on the accused's fitness to stand trial?

Finally, the court and/or Review Board would want to determine that the clinicians have addressed the possibility of malingering unfitness, as it would certainly be in an accused's interest to be declared permanently unfit in order to avoid prosecution for a serious charge.

Ten-Point Review

1) Accused are kept subject to the jurisdiction of the court and the Review Board only so long as they remain unfit to stand trial.
2) Pending an unfit accused's return to court to have the matter retried, any previously made disposition by the court remains operative until the verdict is displaced on a balance of probabilities by the court.
3) The verdict of unfit to stand trial may be reversed only by the court upon a retrial of the issue. The Review Board is merely offering its opinion to the court that the accused may now be fit, which will trigger a retrial of the issue.
4) Within every two years after a verdict of unfit to stand trial, the Crown must demonstrate that it remains in a position to prosecute the matter (i.e., it must show a *prima facie* case).
5) A court may order a stay of proceedings if it is satisfied, *on the basis of clear information*, that the accused remains unfit, is not likely to ever become fit, and does not pose a significant threat to the safety of the public, and that a stay is in the interests of the proper administration of justice.
6) A Review Board may order an assessment in which evidence as to the accused's mental condition is necessary to determine the matter of a stay of proceedings, as set out in section 672.851.

7) The principles set out in *Winko* are applicable to determine whether permanently unfit accused are a significant threat to the safety of the public.
8) The clinician will, in assessing the accused with respect to a possible stay of proceedings under the provisions of section 672.851, have to assess in a prospective manner not only the issue of "significant threat" but also the "likelihood" that the accused will remain unfit to stand trial.
9) In assessing the "likelihood" that the accused will remain unfit to stand trial, the clinician will review the accused's history with respect to unfitness and the extent to which attempts have been made to address the underlying issues.
10) In most cases, the provisions related to stays of proceedings will be applicable to accused suffering from intractable conditions.

CHAPTER 8

Self-Representation: Fitness and Difficult Accused

Among emerging areas of concern for criminal (and civil) courts are fitness for self-representation; managing difficult, vexatious, or querulous self-represented accused (and civil litigants); and guiding psychiatrically and behaviourally well (enough) but under-informed and inexperienced accused (and civil litigants). Given our focus on mental health issues in the context of fitness to stand trial, we will say relatively little about *unrepresented* accused and much about *self-represented* accused. "Unrepresented accused"—a particular problem in the civil justice system—generally refers to litigants/accused who would prefer to have a lawyer but cannot afford legal representation because of insufficient resources, a wish to preserve limited resources, or because of ineligibility for legal aid. "Self-represented accused" (SRA) denotes accused (or litigants) who, for sound or unsound reasons, choose to represent themselves. The distinction is important. Lack of (legal) knowledge and experience defines the former category, while mental illness and personality issues are much more common in the latter.

Our aim in this chapter is to briefly review the hitherto under-addressed issue of fitness for self-representation and the conundrum that SRAs—particularly mentally ill and querulous SRAs—create for the courts. Foremost, we want to provide judges and lawyers with an overview of the psychopathology found in this group and its effect on accused and their ability to manage the exigencies and complexities of their charge(s), and, importantly, some recommendations for how to think about and manage difficult SRAs.

A. FITNESS TO BE SELF-REPRESENTED: A NEW TEST OR STANDARD?

American courts seemingly entered this discussion before their Canadian counterparts. In *Faretta v California*,[1] the US Supreme Court upheld an accused's right to self-representation. Subsequently, in *Godinez v Moran*,[2] the same court concluded that the standard for waiving right to counsel was the same as the standard for competency to stand trial. Until this point in time, all that criminal defendants needed to do to demonstrate the capacity for self-representation was to show that their decision was made knowingly and voluntarily.[3]

Indiana v Edwards[4] was the first American case to adopt a higher standard for competency for mentally ill defendants to represent themselves (referred to in the United States as "*pro se* competence") than for competency to stand trial. Justice Breyer, who wrote the decision for the majority (7:2 decision) in *Edwards*, noted that an accused who met the test for competency to stand trial (in the United States, most frequently the *Dusky* standard[5]) may not necessarily be capable of performing the functions required for self-representation.

The court's view in *Edwards* was that some criminal defendants fall into a "gray area"—capable of passing the low standard for competency to stand trial but insufficiently mentally capable for self-representation. Justice Breyer noted the following reasons in support of imposing a higher standard for self-representation:

- A lack of capacity may result in an improper conviction.
- The accused's right to self-representation may be outweighed by the state's interest in ensuring the trial's integrity.
- Allowing incapable accused to represent themselves may detract from the appearance of fairness of the trial process.
- Allowing afflicted individuals to represent themselves to their detriment will not affirm their dignity.

---

1 422 US 506 (1975).

2 509 US 389 (1993).

3 Mel Greenlee, "Disorder in the Court: Language Use by 'Gray Area' *Pro Per* Defendants" (2015) 2:1 *Language and Law* 12.

4 554 US 164 (2008) [*Edwards*].

5 Referring to the standard in *Dusky v United States*, 362 US 402 (1960) [*Dusky*].

The state of Indiana suggested that the proper standard was whether the accused could "communicate coherently with the court or a jury," but this criterion was rejected by the majority. The court did not articulate a specific test, formula, or standard, or provide guidelines for how to determine whether a mentally ill defendant is capable of self-representation. In this regard, Justice Breyer stated that, rather than setting out an all-encompassing definition for competency for self-representation, the matter should be left to individual trial judges, whom Justice Breyer stated "will often prove best able to make more fine-tuned mental capacity decisions, tailored to the individual circumstances of a particular defendant."[6]

Justice Scalia, who wrote the dissenting decision, opined that a threat to the orderliness of the trial was the only valid reason for denying an accused the right to self-representation. He found that Mr Edwards had been "respectful and compliant" and had not yet failed an opportunity to represent himself. In this regard, Justice Scalia stated, "the dignity at issue is the supreme human dignity of being master of one's fate, rather than a ward of the State—the dignity of individual choice."[7]

Knoll et al.[8] carried out a pilot survey of US judges' views of *pro se* competence after *Indiana v Edwards*. In descending order of importance, judges regarded cognitive/analytical limitations, lack of legal knowledge and experience, and language difficulties as the most likely stumbling blocks to *pro se* competence.

Indiana v Edwards has received very little attention in most Canadian courts, but it does feature prominently in a Yukon Territorial Court decision, *R v Hureau*,[9] where Justice Lilles refers to it as a "significant development in the evolution of the fitness standard in [the United States]."[10] Justice Lilles noted that the exceptions to the right to self-representation set out in *Edwards*—an accused has no right to avoid compliance

---

6 *Edwards*, above note 4 at 177.

7 *Ibid* at 187.

8 James L Knoll IV et al, "A Pilot Survey of Trial Court Judges' Opinions on *Pro Se* Competence after *Indiana v. Edwards*" (2010) 38 *Journal of the American Academy of Psychiatry and Law* 536.

9 [2014] YJ No 48 (Terr Ct).

10 *Ibid* at para 31.

with the law, to abuse the dignity of the courtroom, or to engage in serious obstructionist misconduct—"also apply to Canadian law."[11]

As in *Edwards*, in *Hureau* the accused was sufficiently fit to stand trial if represented but was incapable of representing himself if he chose to do so. Justice Lilles adopted the reasoning in *Edwards*—that the degree of capacity required of self-represented accused for the often complex tasks of managing their defence in a criminal prosecution is greater than the level of capacity needed to be represented by counsel. Justice Lilles summarized his views as follows:

> 1. The requirements of fitness for a represented accused at trial and an unrepresented one are significantly different.
> 2. The standard in s. 2 of the *Criminal Code* assumes representation by counsel and emphasizes the importance of counsel.
> 3. The articulation of the same standard for represented and unrepresented accused assumes that mental illness is a unitary concept—it is not. It varies in degree and in different ways.
> 4. The right to self-representation at trial will not affirm the dignity of a defendant who lacks the mental capacity to conduct his defence without the assistance of counsel. Instead, it will be a humiliating spectacle.
> 5. The accused's lack of capacity threatens an improper conviction or sentence if he is unrepresented and violates his right to a fair trial.
> 6. To deny an accused the right to a trial represented by counsel when he is capable of instructing counsel, understands the nature and object of the proceedings, understands the possible consequence of the proceedings and is able to communicate with counsel would expose him to indeterminate detention in a psychiatric hospital. Crown counsel advised that a placement in Brockville Ontario was being explored for Mr. Hureau. This is several thousand miles away from his family and home. This could amount to cruel and unusual treatment as prohibited by s. 12 of the *Charter of Rights and Freedoms*.[12]

Justice Lilles's Territorial Court decision was overturned,[13] however, on a *certiorari* application by the Crown, which asserted that Justice Lilles had exceeded his jurisdiction by seemingly creating a category—fit to

11 *Ibid* at para 32.

12 *Ibid* at para 39.

13 *R v Hureau*, 2014 YKSC 48.

stand trial only if represented—not contemplated by section 2 of the *Criminal Code.* The Supreme Court of Yukon concluded that the disjunctive language—that is, use of the word "or"—in section 2 requires that a person be found unfit if they are unable to conduct a defence on their own *or* to instruct counsel to do so. The Yukon Supreme Court quashed that portion of Justice Lilles's decision that found Mr Hureau fit if he was represented by counsel. In the view of the court, if Mr Hureau was unfit to represent himself, he was unfit, period. The court took a binary, not nuanced, approach and did not consider the higher standard for self-representation its lower court colleague had painstakingly sought to introduce.

As regards the existence of an articulated standard for fitness for self-representation in Canada, we cannot assume, based on the decision of the Yukon Supreme Court, that the reasoning in *Edwards* is now extant in Canada.

The autonomy of the accused in the adversarial system requires that the accused should be able to make fundamental decisions and assume the risks involved.[14] Accused who have not been found unfit to stand trial must be permitted to conduct their own defence, even if, in doing so, they may act to their own detriment.[15] If an accused has been found fit to stand trial, that person is entitled to self-representation—that is, is fit to decide whether or not to be represented by legal counsel.[16]

While, presumptively, fit accused have the right to represent themselves, the right to self-representation is not absolute.[17] After being appropriately guided, accused are free to employ poor judgment and make foolish tactical decisions, but they are not free to dominate the proceedings. Courts are not required to tolerate an accused's abusive conduct[18] or delay tactics.[19]

The *choice* some litigants make to forfeit legal representation may be a rational and practical one, or may reflect limitations in judgment and/or an array of psychopathological motivations as its basis. The motivation

---

14 *Lienaux v Nova Scotia Barristers' Society*, [2009] NSJ No 32 (CA); *R v Szostak*, [2012] OJ No 3330 (CA); *R v Waranuk*, [2008] YJ No 48 (SC).

15 *Lienaux v Nova Scotia Barristers' Society*, above note 14; *R v Proulx*, [2011] SJ No 477 (Prov Ct); *R v Szostak*, above note 14; *R v Waranuk*, above note 14.

16 *R v Waranuk*, [2010] YJ No 81 (CA).

17 *R v Mirabi*, [2008] OJ No 867 (SCJ); *R v Violette*, [2008] BCJ No 2778 (SC).

18 *R v Fabrikant* (1995), 97 CCC (3d) 544 (Que CA).

19 *R v Beckett*, [2017] BCJ No 1844 (SC).

underlying the decision of accused to represent themselves—and their cognitive, emotional, and behavioural capacity to do so—are key issues in this discussion.

It is unlikely that many would argue in favour of the proposition that accused are better served representing themselves than they would be with skilled criminal counsel.[20] The inherent limitations of a self-represented criminal accused are captured in the following comments by Madam Justice Fuerst:

> Whatever the reason for his or her status, the self-represented accused is usually ill-equipped to conduct a criminal trial. He or she comes to court with a rudimentary understanding of the trial process, often influenced by misleading depictions from television shows and the movies. His or her knowledge of substantive legal principles is limited to that derived from reading an annotated *Criminal Code*. He or she is unaware of procedural and evidentiary rules. Even once made aware of the rules, he or she is reluctant to comply with them, or has difficulty doing so. The limitations imposed by the concept of relevance are not understood or are ignored, and the focus of the trial is often on tangential matters. Questions, whether in examination-in-chief or cross-examination, are not framed properly. Rambling, disjointed or convoluted questions are the norm. The opportunity to make submissions is viewed as an opportunity to give evidence without entering the witness box.[21]

B. UNREPRESENTED ACCUSED

The principle that accused generally have an autonomy-based right to represent themselves, although previously not of itself a contentious notion, was brought to the fore in the Supreme Court of Canada in *R v Swain* in 1991. In that decision, Lamer CJ stated:

> An accused person has control over the decision of whether to have counsel, whether to testify on his or her own behalf, and what witnesses

20 David Berg, "An Inconvenient Right: An Overview of the Self-Represented Accused's Autonomy" (2015) 62:4 *Criminal Law Quarterly* 503.

21 Madam Justice M Fuerst, "The Self Represented Accused: The Trial Judge's Perspective" (2007), quoted in *ibid* at 503–4.

to call. This is a reflection of our society's respect for individual autonomy within an adversarial system.[22]

Courts are required to assist unrepresented accused in presenting their defence throughout the trial.[23] Managing this task puts judges in the difficult position of walking the fine line between sufficiently educating the accused so as to level the playing field and make up for the deficit of lack of representation on the one hand, and avoiding bias and undue interference in the process on the other.[24] This challenge is described in the following excerpt from *R v Romanowicz*:

> The delicate task must be undertaken without compromising the court's impartiality. The duty to ensure a fair hearing will require various types of assistance as the proceeding progresses. This may involve re-instruction regarding procedures explained at the outset of trial or such as may arise as the trial unfolds. In rendering assistance to the accused, the court is obliged to take into account the totality of the circumstances, including the sophistication of the accused, the gravity of the offence charged, the nature of the defence and the complexity of the issues at hand. At the end of the day, however, the unrepresented accused has the right to make strategic decisions and to defend himself or herself at whatever level of competence and effectiveness the accused brings to the case.[25]

In *R v Gonsalves*,[26] the Court of Appeal concluded that an unrepresented accused did not receive a fair trial because of the trial court's failure to:

- provide him with an explanation of how the case would unfold;
- help him understand that he was entitled to object to evidence led by the Crown;
- make him aware of how to use the transcript from the preliminary hearing in cross-examination;
- explain the purpose of cross-examination of a witness, and how to conduct it;

---

22 *R v Swain*, [1991] 1 SCR 933 at para 36.

23 *R v McGibbon* (1988), 45 CCC (3d) 334 (Ont CA).

24 Determining where to set the bar is complex and needs to be done on a case-by-case basis. Donalee Moulton, "Courts Must 'Bend Over Backwards' for Self-Represented Litigants" *Lawyers Weekly* (28 October 2011) 11.

25 *R v Romanowicz*, [1998] OJ No 12 at para 34 (Ct J).

26 [2005] OJ No 1238 at para 3 (CA).

- explain the purpose of *voir dires* dealing with various issues; and
- explain the considerations the accused ought to have borne in mind before testifying on his own behalf.

The legal (and moral) obligation to ensure that unrepresented and self-represented accused and litigants are treated fairly does not start and stop with the courts. Martin[27] notes a stream of caselaw, culminating in the Supreme Court of Canada's endorsement in *Pintea v Johns*[28] of the "Statement of Principles on Self-Represented Litigants on Accused Persons," set out by the Canadian Judicial Council.[29] The guidelines therein, as well as caselaw and the rules of provincial law societies,[30] make it abundantly clear that there is a positive obligation on lawyers to make their position of adversary acting in the interests of the opposing party impeccably clear to unrepresented individuals.

Langan[31] has reported on a marked increase in unrepresented litigants in family court. The reasons here vary, but, unlike the case of self-represented accused in criminal courts, individuals who represent themselves in family court often do so because their socio-economic status and life circumstances have left them in the position of being unable to afford legal representation but ineligible for legal aid. A review of the issues involved in managing self-represented accused where socio-economic factors, and not a mental disturbance, account for lack of representation is beyond the scope of this chapter. However, a study by Hann et al[32] of unrepresented accused in nine provincial criminal courts across Canada has demonstrated that self-representation put these accused at high risk of having their interests compromised. The key findings of the study, with respect to the impact of

27 Bronwyn Martin, "Fair Play: How to Be an Advocate with a Self-Represented Opponent" (2017) 36:3 *Advocates' Journal* 31.

28 [2017] 1 SCR 470.

29 Canadian Judicial Council, "Statement of Principles on Self-Represented Litigants on Accused Persons" (Canadian Judicial Council, September 2006), online: www.cjc-ccm.gc.ca/cmslib/general/news_pub_other_PrinciplesStatement_2006_en.pdf.

30 See the Law Society of Ontario's *Rules of Professional Conduct*, online: www.lsuc.on.ca/lawyer-conduct-rules.

31 Anne-Marie Langan, "Threatening the Balance of the Scales of Justice: Unrepresented Litigants in the Family Courts of Ontario" (2004–2005) 30 *Queen's Law Journal* 825.

32 RG Hann et al, *Court Site Study of Adult Unrepresented Accused in the Provincial Courts* (Ottawa: Robert Hann & Associates Ltd and ARC Applied Research Consultants, prepared for the Department of Justice Canada, 2002).

unrepresented accused on the accused themselves as well as on courts and court officers, and some recommendations to manage these difficulties, are discussed in the following sections.

1) The Impact of Lack of Representation on the Accused

According to the informants in Hann et al's study, unrepresented accused experience serious consequences with respect to the final disposition of their case in court.

- In some situations, depending on the jurisdiction and the stage at which a plea was entered, well in excess of 50 percent of accused who lack the benefit of legal representation are convicted.
- In some situations, depending on the jurisdiction and the type of offence, up to 30 percent of those convicted without benefit of legal representation receive custodial sentences.
- Most key informants believed that unrepresented and under-represented accused suffer negative consequences due to a large number of poor choices and unexploited opportunities during the court process, including the following:
  - At most sites, significant numbers of accused plead guilty "just to get it over with," without understanding the strength of the Crown's case, the options regarding dispositions (e.g., discharges versus convictions), and/or likely and possible sentences.
  - Unrepresented accused (and, at some sites, accused represented by duty counsel) may proceed without having seen the disclosure.
  - The Crown generally will not plea bargain with unrepresented accused, who thus do not benefit from reduced or dropped charges.
  - Accused often do not present relevant information that would influence decisions made during the court process (e.g., regarding bail), including at trial and sentencing.
  - Accused often go through the criminal justice process to disposition and sentencing without understanding what is happening to them (e.g., accused agreeing to, or at least not arguing against, bail or sentencing conditions without understanding their legal and/or socio-economic impact).

- Unrepresented accused often have no idea how to introduce evidence, examine witnesses, or speak to sentence in an appropriate manner, let alone how to do so to their own advantage.
- Accused may plead guilty—even when they have a legal defence—because they are ashamed or embarrassed and want to minimize the shame and publicity.
- Accused plead guilty because they could not live with their bail restrictions or afford the time for numerous court appearances and a trial, given the impact of these restrictions on their ability to fulfil family responsibilities (e.g., obligations to take their children to school) or to retain jobs.
- Accused who plead guilty do not understand the social and economic consequences of carrying a criminal record (e.g., the impact on job prospects, entering foreign countries, or enlisting in the military; possible deportation; driving prohibitions, and so on).

2) The Impact of Lack of Representation on Courts and Court Officers

The justice system is based on the principle that the accused should have a fair hearing. Where the accused does not have legal representation, informants in Hann et al note that judges and other officers of the court must do their utmost to avoid improper situations and compensate for the accused's lack of counsel. In addition, court administrative personnel report significant numbers of requests for information and advice from unrepresented accused. As a result of these factors, key observers believe that cases involving unrepresented accused are particularly stressful for all parties and for the court.

Judges and other court officers must go out of their way to shepherd the case of an unrepresented accused through to completion. Interestingly, while the perception is often that these matters take a greater amount of time (no doubt because of the "pain" involved), in actuality the trials of unrepresented accused take *less* time to conclude, and such accused make *fewer* appearances than accused who have representation. This is no doubt due to the fact that, at each juncture, points are not argued, or are not argued as vigorously as they would be in a trial with counsel assisting. A self-representing accused may not obtain or adduce relevant evidence or even recognize such evidence as helpful.

This may be particularly so with scientific evidence. While all involved in the court process appreciate having matters move expeditiously, this should not be confused with "ineffectively" or "incompletely."

C. ADDRESSING PROBLEMS POSED BY UNREPRESENTED ACCUSED

The informants interviewed by Hann et al list a large number of solutions for addressing problems associated with unrepresented accused. These include the following:

- *Relaxing the eligibility guidelines for legal aid*
  - relaxing financial eligibility criteria to assist more of the working poor with obtaining counsel
  - relaxing coverage provisions, particularly to provide service for first-time offenders, to prevent them from acquiring a criminal record
- *Enhancing the role of duty counsel*
  - expanding the availability of duty counsel
  - providing access to duty counsel, with no consideration of financial eligibility, for all accused, both in-custody and out-of-custody
  - using expanded duty counsel, whereby the duty counsel lawyer retains clients from first appearance to disposition, within the limits of workload
  - having legal aid offices or "advice duty counsel" in court buildings, to provide "information, advice, and assistance" to accused
- *Increasing resources available to legal aid*
  - increasing funding for legal aid
  - increasing the tariff provided to private lawyers accepting legal aid work
  - using paralegals to assist legal aid staff lawyers and duty counsel (e.g., in arranging sureties for bail, researching diversion or sentencing options, etc.)
- *Improving awareness of, and application procedures for, legal aid services*
  - providing information and advice regarding legal aid to unrepresented accused at the earliest possible opportunity.

Methods should recognize the significant literacy handicaps of many accused.

- providing legal aid application officers in the court to expedite matters being stood down pending the assignment of legal counsel, among other factors

- *Enhancing, and improving co-ordination with, other court services and functions*
    - improving co-ordination, in sites with Aboriginal court workers, of services offered by duty counsel and Aboriginal court workers
    - improving access to disclosure
    - instituting better court case and case-flow management procedures that would, *inter alia*, emphasize earlier resolution of cases and reduce the number of "unproductive" court appearances

D. DIFFICULT SELF-REPRESENTED ACCUSED AND THEIR MANAGEMENT

This section[33] focuses on dealing with the difficult self-represented accused (DSRA) in the criminal courts. It is intended to provide judges and lawyers with both a clearer understanding of the psychopathology implicated in accused's decision to represent themselves, as well as some tools to assist in managing frequently ensuing difficulties. Although judges control the legal process and the courtroom itself, some knowledge of the psychological phenomenology being played out with respect to a difficult self-represented accused can enhance that control; such knowledge is one of the factors that influences the way in which a judge will handle DSRAs, as illustrated in Figure 8.1.

FIGURE 8.1. FACTORS THAT AFFECT HOW JUDGES HANDLE DSRA

SUCCESS IN MANAGING DIFFICULT SELF-REPRESENTED ACCUSED

=

Judge's mindset/ personality style	+	*Life experience and courtroom experience*	+	*Use of judicial guidelines/ caselaw*	+	*Understanding accused's psychological difficulties*	+	*Use of strategies aimed at the problem*

1) Why Do Some Accused Reject Legal Representation?

The starting point for this discussion is consideration of the mindset or capacity that allows any person to put themselves into the hands of a lawyer and trust that lawyer and the legal system to do the right thing. Antithetically, one could consider what could possibly motivate an accused to forfeit legal representation. Rejecting legal representation seems counterintuitive when the accused is involved in a proceeding that puts loss of liberty, relationships, status, and perhaps other fundamental states of being at stake.

Tip 1: *Develop a hypothesis concerning the accused's motivation. Why do they not wish legal representation, and why are they being so difficult?*

There are numerous possible reasons why some "fit" but evidently disturbed accused may not wish to be represented by a lawyer. These may include the following:

1) Paranoid accused might believe that nobody around them can be trusted, let alone the lawyer who purports to represent their interests.
2) Narcissistic or psychopathic accused might not feel that a lawyer can represent them as well as they can represent themselves. A lawyer would not understand what they see as their higher agenda.
3) Hypomanic accused (i.e., those who are less than fully manic) might want an opportunity to grandstand; having a lawyer would muzzle them.
4) Delusional accused might be seeking vindication for something or might have another agenda that they would prefer the court to focus on.
5) Accused with severe personality disorders might have as their primary objective the gratification of retributive or even sadistic fantasies by

confronting and attacking witnesses in the potentially theatrical environment of a courtroom.

6) Accused who have had bad experience(s) with lawyers in the past, based either on the accused's psychopathology or some other reason, might be fearful of something bad happening if they put their trust into someone's hands again.

2) Managing DSRAs with Major Mental Disorders and Sub-threshold Conditions

It may not be very long into the proceeding before self-represented accused present challenges to the court's control and convey through their appearance, demeanour, behaviour, and/or utterances that something is amiss with their psychological, emotional, and/or cognitive functioning. It is reasonable at this point for judges to ask themselves "What am I seeing?"

Tip 2: *Characterize the accused's presentation, behaviour, and emotional state*

Oddities in the accused's presentation may have already caused a judge to hypothesize that fitness was going to emerge as an issue in the case. This consideration and whether reasonable grounds exist to order a psychiatric assessment may already have been canvassed and answered in the negative. With no psychiatrist present to address what is being played out in court, the judge will invariably be put in the position of wondering about the state of the accused. Although a judge does not have to pinpoint a condition with great precision, it is useful to identify and have a general understanding of broad categories of behaviour that the accused is exhibiting. For example, is it confusion, intellectual limitation, mood fluctuations, hypersensitivity, a tendency to misinterpret, argumentativeness, suspiciousness, obsessiveness, grandiosity, or a strong sense of entitlement? Is the accused someone who cannot be reassured or directed? Is there more than one aberrant behaviour or process being enacted? The following subsections focus on a number of mental illnesses, personality pathologies, or other psychopathological processes implicated in problematic and disruptive behaviour in self-represented accused, along with suggestions for how to manage self-represented accused with those problems.

3) Delusional Disorder and DSRAs

Delusional disorder is less common than schizophrenia. In delusional disorder, individuals exhibit a generally non-bizarre delusional belief system: they believe things that are theoretically possible but highly unlikely (e.g., government conspiracies targeting them) but without all of the other symptoms associated with schizophrenia (e.g., hallucinations or disorganization).

Many individuals with delusional disorder function perfectly well outside their often highly complex delusional system. The most common delusional belief is persecutory, in the form of extreme paranoia. Examples might include a belief in a pervasive government conspiracy; that a specific individual or group is conspiring or taking steps to cause them personal harm; or that some agency or individual is tampering with their thoughts through transmitters, computers, or other electric paraphernalia. Delusions can insidiously infiltrate a number of domains of the individual's life, but, unless the subject matter of the delusion is specifically examined, the person may appear otherwise *normal*.

Some delusions are of particular interest in the criminal arena. For example, erotomanics believe that a person, usually of elevated social status, such as an actor, politician, physician, or judge, is in love with them, and this drives them to pursue that person. The condition is often the basis of stalking behaviour and criminal harassment charges.

Delusional individuals are rigid, concrete, and obsessional thinkers. They are righteous and indignant, with no sense of humour. They perceive slights and threats everywhere. They are consumed by a notion (delusion), which they may research, present, and discuss in pedantic detail. They are not easily distracted from pursuing vindication, proving the blameworthiness of others, or pursuing some other idea consistent with their very personal sense of justice. The case of *R v Fabrikant*[34] provides an example of such characteristics and tendencies. Professor Fabrikant's trial may not have been so much about defending himself on murder charges as it was about proving that he had been the object of a well-conceived and complex conspiracy that drove him, as it would have driven anyone, to the brink.

34 Above note 18.

In terms of their orientation towards the legal process, delusionally disordered individuals may rigidly adhere to the letter of the law and misperceive its application to their needs and cases. The spirit of the law, a larger abstraction that involves a mindset that embraces the possibility that the justice system is well intended, may be lost on them.

a) Managing Delusional Disordered DSRAs

Delusional accused do not generally behave bizarrely or lose control, but, when they do, it is probably best to let them vent for a brief time, maintaining eye contact and a sympathetic manner. As is the case with most anyone, mentally ill or otherwise, disturbed individuals want and need to be heard. A very agitated delusional accused will find a short rant to be cathartic, after which the pent-up aggression is more likely to be spent. (This in contrast to the case of an individual with a personality disorder, where the behaviour might persist. See Section 7 below.)

Therapists either avoid confronting delusional individuals about their core delusional beliefs or are very careful about doing so. For one thing, delusional individuals believe they are the authority on the subject matter of their beliefs, have often done a great deal of research on it, and can cite chapter and verse. It is consequently best to stand outside the accused's delusional system and to avoid engaging the accused about its subject matter. Where possible, the court should attempt to direct delusional accused away from their delusional ideation and conscript them into assisting with a pragmatic issue before the court.

It is important for the judge to create and maintain temporal boundaries for the proceedings in court. Implanting the idea that things should best happen within a certain time frame may provide a measure of self-governance that the accused before the court would not have considered but for the judge's direction. This individual should be assured that they will be heard fully, but that the process needs to unfold in an orderly manner with all participants taking their turn.

4) Bipolar Disorder: Mania and DSRAs

Bipolar mood disorder affects 1 percent of the population and is characterized by extreme highs (mania) and extreme lows (depression). Mania is more likely than depression to be the source of legal troubles.

Mania is characterized by at least one week of extremely elevated mood. When in a manic episode, individuals require almost no sleep but still feel energized. Their speech is rapid and difficult to interrupt and they can express grandiose ideas—they feel and portray themselves as very powerful or influential or as having abilities others do not have.

Thinking, speech, and communication characteristic of bipolar disorder are readily identifiable. When their mood is elevated, manic individuals can be very gregarious; however, this can either be replaced by or oscillate with an irritable mood. Their thought processes and speech may be scattered and unduly accelerated, marked by tangential thinking, loose associations, and flight of ideas. Their behaviour may be disorganized. They may forfeit legal representation because they feel above or impervious to the legal process or because they are paranoid and cannot trust anyone.

What can lead to legal difficulties is the risk taking that manic individuals can engage in—provoking fights while believing that they are indestructible, maxing out their credit cards, having unprotected sex with strangers, binging on drugs, reckless driving, and so on.

a) Manic Communication Style

Manic accused may find it very difficult to focus on the courtroom process, raising concerns about their fitness to stand trial. Their speech can be rapid and difficult to interrupt (called pressured speech). Although one can expect them to be hyper-talkative and attempt to dominate the airspace, they can occasionally be non-communicative.

b) Managing Manic DSRAs

In essence, the task in managing manic or hypomanic accused may come down to a battle for control in the courtroom, and this may certainly tempt the judge to be more forceful and wield power and authority—and, in some instances, this may be the most reasonable approach. Hypomanic/manic accused need to be patiently reined in. Having a sense of their mental state may assist the judge in keeping them focused. These accused should receive some positive feedback for staying on issue and abiding by the procedural rules and expectations that the judge has set out at the beginning of the matter. Positive feedback—if expressed sincerely—is generally part of a winning formula for dealing with most people. These accused will often "play well" within a set of rules if they feel that they have struck a good deal with the judge and are "being heard."

5) Depressive Disorder and DSRAs

Depression on its own is a very common illness, affecting 10–15 percent of the population. It is characterized by a depressed mood or loss of interest that lasts at least two weeks and is associated with symptoms such as:

- loss of interest in previously enjoyable activities
- neurovegetative signs and symptoms
- increased or decreased appetite and/or sleep
- low energy and poor concentration
- excessive guilt and hopelessness
- suicidal ideation and, depending on the severity of symptoms, the presence of hopelessness, which is a significant risk for suicide
- deteriorated self-care
- psychomotor agitation or slowing

A small subset of depressed people will develop a psychotic depression (i.e., one that involves a full break with reality), in which they can experience hallucinations or delusions. These states may have implications for their criminal responsibility for the act with which they are charged, if they were psychotically depressed at the time it was committed.

a) Depressive Communication Style

Depressed patients also have a characteristic style of communication. They are often withdrawn and slow in their movements and speech. They may convey guilt, generalized apathy, and lack of interest in the outcome of their proceedings (and may perhaps even invite punishment) to an extent that could raise a question about their fitness to stand trial. In addition, they have difficulty focusing on court proceedings.

b) Managing Depressed DSRAs

Depressed DSRAs are more likely to respond to a patient and supportive approach. The judge needs to be aware that depressed accused's pathological guilt can drive them towards poor decision-making and impair their ability to mount a defence. Depressed accused's lack of combativeness and/or lack of interest may make it easier for the judge to direct them to psychiatric assessment and/or intervention pending resumption of the proceedings. Alternatively, the depressed DSRA may be amenable to a renewed suggestion that counsel may be of assistance.

6) Intellectual Disability and DSRAs

Intellectual development disorder (IDD), formerly called mental retardation, is very common in offending populations, either on its own or in combination with other disorders such as major mental illness, substance use, or personality problems. Individuals with IDD have significantly sub-average intelligence (e.g., an IQ that is under 70), although the disorder is stratified depending on its severity, from mild to profound. A mildly afflicted accused has the intellectual capacity of a child in Grade 4, while a person with severe IDD generally has the intellectual capacity of a four-year-old. The more severe the IDD, the more assistance individuals will require attending to their daily activities (e.g., banking, cooking, or even basic tasks like bathing). An individual with intellectual disability disorder is normally diagnosed before the age of eighteen; if IDD is detected after that age, it is almost always another "acquired" condition. Like personality disorders, IDD can often underlie more acute illnesses such as schizophrenia.

IDD is a permanent condition that affects all domains of functioning. Its features include the following:

- limitations in communication and social skills
- emotional dysregulation and vulnerability to stress
- limited ability, or inability, to live independently
- limitations in cognitive abilities (e.g., rigid and concrete thinking; poor information processing, logical thought, and memory; limited ability to engage in abstract thinking)

a) IDD Communication Style

The communications and manner of accused with IDD will reflect the various limitations noted above. With respect to communication, the court may see any of the following:

- variable reliability and consistency of testimony

- emotional outbursts due to stress
- reluctance to say "I don't know" because of a wish to please and concern about being thought of as "dumb"
- failure to understand court proceedings
- inability to behave in accord with specific instructions regarding procedure
- susceptibility to being led in testimony or statements (i.e., a high level of suggestibility)
- vulnerability to environmental stimulation/distraction

b) Managing DSRAs with Intellectual Development Disorder

Accused with IDD will likely respond best to the use of simple and concrete language (abstraction and metaphors should be avoided). In certain situations, their suggestibility may work to their and the court's favour, in that they may more readily accept direction, as well as advice to secure legal representation. If they end up representing themselves, accused with IDD need a close and detailed play-by-play of the proceedings, provided in concrete terms, and they need to be informed when there is a shift from one topic to another. They should be advised that it is acceptable (if not commendable) to say "I don't know" when the circumstances merit it. Judges would be well advised to check the accused's comprehension on a regular basis, and, because of characteristic distractibility, to do their utmost to reduce sensory overload in the courtroom.

It is recommended that the structure of the trial process that will unfold be explained clearly so that there are no "surprises." If, for example, the accused knows that someone's turn to speak is coming, there will be less likelihood of interruptions. A clear and explicit road map is necessary. Finally, as noted, individuals with IDD can be highly suggestible and, consequently, easily led to their detriment. The court should be vigilant with respect to aggressive cross-examinations employing leading questions that amounts to badgering.

7) Personality Disorders and DSRAs

Accused with personality disorders exhibit pervasive patterns of interacting with others and experiencing their environment that are usually maladaptive and inflexible. They exhibit difficulties in a number of domains, including the regulation of emotion and impulse control, or in the interpersonal sphere, and their limitations are sometimes associated with distortions in cognition. According to the fifth edition of the *Diagnostic and Statistical Manual of Mental Disorders* (DSM-5),[35] to reach diagnostic threshold, their disorders need to either cause them personal distress or social or occupational dysfunction. The various personality disorders for which DSM-5 sets out criteria are listed below. Note that only some of these personality disorders may be associated with the DSRA problem.

- Cluster A—"Mad"
  - paranoid
  - schizoid
  - schizotypal
- Cluster B—"Bad"
  - antisocial
  - narcissistic
  - borderline
  - histrionic
- Cluster C—"Sad"
  - avoidant
  - dependant
  - obsessive-compulsive

Patients with personality disorders exhibit just that—problematic personality functioning. They are generally not psychotic or depressed, although they can have co-existing psychiatric disorders of those kinds, and these may be complicated by substance use. As a general rule, personality pathology is worsened or brought to the fore by stressful situations.

a) DSRAs with Paranoid Personality Disorder

Paranoid personality disorder is said to exist when an individual exhibits a recurrent pattern of suspicions without justification and paranoia about the intentions of others. These individuals tend to bear grudges and read hidden meanings into benign remarks. Due to their lack of trust in others, they typically have few if any confidants. They are very sensitive to criticism and rejection, with a tendency to react quickly to

35 American Psychiatric Association, *Diagnostic and Statistical Manual of Mental Disorders*, 5th ed (Washington, DC: American Psychiatric Association, 2013).

perceived attacks or insults. They are very rigid in their thinking; consequently, it is very difficult to reason with them. Their documentation or written materials demonstrate an obsessional and detail-oriented approach.

The key clinical features of paranoid personality disorder include the following:

- aloofness
- difficulty in being directed
- lack of empathy
- lack of rapport with others
- a tendency to bear grudges
- distrust (e.g., recurrent suspicions without justification)
- no sense of humour
- low tolerance for frustration (e.g., quick to react angrily to perceived attacks)
- hypersensitivity to criticism and rejection
- tendency to read hidden meaning into benign remarks
- rigidity in thinking
- obsessional behaviour
- litigiousness (e.g., questioning everything)

i) Paranoid Communication Style

In the courtroom, paranoid individuals can often come across as argumentative, distrustful of everyone, and confrontational. They will not easily accept what is being said to them and will demand evidence or proof. The paranoid accused may choose to represent themselves as a result of their profound distrust of others.

ii) Querulous Paranoia: The Classic Vexatious Accused

Querulous paranoia in vexatious accused/litigants[36] and persistent complainers is more a problem in civil law than in the criminal arena, but the disorder is worth reviewing briefly, particularly because of such individuals' indefatigability as litigators. Every failure in court enlivens and legitimizes their cause and leads to yet another vexatious course of

36 For a recent review of the legal and psychiatric dimensions of vexatious and querulous litigants, see Gary M Caplan & Hy Bloom, "Litigants Behaving Badly: Querulousness in Law and Medicine" (2015) 44:4 *Advocates' Quarterly* 411.

action.[37] Such individuals also crop up as accused on the criminal landscape. In such cases, although they might have been arrested for minor matters, they might seize on the criminal court process—as one process in many different legal (and other) forums—to bring their issues and concerns to the light of day. Morissette cautions that the querulous litigant ought not to be confused with litigants who tenaciously pursues their rights and interest and, further, that querulousness and some form of psychiatric condition are not synonymous.[38]

Mullen and Lester state that querulous paranoia and behaviour (in the civil context) have been increasing, "bringing with it suffering for the querulous and disruption to the organizations through which they seek their vision of justice."[39] Apart from describing the condition in great detail—its clinical features, cognitive styles, and distortions—Mullen and Lester review the phenomenology of the condition in terms of its diagnostic implications. Querulous litigants (and, by extension, querulous accused), however difficult, can at times present their views in a rational and orderly way and may be clear that there is some kind of rational basis for or element of truth to their claim. Unlike truly deluded patients, querulous litigants/accused do not generally proceed on beliefs that are entirely out of keeping with reality-based events. On the contrary, they might seem quite logical in their presentation of the legitimacy of their action: their *interpretation* of the events is more of an issue. On the other hand, some querulous litigants/accused may be obviously deluded, and sometimes "they appear to inhabit that borderline that is captured in such terms as overvalued ideas and delusion-like ideas."[40] Querulous litigants/accused are obviously preoccupied with the subject matter of their interests, paying pedantic attention to the minutiae of their case. This suggests an obsessional dimension, but, unlike true obsessional personalities, querulous litigants/accused do not regard their core beliefs and behaviour as absurd.

37 Yves-Marie Morissette, "Abus de droit, quérulence et parties non représentées" (2004) 49 *McGill Law Journal* 23.

38 *Ibid.*

39 PE Mullen & G Lester, "Vexatious Litigants and Unusually Persistent Complainants and Petitioners: From Querulous Paranoia to Querulous Behaviour" (2006) 24 *Behavioral Sciences and the Law* 333 at 333.

40 *Ibid* at 340.

iii) Written Communications from Querulous Accused

It is not uncommon that the materials querulous accused present in court are obsessive in detail, extensive, over-inclusive, and often irrelevant. Such accused use a characteristic style, overemphasizing points that they see as important by use of highlighting or underlining. The content might be repetitious, rambling, or contain covert, or even overt, threats. In addition, such communications are often characterized by the following:

- rambling prose (e.g., repetition) and a pedantic failure to clarify
- rhetorical questions
- misuse of legal, medical, and other technical jargon
- references to self in the third person
- inappropriately ingratiating statements
- ultimatums
- threats (usually indirect or oblique) of violence to self or others
- threats (usually indirect or oblique) of violence directed at individuals or organizations
- curious formatting
- vastly excessive amounts of material
- odd or irrelevant schedules and appendices (e.g., copies of letters from others, legal decisions, the United Nations Declaration of Human Rights), frequently extensively annotated
- multiple methods of emphasis, including multicoloured highlighting, underlining, and/or capitalization
- repeated overuse of punctuation (e.g., ???, !!!)
- numerous footnotes, marginal notes, and/or endnotes[41]

iv) Managing Paranoid DSRAs

The paranoid individual can often induce frustration and exhaustion in others. Transparency about the process and decisions being made may help to minimize communication difficulties and allow for more effective courtroom management. If possible, the court should avoid sidebars, and the prosecution should avoid taking others aside to discuss matters in private: such private discussions will only enhance the accused's paranoia.

41 *Ibid* at 336.

Some suggestions to consider in managing paranoid DSRAs in the courtroom include the following:

- The accused's hot-button issues should be avoided.
- Procedures and rulings should be explained simply, concretely, and unchangingly.
- Selective asides should be avoided, and the accused included in all discussions, if possible.
- Clarity and transparency should be sought, to the extent possible, and ambiguity avoided.
- Close attention should be paid to procedure, as this group fixates on procedural irregularities and will seize on each of them as the subject matter of the next course of action.
- Written submissions should be received with an acknowledgment of the diligent effort taken to create them, but should be tactfully set aside for the time being.

b) DSRAs with Antisocial (Psychopathic) and Narcissistic Personality Disorders

Individuals suffering from antisocial personality disorder (ASPD) are often the everyday criminal whom judges have come across countless times. Individuals with ASPD have shown characteristic traits since their early adolescence—they were rebellious and rule-defying children and adolescents. In adulthood, they continue to demonstrate antisocial behaviour and values that bring them to the attention of the authorities. They disregard the safety or rights of others and engage in repeated acts of aggression. They perceive themselves in grandiose terms. Accused with ASPD are perpetually irresponsible. They fail to accept responsibility for their actions; rather, they externalize blame, projecting it onto others. They are impulsive, and they exhibit manipulative or conning behaviour, as well as a lack of remorse for their actions and a lack of empathy for others.

Like individuals with antisocial personalities (roughly equivalent to psychopathy, which is not recognized by the American Psychiatric Association in the DSM-5), narcissistic individuals are grandiose (a core trait) in the way they perceive themselves. They lack empathy for others, can be exploitative or manipulative, and lack remorse for their actions. They are focused on their self-importance: they believe they are unique and should associate with individuals of high status. Their personality style is rooted deeply and involves talking incessantly about themselves, turning conversations around to make themselves the topic, perpetually seeking compliments, diminishing the achievements of others in an attempt to bolster themselves, and believing that others are envious or jealous of them. They come across as arrogant, self-important, and entitled. They require excessive admiration, become easily defensive, and are prone to re-attribution of blame.

Narcissistic DRSAs can be the most challenging accused. They are concerned about being seen as inferior. They are conflict-prone due to their attitudes towards others. Their inability to appreciate other viewpoints and their disregard for how their behaviour impacts their environment make them uniquely challenging to manage in the courtroom. These individuals lack insight into their shortcomings, behaviour, and motivation, and feel they are above the law, or, in the extreme, that they *are* the law. Judges should be aware that these individuals routinely evoke negative feelings—anger, frustration, helplessness, and so on—in others.

i) Antisocial (Psychopathic) and Narcissistic Communication Style

The antisocial (psychopathic) and narcissist communication styles can overlap and create similar communication problems in court. Both groups are likely to engage in power struggles as a result of their wish to dominate or control the process. To facilitate their need to feel superior, they may try to put others down by pointing to perceived ineptitude, thus generating frustration or anger in others. Their lack of empathy renders them either oblivious and/or indifferent to the impact their communications have on others. They present as pseudo-intellectual, grandiose, and condescending. If their communications result in repeated infractions or violations of the rules of the courtroom, they likely have no remorse and may, indeed, sometimes flout the rules intentionally.

Some narcissists and psychopaths are, in fact, very skilled communicators, a talent that is often used in the service of getting their needs met or evading punishment. In the courtroom, they may present as slippery and glib, and are likely to proffer facile excuses for most anything, delivered with potentially convincing emotional punctuation. Further probing reveals that the accused's emotions lack depth and sincerity: they are not truly remorseful for their behaviour.

ii) Managing Antisocial (Psychopathic) and Narcissistic DSRAs

In dealing with antisocial (psychopathic) and narcissistic DSRAs, it is important that judges maintain firm boundaries and remain in control. Judges should not deviate from the usual limits set out in their courtroom. The rules of the courtroom, as well as the consequences of violations, should be set out in advance in clear terms, and then should be enforced inflexibly. Although a useful tactic for managing such individuals can be to play up to their need to be admired, by using praise or stroking the ego of the accused, this tactic should not be used at the sacrifice of the judge's own authority or power. A sense of defeat or submissiveness will only empower these accused.

Antisocial and narcissistic accused need both set limits and positive feedback. In the courtroom, judges should:

- avoid "taking the bait" and becoming angry, flustered, helpless, defeated;
- listen empathetically;
- remain in control and convey a clear sense of that control;
- define any procedural and other limits; and
- commend accused and positive feedback for their strengths and accomplishments and for staying within the court's bounds.

c) Histrionic and Borderline Personality Disordered DSRAs

Individuals with histrionic personality disorder are prone to melodrama and seem to always need to be the centre of attention. Their emotional state impresses as being shallow and changes rapidly. Often, in an attempt to garner the attention of others, their mannerisms, physical appearance, and demeanour are inappropriately seductive or provocative. Their behaviour is often dramatic and theatrical. Histrionic individuals are easily suggestible and are influenced by others and by the circumstances they are in. They often consider relationships to be more intimate than they actually are—for example, a person they met just a week ago is their new best friend or their lifelong soulmate. Accused with histrionic personality disorder:

- seek attention to avoid fear of being ignored;
- are often inappropriately seductive, provocative, or flirtatious;
- exhibit rapid shifts of shallow emotions;
- use physical appearance to draw attention to themselves;

- present as dramatic, colourful, and superficial in court;
- tend to represent a problem or issue in a way that is out of proportion to the reality of the situation; and/or
- are prone to exaggeration and fabrication.

Borderline personality disorder is notable among personality disorders for the degree of instability of its sufferers and extent of chaos they can produce. Borderline individuals are often driven by a fear of abandonment. Relationships tend to be unstable and intense, with marked oscillations between idealization and devaluation of another person. In the courtroom, this could result in the judge being idealized one day and then denigrated on another. Borderline patients can also be manipulative and seductive.

Other criteria that define the condition of borderline personality disorder, according to DSM-5, include chronic feelings of emptiness, a disturbance in identity, and impulsivity in at least two potentially self-damaging areas (e.g., spending to excess, sexual behaviour, substance abuse, binge eating, or reckless driving). Borderline individuals often engage in suicidal gestures or threats or in self-mutilating behaviour. Their mood is unstable, with marked fluctuations between depression, irritability, and pronounced anger (they can fly into rages). They may also experience transient stress-related paranoid ideation and/or dissociative symptoms. Although not strictly a diagnostic criterion for the condition, boundary violations are common.

i) Histrionic and Borderline Communication Style

Borderline and histrionic accused are particularly prone to intense displays of emotion in court (these might be most evident in family court settings). Feelings of rejection or abandonment might evoke threats of self-harm. Particularly in the case of borderline accused, their feelings about and consequent communication to all participants in the legal process can oscillate dramatically from day to day (without provocation or evident cause). Such individuals' view of a judge may range from adoring them and characterizing them as the best judge on the planet on one day and cursing the ground they walk on the next. For people with these disorders, there is no in-between: people are black or white, there are no shades of grey.

Patients with borderline and histrionic personality pathology may display any one or a number of the following communication-related behaviours in court:

- high emotional intensity—that is, prone to intense experiences and outbursts due to anger and impulsivity (especially borderline DSRAs)
- rapid shift in mood and angry outbursts (especially borderline DSRAs)
- dramatic/theatrical speech (especially histrionic DSRAs)
- misrepresentation and exaggeration (especially histrionic DSRAs)
- inability to stay focused (especially histrionic DSRAs)

ii) Managing Histrionic and Borderline DSRAs

Managing borderline and histrionic accused can be extremely challenging, as they evoke strong feelings in anyone with whom they come into contact. This is likely to be accentuated in the dramatic environment of the courtroom, although it may take some time for the behaviour to become visible. Initially, borderline and histrionic accused can be quite effective in drawing others into their drama and difficulties, evoking sympathy, and engendering a wish to help or even save them from their difficulties. It soon becomes evident, however, that there is no easy remedy to satisfy their need. In the case of borderline accused in particular, their need is the proverbial "bottomless pit." Efforts to be of assistance, and a strong risk of failure in that regard, often induce a sense of ineptness, helplessness, and frustration in those who try to help.

These accused respond well to genuine empathy—they are astute at detecting insincerity in this regard. Empathic statements are likely to be most effective when they are linked to the source of the emotional outburst (e.g., in a criminal law context, "I can see how upset you are; you're no doubt terrified that you may be convicted and sentenced to a period of incarceration, which would cause you to lose your job and put your children in peril"). Although empathy is an effective tool, it is important that judges convey—clearly and authoritatively—that accused are responsible for their own behaviour and what the consequences are likely to be if the disruptive behaviour continues. Further techniques to manage these difficult accused include the following:

- when possible, using strategic breaks to allow the person a moment to collect themselves;
- focusing discussion and redirecting the attention of the accused;
- giving them manageable tasks; and
- establishing clear boundaries in a calm but authoritative tone.

8) Situational Stress

Tip 3: *Recognize and manage situational stress.*

Problematic behaviour is not necessarily the result of any significant underlying major mental disorder or personality pathology. It is often said that stress can bring out the worst in people; and the stress of dealing with the legal process is particularly noxious. Self-representing accused (and litigants in civil contexts) may be experiencing situational stress in one or more domains of their personal life. Background stress (e.g., financial limitations) may, in fact, have been one of the motives driving the choice accused have made to represent themselves.

Stress can worsen any underlying personality pathology (or personality traits short of a personality disorder) and cause a variety of transient disturbances in emotion (e.g., emotional lability, inappropriate intensity, anger), behaviour (e.g., uncharacteristic outbursts, poor judgment), or cognition (e.g., confusion and difficulty processing information). Clinicians often use the diagnostic term "adjustment disorder" when referring to depressive, anxious, and/or behavioural symptoms that, although exhibited in response to an identifiable stressor, are excessive and impairing.

Some awareness of the circumstances the accused is going through would undoubtedly be an asset to the judge and would probably assist in understanding what needs to be addressed in order to help both the accused and the proceedings move forward. An empathic approach and subtle recommendations for, or guidance towards, help and support are of great value in these circumstances.

Tip 4: *Consider that much of what happens between people in a number of situations is brought about or influenced by unconscious processes.*

Psychiatrists and psychologists generally believe that what happens in the conscious world—in terms of what motivates people—is the tip of the iceberg. Clinicians appreciate that a wealth of forces operate at an unconscious level, which—at a minimum—influence the individual's feelings, actions, and long-term course, and sometimes drive these processes outright, regardless of the individual's conscious awareness. Accused (and lawyers) before the court may resist, subvert, grandstand, or act aggressively because of some unresolved issue in life brought to the fore by something occurring in court, and yet may be entirely unaware of what the behaviour means.

Although judges are not trained to think about unconscious psychological processes, these processes impact everyday life, no less in the courtroom. It would be worthwhile, then, for judges to consider that unconscious processes (e.g., thoughts, feelings, fantasies, attitudes, wishes, conflicts) exert some force, particularly in the interpersonal sphere. The authors suggest that this view can be held without necessarily subscribing to all the principles and notions associated with the larger field of psychoanalytic thought.

9) Transference

Every person is the product of a unique upbringing, with experiences, interactions, emotions, and relations that are specific to them and no other. A person's unique set of experiences inevitably leads to them experiencing life and other people through a filter that is biased by these experiences.

"Transference" is the mental process whereby a person transfers patterns of feelings, expectations, and behaviour that had previously been associated with important figures, such as parents, onto another person. It is a psychoanalytic term that, in the context of psychotherapy, refers to a patient's emotional response to their therapist. For example, a patient with a chaotic background, whose parents abandoned them at a young age and who has never had a stable home or a reliable adult figure in their life, might experience their therapist as someone who will also inevitably disappoint and abandon them, causing them to be hostile and angry towards the therapist for no obvious reason.

The parallel in court might be an accused who experiences the judge as a punitive and unjust parent, even before the judge has made a final decision. Characteristics the accused sees in common between the judge and a past important figure can be particularly evocative. The reaction of an accused—and especially a DSRA—may be a product of their personal past experiences with a difficult parent, and not based on real-life interactions with the judge.

10) Countertransference

"Countertransference" is a psychoanalytic term that refers to the feelings and attitudes the patient evokes in the analyst or therapist. It is, to some extent, the mirror image of transference. In the context of judge and accused, countertransference may provoke the judge's unconscious feelings about important past figures evoked by the accused's actions or representational qualities. However, such countertransference is not invariably based on the judge's past experiences, but might represent a reaction to an accused who exhibits strong transference with respect to the judge. If countertransference is at play (and many clinicians and writers in the field of mental health would argue that transference and countertransference are invariably at play in all relationships), then the judge's response to the accused might be based on one of the following:

- the judge's "realistic" emotional reaction that anyone would have in the same situation;
- the judge's own irrational feelings founded in personal experience; and/or
- the emotional response evoked by the accused's specific reaction/transference to the judge.

Feelings related to countertransference are inevitable in a judge dealing with a DSRA. While it may be true that a difficult accused would evoke a negative response in anyone, countertransference runs deeper and subsumes feelings the judge may harbour about a number of other people in their life of whom the accused is reminiscent.

a) Impact of Unchecked Countertransference in the Courtroom

Countertransference can impede judges' ability to be objective, impartial, and unbiased. As well, the most basic ramification of a strong countertransferential reaction to a DSRA is to potentially misdirect the judge away from the course of action they might have taken, but for the strong reaction.

Generally, there are two types of countertransferential reactions: the first is to react with aggression; the second is to react by overindulging the accused with more benefits and consideration than the situation merits. It would be unusual for a judge to be overtly angry and aggressive towards an accused; instead, they are more likely to respond in a passive-aggressive manner. Passive aggression is a muted form of aggression in which the individual acts out aggression in a passive way by thwarting, hindering, or otherwise subverting another, and/or by engaging in passive or symbolic behaviour that is punitive and conveys the underlying aggression. This may occur at times when the judge cannot call out the DSRA outright on their poor behaviour; instead, the judge might become more covertly punitive in their decisions than they might otherwise have been.

McEwen[42] gets precisely at this point in her review of the trial of a self-represented accused who was appealing convictions for ten counts of sexual assault. The accused, Henry, was acquitted in 2010 by the British Columbia Court of Appeal because legal errors had been made at trial. Among them, McEwen argues, were marked insufficiencies in the trial judge's management of Henry as a self-represented accused, although these claimed shortcomings were not factors on appeal leading to the acquittal. A key point made by McEwen, in reviewing the trial transcripts, was that "the trial judge allowed his growing antipathy toward Henry to tilt the playing field more sharply than it already was."[43]

In other cases, a judge might be more lenient with an accused, even overindulgent. Some people, judges included, do not like thinking badly of others or seeing themselves as intolerant. They disavow extremely negative feelings in themselves that others have evoked (and might evoke in anyone). When an individual harbouring such negative feelings finds them unacceptable, they unconsciously turn them around, through a process clinicians call "reaction formation." Rather than confronting the individual who has induced the negative feeling, a paradoxically permissive, indulging, or positive response may be adopted. As much as judges might respond in a more tolerant, lenient, and permissive manner towards an accused who has acted in a seductive manner and evoked a positive countertransference feeling, they

42 Joan McEwen, "Ivan Henry: Self-Represented Accused and the Trial Judge's Duty to Assist" (2012) 70:4 *Advocate* 537.

43 *Ibid* at 543.

may also, paradoxically, display the same behaviour towards someone who has evoked negative feelings.

b) Managing Countertransference

Judges are the duly mandated controllers of all that happens in their courtrooms. A difficult accused can induce feelings of helplessness and powerlessness in a judge, and a sense of failure if the judge is unable to bring the accused into line. People who are out of control and feel helpless and powerless can induce those same feelings in others around them.

Difficult self-represented accused have an uncanny ability to get under anyone's skin. In the context of the courtroom, and with no lawyer acting between the accused and the court as a buffer, a DSRA can incessantly challenge the rules and require endless redirection; this cannot but have a fatiguing and ultimately demoralizing effect on the judge. DSRAs may care little about the rules that all courtroom personnel and many accused highly respect. Such accused may berate the judge and anyone else in the courtroom, and discount the process entirely. In the end, they can negatively affect judges and be a source of workplace stress and dysphoria. DSRAs can induce many different feelings and reactions in judges. The long list includes feelings of helplessness, hopelessness, defeat, devaluation, anger/rage, frustration, or manipulation. The judge may feel discarded and devalued or, contrarily, idealized and seduced.

Extremely difficult situations that people are inextricably locked into—like a judge needing to conduct a fair trial with a DSRA—may make them feel as if they are all alone. To combat these negative feelings and outcomes, judges faced with a DSRA could use any of the following techniques:

- Be aware of feelings the accused's behaviour is inducing in them.
- Identify the emotions involved and their impact on their own behaviour.
- Recognize that the accused likely elicits similar feelings in others.
- Form a hypothesis as to why the accused is behaving in a particular way (e.g., personality flaws, stress, cognitive limitations).
- Anticipate communication challenges to help maintain a sense of control.

- Consult a support network and/or senior colleague for catharsis and guidance.
- Recognize when further help is required.
- Read about personality pathology.
- Record courtroom experiences in a journal and share them with colleagues.

*****

Managing difficult self-represented accused is a unique challenge for judges, and one that may be outside the scope of activities that they expect to face when they accepted their jobs. Accused whose choice to represent themselves is either the result of, or is influenced by, some mental disturbance invariably bring elements of their mental difficulties into an already complicated, if otherwise orderly, process. Managing the concerns that they present requires not only the commanding presence and inherent control that judges have over the process and their courtrooms, but an enhanced array of strategies based on understanding of the psychological factors at play. As this chapter has demonstrated, there is overlap between different psychopathological processes and disorders, but disorders also come with specific traits that make certain behaviours more likely. Understanding the differences between disorders and the characteristics and behaviours associated with them will likely work towards improving the acuity of a judge's strategy or management plan.

Addressing issues of this kind is likely to prove personally (emotionally and psychologically) taxing to judges. Many judges will no doubt question how they managed a particularly difficult case. The best way to respond to such questioning is to determine for oneself what worked and what did not. Identifying key factors that enhanced or detracted from the strategies used will allow one to modify future interventions accordingly.

Ten-Point Review

1) Courts are increasingly contending with the dilemma of unrepresented and self-represented accused (and litigants).
2) There is a distinction between unrepresented and self-represented accused: socio-economic factors and lack of knowledge are the bigger

issues for unrepresented accused and litigants; mental illness and personality factors feature more prominently among self-represented accused.

3) Some mentally ill accused may be fit to stand trial, but unfit to represent themselves.
4) The Yukon Territorial Court in *Hureau* adopted the analysis in *Edwards v Indiana* and concluded (among other things) that the requirements for self-representation "are significantly different" than those for fitness to stand trial. That view was not upheld on appeal to the Yukon Supreme Court.
5) Allowing incapable accused to represent themselves can be an affront to both their dignity and that of the courts.
6) Legal status aside, there is no established clinical protocol or tool specifically for assessing fitness for self-representation.
7) The adoption of a higher/different fitness threshold for self-representation could result in more accused being found unfit to represent themselves.
8) Different diagnoses, conditions, and psychopathology are found in the backgrounds of difficult self-represented accused.
9) Having a theory about the psychopathology driving a difficult self-represented accused would likely help a judge better manage the accused and meet the needs of justice.
10) Unconscious dynamics in interpersonal dealings and relationships are ubiquitous and need to be considered in the interpersonal dynamics in court and in managing difficult self-represented accused.

CHAPTER 9

Fitness in the United Kingdom and the United States

A. THE UNITED KINGDOM

1) Fitness to Plead

What is referred to as "fitness to stand trial" in Canada or "competency to stand trial" in the United States is, in England and Wales, known as "fitness to plead." The current test has evolved from the common law and is based principally on the case of *R v Pritchard*, where the judge directed the jury that fitness to plead depended on:

> whether [the defendant] is of sufficient intellect to comprehend the course of proceedings on the trial, so as to make a proper defense—to know that he might challenge [any jurors] to whom he may object—and to comprehend the details of the evidence .... If you think that there is no certain mode of communicating the details of the trial to the prisoner, so that he can clearly understand them, and be able properly to make his defence to the charge, you ought to find that he is not of sane mind. It is not enough that he may have a general capacity of communicating on ordinary matters.[1]

The test is an intellectual one that assesses the accused's level of comprehension and communication as well as their ability to instruct counsel. In *R v Berry*, the court held that a high degree of (mental) abnormality did not mean that the accused was incapable of following a trial, giving evidence, instructing counsel, and so on.[2]

1 *R v Pritchard* (1836), 7 Car & P 303 at 304, 173 ER 135 [*Pritchard*].

2 *R v Berry* (1876), 1 QB 447.

The test in England now focuses on four main areas:

1) the defendant's appreciation of the charges and potential consequences (including the significance of potential pleas);
2) the defendant's ability to understand the trial process;
3) the potential for the defendant to participate in that process; and
4) the ability of the defendant to work collaboratively with counsel on their defence.

The effect an accused's mental condition has on their ability to comprehend proceedings, rather than the mere existence of that condition, is the relevant factor in determining fitness. As in Canada, a "mental disorder" is a necessary but not sufficient condition for a finding of unfitness. Also as is the case in Canada, amnesia with respect to the alleged offence, by itself, would not lead to a finding of unfit, as it would not, by itself, affect the accused's ability to understand the proceedings.[3] If the individual is of insufficient intellect to comprehend the court proceedings, that person is said to be unfit to plead, or "under disability." The decision in *Pritchard* implies that there is a threshold of disability to be met in order to be found unfit to plead. (This level of disability may be measured only in terms of the impact it has had on the accused.) As well, *Pritchard* makes the observation, which can be quite important in other contexts, that there is a distinction to be made between the capacity required to be "fit" and the "general capacity of communicating on ordinary matters."

In England, unlike in Canada, if the issue of fitness is raised by the Crown, the criminal standard (of beyond reasonable doubt) is set;[4] if the issue is raised by the defence, the civil standard of proof (that is, on the balance of probabilities) applies.[5] Evidence from two doctors is required but is not determinative.

If the accused is considered fit to plead, then the court proceedings continue in the usual manner, either to sentencing or to a trial, depending on which plea is then entered. If the court determines that the accused is unfit to plead, then a "trial of the facts" takes place before a jury. This requirement was introduced by the *Criminal Procedure (Insanity*

---

3 *R v Podola*, [1960] 1 QB 325 (CA). See the discussion of *R v Morrissey* in Chapter 3, Section B.

4 *R v Robertson*, [1968] 3 All ER 557 (CA).

5 *R v Podola*, above note 3.

and Unfitness to Plead) Act 1991;[6] that Act ensures that the evidence against the defendant is tested in advance. In Canada, under section 672.25 of the *Criminal Code*,[7] a similar discretion is left with the court. The 1991 Act provided that the trier of fact must be "satisfied ... the accused ... did the act or made the omission charged against him as the offense" before the matter can proceed to "disposal."[8] The criminal standard of beyond a reasonable doubt is used. If a *prima facie* case is not established, the trier must acquit the accused. The accompanying Government Circular to the 1991 Act states that the trial of the facts should not dwell on the accused's intent (*mens rea*).[9] As Exworthy points out,

> [d]ifficulties have arisen because to concentrate solely on the *actus reus* eliminates possible defenses such as self-defense yet to examine both the *actus reus* and *mens rea* makes the trial of the facts indistinguishable from a criminal trial, in which the defendant is unfit to participate. In *Egan*, the Court of Appeal held that "the act" required "proof of all the ingredients of what otherwise would be an offense." This seems to incorporate *mens rea*, because the same physical act can be charged as different offenses depending on the person's intent. The same court later decided that *Egan* had been decided incorrectly and only the *actus reus* need be proved. The House of Lords, in *Antoine*, effectively overruled *Egan* and held that "the jury need only be satisfied ... (of) the *actus reus* of the offense, not the *mens rea*," but added a compromise that the defenses of mistake, accident, self-defense, or involuntariness could be raised.[10]

---

6 *Criminal Procedure (Insanity) Act* 1964 (UK), c 84 [the 1964 Act], as amended by the *Criminal Procedure (Insanity and Unfitness to Plead) Act* 1991 (UK), c 25 [the 1991 Act] and the *Domestic Violence, Crime and Victims Act* 2004 (UK), c 28.

7 *Criminal Code*, RSC 1985, c C-46.

8 The 1991 Act, above note 6, s 2, enacting new s 4A(2) in the 1964 Act.

9 Home Office, *Guidance on the Criminal Procedure (Insanity and Unfitness to Plead) Act 1991, Circular* 93/91 (London: Home Office, 1991).

10 Tim Exworthy, "Commentary: UK Perspective on Competency to Stand Trial" (2006) 34:4 *Journal of the American Academy of Psychiatry and the Law* 466 at 468 [footnotes omitted]. *R v Egan*, [1998] 1 Cr App R 121 and *R v Antoine*, [2000] 2 All ER 208 are referred to by Exworthy. Such defences do involve consideration of the defendant's motivation, but this concession by the House of Lords avoids the absurdity of the trial of the facts, adopting the narrow interpretation of "the act," potentially finding a defendant "guilty of an act that was in fact lawful." See RD Mackay & G Kearns, "The Trial of the Facts and Unfitness to Plead" (1997) *Criminal Law Review* 644.

The consideration of these defences is restricted to the use of objective evidence, thus ensuring that the accused "could not participate in the process when adjudged to be unfit. In *Antoine*, Lord Hutton quoted, with approval, from the judgment in the *Attorney General's* case, that it is not necessary to prove *mens rea* because 'in an insanity case the issue of *mens rea* ceases to be relevant.'"[11]

2) Dispositions After a Trial of the Facts

Exworthy describes the process after a trial of the facts pursuant to the provisions of the 1964 *Criminal Procedure Act*. A finding of unfitness to plead led to a mandatory, indefinite committal of the accused to a psychiatric hospital. This outcome could be quite inappropriate, as the offence might have been rather insignificant relative to the incursion upon the accused's liberty and, further, the condition causing the unfitness might be one for which a hospital could not provide treatment. Amendments to the Act provided a broader range of disposition options that would fit better with the accused's needs.[12]

> In addition, the court may also make a restriction order, under section 41 of that Act, restricting authorization of the person's discharge from hospital to either a Mental Health Review Tribunal or to the Home Secretary, the government minister with political responsibility for such detained patients. The restriction order is a judicial decision, after hearing medical evidence that explicitly addresses the need to protect the public from serious harm.[13]

Curiously, while most trials of the issue of fitness in Canada are conducted at the provincial or territorial court level (where the bulk of criminal prosecutions begin and end), that is not the case in England. In fact, the issue of fitness is (apparently) rarely raised for less serious matters.

Exworthy explains:

> The procedures for determining fitness to plead described herein relate only to the Crown Courts, the higher criminal court dealing with more serious offenses. The overwhelming majority of criminal offenses are

11 *R v Antoine*, above note 10 at 216, cited in Exworthy, above note 10 at 468.

12 Exworthy, *ibid* at 469.

13 Exworthy, *ibid* at 470.

dealt with in the lower, magistrates courts. There is no procedure set out in statute whereby a person's fitness to plead may be determined in these courts. However, various mechanisms are available to resolve such a situation. If the court's jurisdiction encompasses the alleged offense, the Crown Prosecution Service (CPS) may discontinue legal proceedings when consideration of the person's mental health outweighs the "interests of justice." Such an outcome can be combined with the civil admission of the person to hospital under the Mental Health Act.[14]

However, if the public interest demands that a prosecution be pursued but concerns exist over an individual's fitness to plead, these matters can be addressed through the provisions of the *Mental Health Act* that allow the admission to hospital for a finite period while criminal proceedings continue. Taking this course of action assumes that the person's mental disorder and his unfitness to plead are linked and that treating the former will reverse the latter. The need to determine fitness to plead is thus circumvented rather than addressed.

However, it may be that the person's mental disorder proves to be resistant to the treatment and a return to fitness is not anticipated. In these circumstances, the court, when satisfied "the accused did the act or made the omission charged" has the power to make a hospital order without recording a conviction. This provision makes no reference to fitness to plead but repeats the relevant phrase in the 1991 Act, and the power has been considered suitable for the scenario of a defendant's being unfit. Lord Lane, as a former Lord Chief Justice, termed this an "unusual power" that "would usually require … the consent of those acting for the accused if he is under a disability so that he cannot be tried." In that case, the person's mental disorder prevented him from understanding what it meant to consent to trial. This suggests the defense lawyer has to adopt a pragmatic but nonetheless paternalistic approach and decide to accept the facts of the prosecution case without acting on formal instructions from his client to do so. There is no doubt that to escape a conviction can be considered to be in the client's

14 This ability to abort prosecutions for less serious matters once the accused is in the hands of appropriate civil mental health care appears to be very much like what is being accomplished in Canada with its diversion programs. Most provinces have adopted a process where minor matters may be "diverted" out of the criminal courts once the Crown is satisfied that the individual is engaged in appropriate mental health care.

interests (and using this route, there is no possibility of a return to court should the person subsequently become fit to plead again). However, there are consequences, specifically, admission to a hospital.

The Mental Health Act contains an additional power relating specifically to unsentenced prisoners transferred to the hospital for treatment of their mental illness. If it "appears ... impracticable or inappropriate to bring the detainee before the court" a hospital order, with or without an additional restriction order, may be passed on the basis of written or oral medical evidence from two practitioners that the person has a mental illness of the requisite severity, so as to make hospital detention appropriate. The wording of the provision makes no explicit reference to fitness to plead and the court has only to be "of the opinion, after considering any depositions or other documents ... that it is proper to make such an order." There is no requirement to test the strength of evidence against the defendant and this could lead to the hospitalization of someone who might have been acquitted had the matter proceeded to trial. Many would argue this power has become increasingly outdated since the amendments to the 1964 Act. *Kenneally*[15] is the leading authority on this provision. The agreed medical evidence before the court was that Mr. Kenneally, who had schizophrenia, was fit to plead at the time of interview, but his mental state was liable to deteriorate, and his behaviour become disturbed in the courtroom setting. Then, he would be unfit to appear in court. The medical opinions seemed to consider fitness to plead literally and distinguished the ability to enter a plea from the other legal criteria relating to fitness to plead, such as the ability to follow and participate in the trial process.[16]

B. THE UNITED STATES

1) Competency to Stand Trial

In the United States, fitness is referred to as "competency to stand trial." As has been recognized in many US Supreme Court decisions,[17] a requirement of competency to stand trial is of fundamental importance

15 *R (on the application of John Kenneally) v Snaresbrook Crown Court*, [2001] EWHC Admin 968.

16 Exworthy, above note 10 at 470–71.

17 For example, see *Drope v Missouri*, 420 US 162 (1975) and *Riggins v Nevada*, 504 US 127 at 139–40 (1992).

in ensuring that an accused receive a fair trial. The abilities required in order to satisfy the threshold of competency to stand trial include the capacity to understand the nature and object of the proceedings, an ability to consult with counsel, and an ability to assist counsel in the preparation of the defence.

In those American jurisdictions where criminal law is within the jurisdiction of the state, the test (or a variant) established by the US Supreme Court in *Dusky v United States* is used.[18] Milton Dusky was a thirty-three-year-old man charged with assisting in the kidnapping and rape of an underage female. He was clearly suffering from schizophrenia but was found competent to stand trial and was sentenced to forty-five years in jail. He appealed to the Supreme Court of the United States, where it was held that:

> It is not enough for the district judge to find that "the defendant (is) oriented to time and place and (has) some recollection of events," but that the "test must be whether he has sufficient present ability to consult with his lawyer with a *reasonable degree of rational understanding*—and whether he has a *rational as well as a factual understanding of the proceedings* against him."[19]

Clearly, there is sufficient ambiguity in the ruling to provide room for many different interpretations of the decision. What, for example, is "rational understanding"? What is "sufficient present ability"? What is a "factual understanding"? Is there an element of prospectivity in "present ability"?

It has been held without controversy that the trial of an incompetent defendant violates due process.[20] While the defendant must shoulder the burden of proving incompetence by a "preponderance of evidence," it may be, as discussed below, that an otherwise incompetent accused is sufficiently competent with the assistance of counsel to proceed to trial.[21] The threshold that must be met to displace the presumption of

---

18 *Dusky v United States*, 362 US 402 (1960) [*Dusky*]. See also earlier cases such as *Youtsey v United States*, 97 F 937 (6th Cir 1899), where the Court of Appeal reversed the finding of a trial court and found the accused incompetent due to its doubts about his capacity to *appreciate* his legal predicament and *intelligently* instruct his lawyer about his defence.

19 *Dusky*, above note 18 at 402 [emphasis added].

20 *Medina v California*, 505 US 437 at 453 (1992).

21 *Indiana v Edwards*, 554 US 164 (2008).

competency is by a "preponderance of evidence" rather than "clear and convincing evidence."[22]

It is clear that, however defined, in the United States, "rationality," and not just a factual understanding of one's legal predicament, is required to demonstrate competence.[23] The requirement of rationality for competency to stand trial runs deep in American jurisprudence. This was poignantly stated in *United States v Chisolm*:

> It would ... be a reproach to justice and our institutions, if a human being ... were compelled to go to trial at a time when he is not sufficiently in possession of his *mental faculties to enable him to make a rational and proper defense*. The latter would be a more grievous error than the former; since in the one case an individual would go unwhipped of justice, while in the other the great safeguards which the law adopts in the punishment of crime and the upholding of justice would be rudely invaded by the tribunal whose sacred duty it is to uphold the law in all its integrity.[24]

A later decision, *Drope v Missouri*, expanded comments in *Dusky* that indicated that the accused must be capable of consultation with an attorney, adding that the accused must be able to "assist in preparing his defence."[25] In *Godinez v Moran*,[26] the US Supreme Court specifically stated that individual states may adopt criteria for competence in their statutes that are more elaborate than the *Dusky* formulation. For example, a court may require that an accused be able to make choices about whether to have a jury trial, to testify, and to cross-examine witnesses. Before trial, accused may have to decide whether and how to put on a defence and whether to raise an "affirmative defence." The Court in *Godinez* suggests that the trial courts may have to evaluate at least some of an accused's decision-making abilities when judgments about competency are being made.

The Court in *Godinez* indicated that competency to plead guilty, to waive counsel, or to stand trial should be considered to be the same,

---

22 *Cooper v Oklahoma*, 517 US 348 (1996).

23 This is in contrast to the Canadian test in *R v Taylor*, [1992] OJ No 2394 (CA). See the discussion in Chapter 2, Section B.

24 *United States v Chisolm*, 149 F 284 at 288 (SD Ala 1906) [emphasis added].

25 *Drope v Missouri*, above note 17 at 171.

26 509 US 389 (1993) [*Godinez*].

in that they are all driven by the underlying ability to make "reasoned choice[s]" among available alternatives. In dissent, however, Justice Blackmun found that the ruling of the majority was "contrary to both common sense and longstanding case law."[27] He reasoned that competency must be assessed not in a vacuum but in the context of the particular legal proceedings, indicating that "competency for one purpose does not necessarily translate to competency for another purpose."[28] He noted that previous Supreme Court cases had required competency evaluations to be specifically tailored to the context and purpose of the proceeding.

As in Canada and England, an inability to remember the events leading to the charges does not render an accused incompetent in the United States,[29] even though accused must be capable of consultation with an attorney and of assisting in the preparation of their defence. The cases cumulatively indicate that, in order to be competent to stand trial, the accused must have (1) a factual understanding of the proceedings, (2) a rational understanding of the proceedings, and (3) the ability to consult with counsel.[30]

With respect to the consequences and aftermath of an incompetency verdict, the process varies from state to state and is therefore beyond the scope of this chapter. Depending upon the nature of the charge (misdemeanour or felony), the outcomes range from an acquittal if the defendant has not become competent within a certain window of time (in the United States, this is most often referred to as "competence restoration") to involuntary committal to hospital with or without reviews by a court or a specialized tribunal.

While the broad form of concern and rationale for the fitness rules is essentially the same in the United States as it is in Canada, there are subtle variations from state to state.

---

27 *Ibid* at 409.

28 *Ibid* at 413.

29 *United States v Andrews*, 469 F3d 1113 (7th Circ 2006); *United States v Stevens*, 461 F2d 317 (7th Circ 1972).

30 RK Otto et al, "Psychometric Properties of the MacArthur Competence Assessment Tool: Criminal Application" (1998) 10:4 *Psychological Assessment* 435; R Rogers & N Grandjean, "Competency Measures and the *Dusky* Standard: A Conceptual Mismatch" (2000) 41 *Biennial Conference of the American Psychology–Law Society/APA Division*.

Ten-Point Review

ENGLAND

1) The test for "fitness to plead" is an intellectual one based upon the accused's abilities with respect to comprehension, communication, and ability to instruct counsel.
2) As in Canada, the evidence against the accused is tested before a verdict of unfit to plead can be entered.
3) In a trial of the facts, proof of the act requires proof of all elements otherwise required to obtain a conviction.
4) If the issue of fitness is raised by the Crown, the test is one of beyond a reasonable doubt.
5) The issue of fitness is rarely raised in less serious matters.

THE UNITED STATES

6) The test for "competency to stand trial," as articulated by the Supreme Court in *Dusky*, requires that the accused have a rational as well as a factual understanding of the proceedings.
7) The *Dusky* test permits a range of interpretations.
8) The *Dusky* test requires that accused be able to assist in preparing their defence.
9) Individual states may adopt more elaborated criteria for competency.
10) Some states may require that, to be found competent, an accused have the ability to assist with trial tactics.

Conclusion

Canadian courts insist that an accused be fit to stand trial because the common law demands that a trial, in order to be valid, must be "fair." And, for a trial to be fair, an accused cannot be prosecuted when they are unable to conduct a defence on account of mental disorder. Across Western jurisdictions, there is very little debate that fairness demands fitness. Prosecutors, as "ministers of justice," should take no pleasure in, or have any appetite for, a trial process that is not fair. Unlike the other major psycholegal issue—"criminal responsibility"—the basic concept of a fairness-based need for an accused to be fit is largely uncontroversial and most often non-adversarial. The authors are not aware of any Western jurisdiction that has decided to do away with the fitness requirement.

Yet, while the objectives of ensuring a fair trial are common and have their roots in antiquity, some considerable debate nonetheless remains about the fitness rules that we have covered in the preceding chapters. How fit does the accused have to be? For how long does the accused have to be fit? Does an accused have to be fit to have a bail hearing? Can others fill in gaps or assist in order to make an otherwise unfit accused fit? We have tried to consider all sides of such issues and have come to a number of conclusions.

First, we are of the view that specifically not requiring accused to have a rational understanding of their legal predicament was, prior to *R v Taylor*,[1] unprecedented. We would argue that rationality is required for

1 [1992] OJ No 2394 (CA).

fitness, in that it enables the accused to meaningfully participate in the trial process. To have any lower standard departs from the purpose of the rules in the first place. To have an accused respond to the state while not rational is to travel back several hundred years to a time when the accused's physical presence alone was sufficient. It is apparent that courts have recently been supporting the view that meaningful participation is required of the accused in order to meet the threshold for fitness, and that rationality is part of that requirement.

Meaningful participation includes not just a rudimentary factual understanding of one's legal predicament but an ability to respond to the state with a modicum of rationality. An accused's right to autonomy should not permit that individual to make foolish decisions and suffer disadvantage as a result of an untreated mental disorder. After all, making foolish or counterproductive responses to the state's prosecution may be worse than not attending or responding at all—a situation the law decided was unacceptable several hundred years ago.

Second, we are of the view that, if accused are able to compensate for "inabilities" that might otherwise render them, standing alone, unfit, then they should be able to proceed if a fair trial would ensue. The fitness rules should be, as originally conceived, protective, but not an obstruction if circumstances can be modified to achieve the fitness goal (i.e., a fair trial). Borrowing by analogy from the tests surrounding criminal responsibility, we learn that, in considering the jurisdictional threshold, the issue of "significant threat" must include an assessment of accused in their natural state—that is, with all the supports and assistance that one might assume would remain in place. Similarly, in assessing fitness, accused should be assessed not in a vacuum but rather with all of the supports and assistance that might fortify their ability to conduct a defence.

Third, it would appear to be entirely consistent with common law pre-dating our statutory definition of "unfit to stand trial" (which was proclaimed in 1992), and with the general objective of fairness, that an accused must be fit in order to be sentenced. Most criminal matters are resolved by way of a guilty plea. An accused must be fit to be arraigned and fit to participate in the sentencing process, which may vary with respect to its complexity and duration as well as the required participation of the accused.

Fourth, we are of the view that unfitness *per se* should not be a bar to judicial interim release. It is recognized that psychiatric issues may be relevant to either the primary or secondary ground—that is, the probability of the accused (1) attending court as required and (2) reoffending if released (see Chapter 3, Section J)—but that unfitness to stand trial should not preclude a bail hearing or the making of a judicial interim release order. In Ontario, it has never been the practice to prevent an unfit accused from participating in a bail hearing or to deny judicial interim release where the primary and secondary ground concerns can be adequately addressed.

Fifth, it seems clear and logical that a self-represented accused needs to have greater legal (and other) wherewithal than an accused who is represented by counsel. Although we have noted the arrival of disparate tests for fitness to stand trial and fitness for self-representation, as articulated in *Indiana v Edwards*,[2] into Canada by way of *R v Hureau*,[3] Canadian forensic psychiatry has yet to address how, if at all, the clinical assessment of an accused's fitness for self-representation differs from assessing an accused for fitness to stand trial.

Finally, we are of the view that an accused's fitness to stand trial must be assessed contextually. So long as the accused, mental disorder notwithstanding, are able to conduct their defence with or without representation and the circumstances are such that a fair trial will result, the accused should be permitted to proceed. Fairness must be the touchstone.

---

2 554 US 164 (2008).

3 [2014] YJ No 48 (Terr Ct).

Canadian, British, and American Case Summaries

CANADIAN CASES

Calvert (Litigation Guardian of) v Calvert (1997), 32 OR (3d) 281 (Gen Div)
A fit litigant may have the capacity to make decisions regarding only certain aspects of a plan rather than all of them.

Canada (Attorney General) v Savard, [1996] YJ No 4 (CA)
With respect to the mandatory appointment of counsel for unfit accused pursuant to the provisions of section 672.24(1) of the *Criminal Code*, the court, notwithstanding the provisions of section 672.24(2), does not have the authority to order the attorney general of Canada to pay counsel who represents an accused as a result of an order made under that section.

Desmarais v R, [2017] QJ No 3864 (Sup Ct)
Upon the earlier decision from the Court of Appeal in this matter finding, *inter alia*, that an accused had to be fit to stand trial in order to have a bail hearing, the Superior Court granted the accused's application for a stay of proceedings as a result of the "Kafkaesque procedural nightmare" experienced by the accused (at para 1). The accused, who suffers from a mental disorder, was in custody for over four years without a bail hearing while the matter of his fitness to stand trial was being batted about. (NOTE: Unfortunately, as a result of the stay, the rather remarkable decision of the Court of Appeal remains intact.)

Evers v British Columbia (Adult Forensic Psychiatric Services), [2009] BCJ No 2450 (CA)
The provisions of section 672.49 of the *Criminal Code* pertain only to initial hearings (section 672.47). Accused, other than those at an initial hearing, maintain their disposition, which remains undisturbed by a Review Board's determination of fitness.

HH (Re), [2007] BCRBD No 21
A "keep fit" order was made where the accused, presently fit, was prone to decompensation.

Italy v Seifert, [2003] BCJ No 726 (SC)
The concept of fitness to stand trial was considered at an extradition hearing. The court found that an extradition hearing is not a trial and that the same level of fitness is not required.

Law Society of Upper Canada v Tollis, [2011] LSDD No 236
The standard that is applied when an appellant relies on mental disorder to invalidate a plea because of involuntariness is the same test that is used to determine the fitness of an accused to stand trial.

Murphy (Re), [1998] AJ No 826 (Prov Ct)
There was, in respect of the accused's fitness, a question as to whether his "amnesia" was due to post-traumatic shock or a suicide attempt. Regardless, the accused could communicate with counsel and understood the nature and object of the proceedings and was therefore considered to be fit. (NOTE: Compare *R v Morrissey* which found that amnesia is of no consequence with respect to fitness to stand trial.)

Ohenhen (Re), 2018 ONCA 65
The capacity required to consent to a condition under section 672.55(1) of the *Criminal Code* is the ability to understand all information relevant to the operation of the condition and to appreciate all reasonably foreseeable consequences of agreeing to the condition.

Pintea v Johns, [2017] 1 SCR 470
An unrepresented litigant must be made aware of role played by opposing counsel.

R v Adam, [2013] OJ No 222 (SCJ)
A test for fitness should focus not so much on the individual's exercise of good judgment or ability to make the "right choice," as on whether the accused's capacity to judge and choose has not been fettered by mental illness: "For an accused person in a criminal trial, meaningful participation can only mean the ability to defend oneself" (at para 29).

R v Amey, 2009 NSPC 29
An accused's inability to remember the events leading to the charge as well as an inability to remember the course of the trial led to a finding of unfitness, as, in the instant case, these elements were important to the ability of the accused to give instructions to counsel.

R v Bain, [1994] NSJ No 194 (CA)
That the accused's evidence was totally at odds with the instructions defence counsel received, without more, does not constitute reasonable grounds for believing the accused to be unfit to stand trial.

R v BB, [2009] OJ No 863 (SCJ)
Where the expert opinion is that the accused is choosing not to answer questions regarding the trial process and is generally uncooperative with counsel, and while there is no indication of a mental disorder, the threshold for ordering an assessment has not been met.

R v Bernardo, [1994] OJ No 4382 (Gen Div)
A court may order an assessment where it has "reasonable grounds to believe" an accused may be unfit. There is no requirement that reasonable grounds be founded on expert evidence. (NOTE: Indeed, where would one get the expert evidence to found the reasonable grounds if reasonable grounds based upon expert evidence were necessary to get an assessment?)

R v Blackjack, [2010] YJ No 120 (Terr Ct)
The caselaw made evident that the application of the limited cognitive capacity test enunciated in *Taylor* cannot be a simplistic exercise. It is not simply a matter of determining whether an accused demonstrates a rudimentary understanding of the legal proceedings. That in and of itself is not enough. The level of understanding, while not required to be comprehensive and nuanced, must be sufficient to enable the accused to participate in his or her own defence in a meaningful way. (at para 16)

R v Brideau, [2015] NBJ No 59 (QB)
The jury conducting the trial of the issue of fitness should be apprised of the nature of the allegations.

R c Brigham, [1992] JQ no 2283 (CA)
"If Mr. Brigham was convicted though unfit, he was in effect not 'present at his trial' . . . If he was fit, but not called, he was deprived of his right to testify in his own defence" (at Conclusions).

R v Budic, [1977] AJ No 516 (SCAD)
Any declaration made by counsel that a client is unable to instruct counsel raises an issue that calls for close scrutiny. Section 672.23(1) of the *Criminal Code* requires the court to have "reasonable grounds" to believe that the accused is unfit to stand trial. "Mere suspicion" will not suffice. While the representation of trial counsel may not have been sufficient to allow the trial judge to conclude that the accused was unfit to stand trial,

there was sufficient evidence to require a more thorough inquiry so as to ensure that there would be no miscarriage of justice.

R v Conception, [2014] 3 SCR 82

> The hospital's consent is required in relation to all the aspects of the disposition order made under s. 672.58 [of the *Criminal Code*] and, absent that consent, the court may not make the order.
>
> ...
>
> That said, although we think it would be exceedingly rare. A judge proposing to make a disposition is entitled to consider, in an appropriate case, whether a refusal of consent will have the effect of unconstitutionally limiting the accused's rights to life, liberty or security of the person in a fashion that does not accord with the principles of fundamental justice. If so persuaded, the judge would also be entitled to consider whether ordering an immediate admission would constitute an appropriate and just remedy for that breach. While we think the circumstances under which this inquiry is appropriate will be rare, *the* Charter *assures that judges and not the person in charge of the hospital where the accused is to be treated will have the last word in terms of the disposition order where the accused's* Charter *rights would otherwise be compromised.* (at paras 40 and 43; emphasis added)

R v Cooper, [1980] 1 SCR 1149
Disease of the mind "embraces any illness, disorder or abnormal condition which impairs the human mind and its functioning" (at 1159).

R v Couture (1947), 4 CR 323 (Que BR)
The court will exercise its discretion to try the issue of fitness to stand trial when there is good reason for doubting that the accused is then, because of insanity, in a condition to conduct his defence (at para 11).

R v Demers (2004), 185 CCC (3d) 257 (SCC)
Permanently unfit accused cannot be held indefinitely, pursuant to the provisions of Part XX.1 of the *Criminal Code*, unless they constitute a significant threat to the safety of the public. (NOTE: This decision gave rise to the provisions contained in section 672.851 of the *Criminal Code*, which came into effect in 2005.)

R v Desmarais (17 November 2016), No 500-36-008237-169 (Que Sup Ct)
The definition of "unfit to stand trial" contained in section 2 of the *Criminal Code* pertains exclusively to an accused's ability to conduct a defence before a verdict is rendered. It may be that the accused is never called upon to conduct a defence. The accused's appearance before the court at the time of the bail hearing is not for the purpose of conducting a defence. Rather,

it is limited to a consideration of the three grounds set out in section 2. Further, section 11(e) of the *Charter* guarantees reasonable bail to *any person* (fit or unfit) without just cause being shown. The accused (fit or unfit) is presumed to be innocent. The fitness rules do not have the effect, nor should they have, of depriving unfit accused of their fundamental right to reasonable bail. While there is no explicit provision for the unfit accused to have a bail hearing, there is nothing in the *Code* to *prevent* such a hearing.

R v Desmarais (4 July 2017), No 500-10-006286-163 (Que CA)
The Court of Appeal overturned the decision of the Superior Court that an unfit accused cannot have a bail hearing. The court found that, in respect of whether or not an accused is able to "conduct a defence," a bail hearing is included within the ambit of "any stage of the proceedings." The Court found, *inter alia*, that an accused "is not a person charged with an offence when a verdict confirms he or she is unfit to stand trial" (at para 29). Therefore, the provisions of section 11(e) of the *Charter* do not apply.

R v Eisnor, [2013] NSJ No 584 (SC)
To be fit to stand trial, it is not necessary for the accused to be able to remember the events that gave rise to the charges. (NOTE: Follows *R v Morrissey*.)

R v Eisnor, 2015 NSCA 64
Amnesia *simpliciter* does not justify a finding of unfitness to stand trial.

R v Ejigu, [2012] BCJ No 910 (SC)
The accused was found fit to stand trial. She appeared to understand that the consequences of the proceedings would be either a prison term or committal to a mental institution. She would not be unable to communicate with counsel if the meetings took place in the hospital or to decide whether to give evidence when the trial resumed.

R v Esseghaier, 2015 ONSC 5855
Although mentally ill, the accused nevertheless had the requisite limited cognitive capacity to understand the trial process and to communicate with counsel.

R v Fabrikant (1995), 97 CCC (3d) 544 (Que CA)
The right of an accused to make full answer and defence entitles the accused to adduce relevant evidence, to advance legal argument, and to address the court. It carries with it no licence to paralyse the trial process by subjecting an endless stream of witnesses to interminable examination on irrelevant matters.

R v Faraz, [2006] OJ No 5612 (Ct J)
When considering whether the timeline has been exceeded such that loss of jurisdiction may result, the court will likely consider the following: prejudice to the accused caused by the delay, which will in part be a function of the length of delay, versus the public's interest in disposing of the case on the merits, which will be informed by, *inter alia*, the seriousness of the allegations.

R v Flowers, [2008] OJ No 4642 (SCJ)
Prior to raising the issue of fitness, the trial judge must be satisfied that the "Crown is in a position to establish that the accused committed the act alleged or, ... that there is some basis to put that accused on trial" (at para 7). The court proceeded to hear a *Charter* application to dismiss charges for delay even though the accused was presently unfit to stand trial.

R v Fortune, [2009] OJ No 5135 (SCJ)
What must be established is the ability of the accused to meaningfully participate in the proceedings or to assist counsel in conducting a defence. Also required is the ability of the accused to rationally communicate and converse with counsel or to make critical decisions based on counsel's advice.

R v GB, [2003] OJ No 784 (SCJ)
The accused was found to be unfit after conviction but prior to sentencing. The definition of "unfit" pertains at any time in the prosecution up to the verdict. Sections 2 (defining "unfit to stand trial") and 672.23(1) of the *Criminal Code* violated GB's *Charter* rights, not justified by section 1 of the *Charter*. The court "read-in" to the section 2 definition of "unfitness" the words "at any stage of the proceedings before a verdict is rendered or sentence imposed."

R v Gero, [2000] AJ No 945 (CA)
There is a miscarriage of justice where there is a failure to conduct a proper inquiry on the issue of fitness to stand trial.

R v Gibbons (1946), 86 CCC 20 (Ont CA)
The court used as criteria for fitness to stand trial "whether the man can understand the nature of the proceedings ... comprehend the evidence and be able to adequately instruct counsel." (at para 36)

R v Gonsalves, [2005] OJ No 1238 (CA)
The Court of Appeal concluded that an unrepresented accused did not receive a fair trial because of the trial court's failure to:

- provide him with an explanation of how the case would unfold;

- help him understand that he was entitled to object to evidence led by the Crown;
- make him aware of how to use the transcript from the preliminary hearing in cross-examination;
- explain the purpose of cross-examination of a witness, and how to conduct it;
- explain the purpose of *voir dires* dealing with various issues; and
- explain the considerations the accused ought to have borne in mind before testifying on his own behalf.

R v Halfyard, 2010 NSPC 46
The court ordered on its own motion an assessment of the accused's fitness to stand trial when the accused was observed to have a "serious emotional breakdown" (at para 4) in the courtroom.

R v Hogan, [1985] BCJ No 195 (Co Ct)
The court conducted one fitness hearing and, at its conclusion, found that the accused was fit to stand trial in respect of charges on two different informations. (Note: We submit that, while, upon consent and other exigencies that may exist, such a procedure might be appropriate, it is not generally sound. Where there are to be separate "trials," there must be separate considerations of fitness. The substance of the trials, their complexity, the role the accused must play, and the timing of the matters might all be quite different, such that the accused at a particular point in time is fit in respect of one matter but unfit in respect of another.)

R v HSR, [1994] OJ No 1131 (Gen Div)
Counsel will be able to put the same questions to prospective jurors trying the issue of fitness as they would to prospective jurors in respect of the trial proper.

R v Hubach, [1966] 4 CCC 114 (Alta SCAD)
The court, relying on *HM Advocate v Robertson*, found the accused unfit to stand trial where he "could not give any reasonable instructions for his defence and would not have been able to follow the evidence and its details rationally" (at para 26).

R v Hureau, [2014] YJ No 48 (Terr Ct)
The court adopted the reasoning in the US Supreme Court decision in *Indiana v Edwards*. Further, the court found that there is nothing in the *Criminal Code* prohibiting different standards depending upon whether the accused has counsel or not.

R v Hureau, 2014 YKSC 48
The appeal court reversed the trial court's decision and found that, if an accused is unable to conduct a defence on their own, they are unfit. It is irrelevant that the accused might be able to instruct counsel to conduct a defence.

R v Huruy, [2015] OJ No 6502 (SCJ)
The accused's unwillingness to cooperate or collaborate with counsel and propensity to disruptive outbursts did not, by themselves, render the accused unfit to stand trial.

R v Isaac, [2009] OJ No 5804 (Ct J)
An accused who is deaf and unable to speak cannot be said to suffer from a mental disorder as defined in section 2 of the *Criminal Code* and is therefore not unfit to stand trial on the basis of this limitation alone.

R v Isbister, [2005] AJ No 265 (Prov Ct)
The court does not lose jurisdiction in the holding of a *prima facie* case hearing where no prejudice is demonstrated as a result of the delay.

R v Iyoho, [2009] AJ No 950 (Prov Ct)
The accused was found to be unfit where no meaningful communication with counsel was possible.

R v Jackson, [2016] OJ No 4780 (SCJ)
Judges do not have jurisdiction to vacate an accused's bail on their own motion without cause being shown, regardless of the accused's history of failing to attend court as directed.

R v Jaser, 2015 ONSC 4729
"Meaningful presence" and "meaningful participation," as referred to in *R v Morrissey*, are not meant to signal a new test for fitness to stand trial but, rather, are simply "important values that inform all three branches of the test" in section 2 of the *Criminal Code* (at para 61).

R v JI, [2000] BCJ No 199 (SC)
The Youth Court did not lose jurisdiction over the matter of a *prima facie* hearing in respect of an unfit accused because the accused was about to become an adult.

R v Jobb, [2008] SJ No 764 (CA)
The proper test of fitness is limited to the court's assessment of the accused's ability to conduct a defence and to communicate with and instruct counsel. This would include an inquiry into whether the accused can recount the necessary facts to enable counsel to properly present a defence. (NOTE: Compare *R v Morrissey*, where the court held that amnesia

with respect to the event leading to the charges was not something that could lead to a finding of unfitness.)

R v John Doe, [2011] OJ No 52 (SCJ)
Especially when considering a Crown application for an assessment, great care must be taken prior to the granting of such an order, as great liberty interests are at stake.

R v Jones (1996), 87 CCC (3d) 350 (Ont CA)
It is only the finding of a "mental disorder" that could potentially give rise to a finding of unfitness.

R v Kariimian-Kakolaki, [2016] OJ No 3015 (Ct J)
Evidence that is trustworthy or credible may be considered in determining whether a *prima facie* case has been demonstrated, notwithstanding procedural shortcomings. (Note: Follows *R v Faraz.*)

R v Kearly, [2005] OJ No 5394 (Ct J)
A reading of the Supreme Court's decision in *R v Demers* makes it quite clear that, to the extent possible, a permanently unfit accused who does not constitute a significant threat to the safety of the public should be treated the same as the not criminally responsible (NCR) accused who does not pose a significant threat to the safety of the public. Of course, the NCR accused has obtained a final verdict on the merits after a trial, whereas the permanently unfit accused has not been tried. The permanently unfit accused is still presumed to be innocent, whereas there has been a finding of guilt in respect of the NCR accused.

R v King, 2007 ONCA 713
Even where accused appear to understand the nuts and bolts of the trial process, delusions caused by their mental illness may cause them to believe that they have no part in the process. Such a situation occurred here, as the accused believed that he was "Captain Rod Malak Yah-Wah" and not "Rodney King" (his real name). Such an accused is unfit.

R v Kobzar, [2012] OJ No 2179 (CA)
The provisions of Part XX.1 of the *Criminal Code*, which, upon the Crown's appeal of an absolute discharge, revived the previous disposition, were not in accordance with the fundamental principle of due process, as a not criminally responsible accused person is afforded no procedural safeguards before the automatic suspension of the absolute discharge order took effect and deprived the accused of their liberty. The impugned portion of the provision was contrary to section 9 of the *Charter* and could not be saved by section 1 of the *Charter*.

R v Kolbe, [1974] AJ No 162 (SCAD)
The court is not obligated to direct the jury to try the issue of fitness where there is no evidence called nor any indication from counsel that evidence would be called on the issue.

R v Krivicic, [2011] OJ No 5005 (CA)
The inquiry into the accused's fitness demands an assurance that, despite suffering from a mental disorder, the accused person is able to receive a fair trial.

R v Kurd, [2005] OJ No 2794 (SCJ)
It is not open to the hospital to return the accused to a detention centre while subject to an order pursuant to the provisions of section 672.29 of the *Criminal Code*.

R v Le, [2004] OJ No 3374 (Ct J)
Where an accused disputes the Crown's ability to show a *prima facie* case prior to a trial of fitness to stand trial, this may be done in a relatively informal manner by calling the officer in charge to indicate what witnesses remain ready to testify and the sorts of evidence they will be producing.

R v Lee Kun, [1916] 1 KB 337 (CA)
The test for unfitness is whether the accused is able to understand the proceedings and to instruct counsel.

R v Lessard, [1976] OJ No 74 (CA)
In exceptional circumstances, a trial judge sitting alone may set aside a verdict so as to resume position within the trial.

R v Leys (1910), 17 CCC 198 (Ont CA)
"No person can be rightly tried, sentenced, or executed while insane" (para 1).

R v Lovie, [1995] OJ No 2065 (CA)
Without more, evidence that the accused may be mentally ill is insufficient to provide the court with reasonable grounds to believe that the accused may be unfit to stand trial.

R v LSC, [2003] AJ No 388 (CA)
The Court of Appeal permitted a revisiting of the fitness issue where there was new evidence that trial counsel may not have been aware of the accused's mistaken perceptions and other factors potentially relevant to the accused's fitness.

R v MAW, [2008] OJ No 2738 (CA)
The court gave two reasons for confirming the "limited cognitive capacity test," as set out in *R v Taylor*. The first is "consistency"—that is, as

the Supreme Court of Canada has stated in *R v Whittle*, there should be one standard of mental capacity for decisions at all junctures in the prosecution process. The second reason is that the accused's liberty interests dictate that they should be permitted to conduct their own defence. To impose a higher standard than the limited cognitive capacity test—one that would require the accused to be rational or act in their own best interests—would "smack of paternalism" (at para 35).

R v McIlvride, [1986] BCJ No 634 (CA)

> If at the opening of the trial an inquiry into the fitness of the accused to stand trial is sought, there will in most cases be put before the judge material supporting the submission that the accused is not fit. There may also be material from the Crown indicating that he is fit, or the Crown may agree that such an inquiry should be conducted. The judge may act on the material placed before him, or may direct that a further assessment of the accused be made. It may, in some cases, be necessary for the judge to hear the evidence of psychiatrists and of other witnesses. The judge's role at this stage is to decide if there is "sufficient reason to doubt" the fitness of the accused. It is for the judge to decide how to proceed in order that there will be before the court sufficient information to resolve the preliminary question. (at para 34)

This inquiry never got past the first stage.

R v McLeod, [1983] OJ No 81 (CA)

> It is to be noted that it [a fitness hearing] is a two-stage process. The first stage is for the judge alone to decide whether there is "sufficient reason to doubt the accused is, on account of insanity, capable of conducting his defence" and the second, which is only pursued if the first stage is answered affirmatively, is for the jury to determine "whether the accused is then, on account of insanity, unfit to stand his trial." (at para 12)

R v Michael, 2015 ONSC 148

An accused's disinclination to follow counsel's advice cannot be taken, without more, as the basis for ordering an assessment.

R v Miller, [2011] BCJ No 1801 (SC)

Where the accused may be presently fit to stand trial but nevertheless quite unwell, the issue of fitness to stand trial may be revisited as required during the course of the proceedings.

R v Morrissey, 2007 ONCA 770

Testimonial competence is not a condition precedent to fitness to stand trial. The rationale for the test for fitness is that the accused be able to participate meaningfully in the trial so that minimum standards of fairness are met. Fitness to stand trial deals with the accused's capacity to understand the nature and object of the proceedings, to be aware of the possible punishment, and to communicate with counsel. The key question regarding communication with counsel is whether the accused can seek and receive legal advice. There is no additional requirement that an accused be able to tell defence counsel about the events immediately prior to the offence or have the ability to testify about those events. Moreover, amnesia alone does not render an accused unfit to stand trial.

R v Nehass, [2014] YJ No 117 (Terr Ct)
The court concurred with the view expressed in *R v Blackjack* and emphasized that the test in *R v Taylor* subsumes "a rational understanding [on the part of the accused] of the fundamental tenets of the process and procedure of the criminal case in which he or she is involved" (at para 71).

R v Nehass, 2017 YKSC 4
An accused must be mentally fit to be sentenced. Meaningful presence and meaningful participation are the touchstones of the inquiry into fitness.

The court has the ability to make an assessment order to determine fitness after a verdict and before sentencing, pursuant to both the common law and its inherent jurisdiction. There is good authority for the proposition that, under the common law, a court is entitled and, indeed, bound to be concerned with the mental fitness of an accused during the sentencing phase of a trial.

R v Palamarek, [1992] BCJ No 3077 (Prov Ct)
Notwithstanding a "learned and detailed report from the psychiatrist" (at para 34), the judge remained unshaken in his belief that the accused was and remained unfit to stand trial.

R v Pawlivsky, [1998] AJ No 1092 (QB)
The accused is entitled to cross-examine witnesses or affiants tendered by the Crown in order to establish its post-verdict *prima facie* case.

R v Peepeetch, [2003] SJ No 542 (CA)
The accused sought to adduce fresh evidence that, at the time of his trial, he was unfit to stand trial. The court found that the evidence was inadmissible. The "experts" were not expert, and the facts they relied upon were inaccurate. The court observed that "medical reports based on interviews and testing done long after the event bear little relevance to the ability of the appellant to communicate and instruct counsel at the time of the trial" (at para 16).

R v Penny, 2010 NBCA 49
Where there is no application made with respect to fitness and no evidence before the judge to suggest that the accused may be unfit to be sentenced, there is no error.

R v Pietrangelo, [2001] OJ No 868 (CA)
The court found that the trial judge erred in failing to hold a fitness hearing. The accused's conduct clearly warranted such a hearing, as did the psychiatric report filed by the Crown. Instead, the trial judge merely asked the accused if he was fit to stand trial and, when he answered in the affirmative, directed that the trial should proceed. The appeal court also ruled that, where the accused has obtained a verdict of unfit to stand trial and has made a previous election to be tried by a judge and jury, any retrial of the issue of fitness will be tried by a judge and jury.

R v Pollard, [2007] OJ No 615 (Ct J)
In assessing "significant threat" in the context of section 672.851 of the *Criminal Code*, the court considered, among other factors, four years of good behaviour on the part of the accused and the salutary effect of the discharge on that individual.

R v Proctor, [1993] MJ No 525 (QB)
The determination of fitness by the Review Board may be what provides the court with reasonable grounds to retry the issue of fitness, although a determination by the Review Board is not a prerequisite.

R v Proulx, [2011] SJ No 477 (Prov Ct)
The court held a fitness hearing after guilty pleas were entered and then used the finding of unfitness to set aside the guilty pleas.

R v RCMc, [2011] SJ No 243 (Prov Ct)
In a calm and controlled environment, the accused, at times, met the limited cognitive capacity standard regarding the nature of the proceedings and their possible consequences. The accused had some memory of the events in question but had virtually no ability to participate in the court proceeding in any meaningful way. However, the court found that the accused met the limited cognitive capacity test as enunciated in *R v Jobb*.

R v Reid, [2013] BCJ No 2679 (SC)
The court overlooked the strict wording of section 672.29 of the *Criminal Code*, which refers to jurisdiction arising at a specific juncture in the proceedings—that is, "on delivery of a verdict of fit to stand trial"—to find that an order can be made to preserve fitness even upon the conclusion of an assessment order that the accused was fit to stand trial.

R v Roberts (1975), 24 CCC (2d) 539 (BCCA)

> It is a prerequisite to any criminal trial that the accused be capable of conducting his defence .... [H]e must be physically, intellectually, linguistically and communicatively present and able to partake to the best of his natural ability in his full answer and defence to the charge against him. (at para 12)

R v Rockey, [1999] OJ No 1352 (CA)
In respect of a second trial, there was no need to conduct a fitness hearing where the issue had been tried seven months earlier and the accused was found to be fit to stand trial. There was no evidence that the accused's mental condition had changed since the time of the verdict.

R v Rooney, [1994] PEIJ No 82 (SCTD)

> In my view, the statutory language "... unable on account of mental disorder to conduct a defence ..." must be given meaning and life. That general language is not necessarily confined to the particulars stated in the language of the definition. It is apparent that those particulars do not address the situation that comprises the issue of this proceeding. Understanding the nature and object of the proceeding, and understanding the possible consequences of the proceeding are not in issue. In my view, it is not sufficient to conclude that because the accused does not have counsel, definition clause (c) [of section 2 of the *Criminal Code*] "communicate with counsel" does not apply, and that is the end of the matter. To the contrary, fundamental precepts of our criminal law would indicate that the reasonable meaning to be given to the statutory language enacted by Parliament is that the accused must be able to recount the necessary facts relating to the event in such a way that he can properly present a defence. If that ability to recount is presently blocked by delusions caused by the kind of mental disorder addressed in s. 16 [of the *Criminal Code*], then it cannot be said that an accused is fit for trial. That analysis is entirely consistent with the limited cognitive test. It does not explore whether the accused trusts counsel, or whether the accused can make decisions in his best interest, which are not the proper test. It is not an application of a more liberal "analytic capacity" test. (at para 37)

(NOTE: The court did not advert to the requirement that, if fitness is being considered, there is, arguably, an obligation to appoint counsel.)

R v Rouse, [1996] OJ No 4688 (Gen Div)
The definition of disease of the mind, from the perspective of criminal law, is broad and includes, for example, "mental retardation."

R v Scurvey, 2002 YKTC 48
With respect to the mandatory appointment of counsel for unfit accused pursuant to the provisions of section 672.24(1) of the *Criminal Code*, the court, notwithstanding the provisions of section 672.24(2), does not have the authority to order the attorney general of Canada to pay counsel who represents an accused as a result of an order made under that section.

A court does not lose jurisdiction in the hearing of a *prima facie* where there has been no demonstration of prejudice. Even if jurisdiction were lost, section 485 of the *Criminal Code* would remedy the situation.

R v Sealy, [2010] QJ No 30723 (CQ)
While expert evidence is not necessary to support "reasonable grounds to believe" an assessment is necessary, there must be a clear and/or compelling reason for making the assessment order. It cannot be based upon a whim, wishful thinking, or mere possibilities.

R v Semenovitch, [2010] AJ No 1285 (QB)
Where the matter of fitness is disposed of quickly, and the trial is to proceed, the same jury that tried the matter of fitness may, with the accused's consent, proceed to hear the trial proper.

R v Skyers, [2011] OJ No 6272 (SCJ)
The accused, mental disorder notwithstanding, shall not be denied reasonable bail without just cause. The principles set out in section 515(10) of the *Criminal Code*, the caselaw governing the application of the primary and secondary grounds for detention, and the facts set out in this case did not preclude judicial interim release simply because the accused may be unfit to stand trial.

R v Song, [2008] AJ No 746 (CA)
At the retrial of the issue of fitness, the presumption is that the accused remains unfit to stand trial. This presumption must be displaced on a balance of probabilities.

R v Steele (1991), 63 CCC (3d) 149 (Que CA)

> An accused is incapable of conducting the defence, within the meaning of s. 615 of the *Criminal Code*, if he or she:
> (a) cannot distinguish between available pleas;
> (b) does not understand the nature or purpose of the proceedings, including the respective roles of the judge, jury and counsel;
> (c) does not understand the personal import of the proceedings;
> (d) is unable to communicate with counsel, *converse with counsel rationally* or make critical decisions on counsel's advice; or
> (e) is unable to take the stand, if necessary. (at summary; emphasis added)

R v Stojanovic, [2014] OJ No 4823 (Ct J)
The so-called *Taylor* test requires that accused have only a rudimentary factual understanding of their legal predicament.

R v Sun, [1999] OJ No 2821 (SCJ)
Behaviour that is simply unusual or even unacceptable in a courtroom does not, by itself, constitute a basis for "reasonable grounds to believe" that an assessment order is necessary.

R v Szostak, [2012] OJ No 3330 (CA)
Where counsel is of the view that their client may not be fit to stand trial, there is an obligation to bring the matter to the attention of the court.

R v Talbot, [1996] OJ No 5323 (Ct J)
The court maintains jurisdiction over the accused until the accused is fit. The court retains jurisdiction to hear the Crown's demonstration of a *prima facie* case even though the statutory time lines had been exceeded. The remedies of *habeas corpus* and *mandamus* are not available at the Provincial Court.

R v Taylor (1992), 11 OR (3d) 323 (CA)

> In order to ensure that the process of determining guilt is as accurate as possible, that the accused can participate in the proceedings or assist counsel in his/her defence, that the dignity of the trial process is maintained, and that, if necessary, the determination of a fit sentence is made possible, the *accused must have sufficient mental fitness to participate in the proceedings in a meaningful way*. (at para 50; emphasis added)

Where the Crown's ability to demonstrate a *prima facie* case is disputed by the accused, the trial of the issue of fitness should be deferred until such a demonstration has taken place. As well, a trial of the fitness issue shall not take place until the Crown has made its election as to mode of trial.

R v TJ, [1999] YJ No 57 (Terr Ct)
The Territorial Court of the Yukon anticipated the Supreme Court of Canada's decision in *R v Demers* finding that unfit accused, as is the case with not criminally responsible accused, should not have their liberty curtailed if they are not a significant threat to the safety of the public.

R v Trecroce (1980), 55 CCC (2d) 202 (Ont CA)
The *ratio* of this case is not entirely clear; however, the court, in finding the accused fit, appears to have relied on psychiatric evidence that the accused

> understood the nature of the proceedings and the functions of the persons involved in them. He knew what the issues were and the possible

> outcome of the proceedings ... [and] was able to follow the evidence generally, although he might misinterpret it. [He] was capable of instructing counsel although he might disagree with counsel as to how the case should be conducted, and might not act with good judgment. The appellant did not want to be seen as mentally ill, and was opposed to the issue of insanity being considered by the Court. (at para 41)

R v Verma, [2011] BCJ No 165 (CA)
It could not be concluded that the trial court's failure to order the accused's representation by counsel at the assessment stage of the proceedings and failure to address the fitness issue with counsel present after the assessment was ordered were inevitably harmless and resulted in no prejudice to the accused.

R v Volpini (4 March 2005), ORB File No 4011 (Ontario Review Board)
Although the accused was fit at the moment, his fluctuating fitness and an inability to say that he would be fit at the time of trial rendered him unfit.

R v Walker, [2016] OJ No 2082 (SCJ)
The trial court declined to make a treatment order. The accused had no criminal record, she was facing relatively minor charges, and she had instructed her counsel she would refuse treatment pursuant to the court's order and would prefer to be subject to the provincial civil mental health regime. With a treatment order, counsel argued, there was no right of appeal, whereas, under the civil system, an appeal could be made and his client would have "rights." (NOTE: The argument with respect to right to appeal a treatment order was incorrect: see section 672.72 of the *Criminal Code*.) Upon review at Superior Court, it was held that the trial court had placed too much emphasis on the unfit (and civilly "incapable") accused's instructions to counsel. The Superior Court clearly had difficulty with the extent to which the accused was able to instruct counsel and hence the amount of weight placed upon those instructions. As well, the court found that to accede to the trial court's line of logic would be to "eviscerate the purpose of the provision" (at para 40).

R v Waranuk, [2008] YJ No 48 (SC)
Accused found fit to stand trial are entitled to self-representation—that is, they are fit to decide whether or not to be represented by legal counsel.

R v WH, [2006] OJ No 766 (SCJ)
The accused was found unfit where his communication difficulties were the product of a stroke from which he would not recover.

R v Whittle (1994), 92 CCC (3d) 11 (SCC)
In exercising the right to counsel or waiving the right, an accused must possess the limited cognitive capacity that is required for fitness to stand trial.

R v Williams, [2012] OJ No 4974 (SCJ)
Quigley J noted:

> [T]he evidence of the defence experts is not persuasive on a balance of probabilities that Mr. Williams is not fit to stand trial. The burden of persuasion rests on the defence. They have not discharged that burden. Some accommodations may need to be made for him, or not, but that does not mean he is not fit. For the reasons set out in this ruling, I am not persuaded that he is unfit to stand trial. As such, the presumption of fitness operates, and the application is dismissed. (at para 143)

R v Wisniewski, [2012] AJ No 1010 (Prov Ct)
The accused did not misunderstand questions posed to him, and, although he disrupted proceedings twice, neither interruption established that he did not understand the nature of the proceedings or could not communicate with counsel. The accused's counsel did not seek updated assessments to counter the medical reports, nor did she state that she thought the accused did not know what was going on or could not communicate with her. The accused failed to rebut the presumption of fitness to stand trial.

R v Wolfson, [1965] AJ No 35 (SCAD)
In accordance with section 524(1) of the *Criminal Code*, the trial judge is bound to submit the issue of fitness to the jury where it appears that there is sufficient reason to doubt that the accused is, on account of insanity, capable of conducting a defence.

R v Woltucky (1952), 103 CCC 43 (Sask CA)
"[T]he test on the issue [of unfitness] is whether or not the accused is able to understand the proceedings . . . and to instruct counsel" (at para 7).

R v Wong, [2006] BCJ No 1539 (Prov Ct)
In assessing "significant threat" in the context of section 672.851 of the *Criminal Code*, the court considered, among other factors, that the accused was seventy-two years of age and that he had been stable and non-aggressive for fourteen years.

R v Worrie, (11 September 2015), Court File No Brampton 15-47-42 (Ont Ct J)
The court insisted that the accused be brought to court for the purpose of the hearing of an application for a treatment order where the charges were very serious and a number of the preconditions set out in section 672.59 of the *Criminal Code* had been dispensed with "on consent." The court noted

the serious consequences of the order sought and, quite appropriately, refused to dispense with any procedural or evidentiary requirements.

R v Wride, [1997] MJ No 508 (QB)
The higher threshold to be met in obtaining fitness assessments in respect of summary matters reflects the reality that many offences would attract non-custodial dispositions even were the accused to be convicted.

R v Xu (No 2) (20 April 2007), Court File No 0710000305 (Ont Ct J)
The accused saw the trial process as a vehicle for demonstrating that she was not mentally ill. In the circumstances, it was not possible to move the accused on to relevant dimensions of her case, even though, in an abstract sense, she understood the nature and object of the proceedings.

Re R v Gorecki (No 1) (1976), 32 CCC (2d) 129 (Ont CA)
The accused was not unfit to stand trial where he was able to converse with counsel rationally and make decisions on their advice. The fact that he, because of the consequences of the verdict, insisted that a defence of insanity not be advanced did not render him unfit to stand trial. (NOTE: Perhaps, had the "insistence" been the product of a mental disorder, the decision regarding fitness would have been different.)

BRITISH CASES

Attorney General's Reference (No 3 of 1998), [1999] 3 All ER 40
The court found that it is not necessary to prove *mens rea because, in an insanity case, the issue of* mens rea *ceases to be relevant.*

R v Antoine, [2000] 2 All ER 208 (HL)
It is not open to the accused to raise the defence of diminished responsibility where they have been found unfit to plead. (at 216)

R v Berry (1876), 1 QB 447
The court relied on Hale's *Pleas of the Crown* and *R v Pritchard*. The jury was instructed "to consider whether the prisoner had sufficient intellect to comprehend the course of the proceedings, so as to make a proper defence, to challenge any question he might wish to object to, and to comprehend the details of the evidence; and that if they thought he had not, they should find him not of sane mind" (at 450)—that is, unfit.

R v Beynon, [1957] 2 QB 111
The court directed that the matter of the accused's fitness to stand trial must be considered in advance of the hearing of any evidence as a preliminary matter. (NOTE: Compare *R v Roberts*.)

R v Dashwood, [1943] KB 1
The determination of mental capacity or fitness to stand trial is based on the accused's ability to understand and participate in the trial process.

R v Dyson (1831), 7 C&P 305
The defendant was deaf and had never been able to speak. Even with the use of sign language, she could not understand matters such as her right to challenge jurors. A jury found her "mute by visitation of God," and the court relied on the authority of Hale to require the jury to find her insane. *Per* Lord Hale's *Pleas of the Crown,* the jury was instructed as follows:

> If a man in his sound memory commits a capital offence, and before his arraignment he becomes absolutely mad, he ought not by law to be arraigned during such his phrensy, but be remitted to prison until that incapacity be removed. The reason is, because he cannot advisedly plead to the indictment. And if such person after his plea, and before his trial, becomes of non-sane memory, he shall not be tried; *or if after his trial he become non-sane memory, he shall not receive judgement; or if after judgement he become of non-sane memory, his execution shall be spared;* for, were he of sound memory, he might allege somewhat in stay of judgement or execution. (at 307; emphasis added)

R v Egan, [1998] 1 Cr App R 121
In establishing a *prima facie* case, the Court of Appeal held that "the act" required "proof of all the ingredients of what otherwise would be an offense" (at 124).

Frith's Case (1790), 22 How St Tr 307

> No man shall be called upon to make his defence at a time when his mind is in that situation as not to appear capable of so doing, for however guilty he may be, the inquiring into his guilt must be postponed to that season, when by collecting together his intellects, and have them entire, he shall be able so to model his defence as to ward off the punishment of the law. (at 318)

R (on the application of John Kenneally) v Snaresbrook Crown Court, [2001] EWHC Admin 968
With a hospital order pursuant to the *Mental Health Act*, there is no requirement to test the strength of evidence against the defendant. This could lead to the hospitalization of someone who might have been acquitted had the matter proceeded to trial. The agreed medical evidence before the court was that Mr Kenneally, who had schizophrenia, was fit to plead at the time of interview, but his mental state was liable to deteriorate and his

behaviour become disturbed in the courtroom setting. At that point, he would be unfit to appear in court. The medical opinions seemed to consider fitness to plead literally and distinguished the ability to enter a plea from the other legal criteria relating to fitness to plead, such as the ability to follow and participate in the trial process.

R v Podola (1959,) 43 Cr App R 220 (CA)
The burden of proving unfitness lay with the defence:

> Why is a man to be presumed to be insane when called upon to plead? The presumption is that he is sane. I do not see any sufficient reason for deviating from the old practice. If you suggest that the prisoner is not in such a state of mind as to be able to plead to the indictment, you must give evidence of the fact. (at 236)

"Mental disorder" is a necessary but not sufficient condition for a finding of unfitness. Amnesia with respect to the alleged offence, by itself, would not lead to a finding of unfit, as it would not affect the accused's ability to understand the proceedings. If the issue of fitness is raised by the defence, it must meet the civil standard of proof—that is, on the balance of probabilities.

R v Pritchard (1836), 7 Car & P 303
The court considered three issues:

> First, whether the prisoner is mute of malice [i.e. wilfully mute] or not; secondly, whether he can plead to the indictment or not; thirdly, whether he is of sufficient intellect to comprehend the course of the proceedings on the trial, so as to make a proper defence—to know that he might challenge any of you to whom he may object—and to comprehend the details of the evidence, which in a case of this nature must constitute a minute investigation. (at 304)

R v Roberts, [1954] 2 QB 329
The court has discretion to postpone consideration of the issue of fitness until it is demonstrated that there is a case to meet. (NOTE: Compare *R v Beynon.*)

R v Robertson, [1968] 3 All ER 557, 1 WLR 1767 (CA)
If the issue of fitness is being raised by the Crown, the criminal standard of beyond reasonable doubt is set. (NOTE: This is in contrast to Canada, where the civil standard—that is, on a balance of probabilities—applies if the Crown raises the issue of fitness.)

R v Turton (1854), 6 Cox CC 385
The burden of proving unfitness lays upon the accused.

Rex v Rivett (1950), 34 Cr App R 87 (CA)
It must not be overlooked "that it is for the jury and not for medical men, of whatever eminence, to determine the issue" of insanity in a criminal case and it is quite within the province of the jury to give effect to the evidence of surrounding facts against the expert "opinion of medical men of undoubted integrity and whose qualifications none would question" (at 94).

AMERICAN CASES

Drope v Missouri, 420 US 162 (1975)
An accused must be capable of consultation with an attorney and must be able to "assist in preparing his defence" (at 171).

Dusky v United States, 362 US 402 (1960)

> [I]t is not enough … to find that the defendant [is] oriented to time and place and [has] some recollection of events, but … the test must be whether he has sufficient present ability to consult with his lawyer with a reasonable degree of rational understanding—and whether he has rational as well as a factual understanding of the proceedings against him. (at 403)

Faretta v California, 422 US 506 (1975)
The Supreme Court upheld the accused's right to self-representation.

Godinez v Moran, 509 US 389 (1993)
The court indicated that the competency to plead guilty, to waive counsel, or to stand trial should be considered the same, in that they were all driven by the underlying ability to make "reasoned choice" among alternatives available. However, in dissent, Justice Blackmun found that the ruling of the majority was "contrary to both common sense and long-standing case law" (at 394). He reasoned that competency must be assessed not in a vacuum but in the context of the particular legal proceedings, indicating that "competency for one purpose does not necessarily translate to competency for another purpose" (at 413). He noted that previous Supreme Court cases *had* required competency evaluations to be specifically tailored to the context and purpose of the proceeding.

Indiana v Edwards, 554 US 164 (2008)
The court set out the American Constitution's "mental competence" standard, "forbidding the trial of an individual lacking a rational and factual understanding of the proceedings and sufficient ability to consult with his lawyer with a *reasonable degree of rational understanding*" (at 164; emphasis added).

United States v Andrews, 469 F3d 1113 (7th Circ 2006)
The Seventh Circuit considered whether the accused's amnesia would prevent him and his lawyer from reconstructing the events of the alleged offence and raising any possible defences to the evidence against him, and concluded it would not.

United States v Hemsi, 901 F2d 293 (2d Cir 1990)
The accused was found incompetent to stand trial where he was incapable of making rational decisions regarding his defence. His mental disorder prevented him from focusing upon his legal needs and from acting effectively. He was incapable of cooperating rationally in his defence.

United States v Lawrence, 26 F Cas 886 (DC Cir 1835)
The accused, who had tried to assassinate President Andrew Jackson, spent his life in jail after a finding of incompetent to stand trial. (at 891)

United States v Stevens, 461 F2d 317 (7th Circ 1972)
The court concluded that amnesia did not bar prosecution of an otherwise competent defendant.

Wilson v United States, 391 F2d 460 (DC Cir 1968)
The court considered six factors that determine whether amnesia renders an accused incompetent.

Youtsey v United States, 97 F 937 (6th Cir 1899)
The Court of Appeal reversed the finding of a trial court and found the accused incompetent, due to its doubts about the accused's capacity to appreciate his legal predicament and intelligently instruct his lawyer about his defence.

Form 48: Assessment Order of the Court

This form is contained in the *Criminal Code*. It has been modified slightly in order to permit the administrator of the hospital to return the accused to court earlier than anticipated if the assessment is complete prior to the return date on the information.

When an accused is to be returned to court earlier than anticipated, the administrator issues a letter that authorizes the wagon to pick up the accused and take them to court. The administrator contacts the court clerk at the court, who adds the information to the list. Duty counsel will notify counsel if the accused has retained counsel or, alternatively, will take instructions.

FORM 48
(Section 672.13)
ASSESSMENT ORDER OF THE COURT

Canada,
Province of
(*territorial division*)

Whereas I have reasonable grounds to believe that evidence of the mental condition of (name of accused), who has been charged with ________, may be necessary to determine*

- ☐ whether the accused is unfit to stand trial
- ☐ whether the accused suffered from a mental disorder so as to exempt the accused from criminal responsibility by virtue of subsection 16(1) of the *Criminal Code* at the time of the act or omission charged against the accused
- ☐ whether the balance of the mind of the accused was disturbed at the time of commission of the alleged offence, if the accused is a female person charged with an offence arising out of the death of her newly-born child
- ☐ if a verdict of unfit to stand trial or a verdict of not criminally responsible on account of mental disorder has been rendered in respect of the accused, the appropriate disposition to be made in respect of the accused pursuant to section 672.54 or 672.58 of the *Criminal Code*
- ☐ if a verdict of unfit to stand trial has been rendered in respect of the accused, whether the court should order a stay of proceedings under section 672.851 of the *Criminal Code*

I hereby order an assessment of the mental condition of (name of accused) to be conducted by/at (name of person or service by whom or place where assessment is to be made) for a period of ____ days.

This order is to be in force for a total of ____ days, including travelling time, during which time the accused is to remain*

- ☐ in custody at (place where accused is to be detained)
- ☐ out of custody, on the following conditions: (*set out conditions, if applicable*)

* Check applicable option.

Dated this _____ day of ____________ A.D. ______, at __________ .

____

(Signature of justice or judge or clerık of the court, as the case may be)

Form 48.1: Assessment Order of the Review Board

This form is contained in the *Criminal Code*. It appeared for the first time with the proclamation of Bill C-10. It may be used by the Review Board to order the assessment of the accused pursuant to the provisions of section 672.121 of the *Criminal Code*.

FORM 48.1
(Section 672.13)
ASSESSMENT ORDER OF THE REVIEW BOARD

Canada,
Province of
(*territorial division*)

Whereas I have reasonable grounds to believe that evidence of the mental condition of (*name of accused*), who has been charged with ______, may be necessary to*

- □ if a verdict of unfit to stand trial or a verdict of not criminally responsible on account of mental disorder has been rendered in respect of the accused, make a disposition under section 672.54 of the *Criminal Code*
- □ if a verdict of unfit to stand trial has been rendered in respect of the accused, determine whether the Review Board should make a recommendation to the court that has jurisdiction in respect of the offence charged against the accused to hold an inquiry to determine whether a stay of proceedings should be ordered in accordance with section 672.851 of the *Criminal Code*

I hereby order an assessment of the mental condition of (*name of accused*) to be conducted by/at (*name of person or service by whom or place where assessment is to be made*) for a period of ________ days.

This order is to be in force for a total of ________ days, including travelling time, during which time the accused is to remain*

- □ in custody at (*place where accused is to be detained*)
- □ out of custody, on the following conditions: (*set out conditions, if applicable*)

* Check applicable option.

Dated this ________ day of ________________ A.D. ____ , at ________ .

____

(Signature of Chairperson of the Review Board)

Treatment Order (Section 672.58)

This form is not contained in the *Criminal Code*. The following form is a creation of one of this book's authors, Richard Schneider. It is a modified version of a form produced by the Ontario Ministry of the Attorney General. It has been modified slightly in order to permit the administrator of the hospital to return the accused to court earlier than anticipated if the treatment has been successful, and the accused rendered fit, prior to the return date on the information.

When an accused is to be returned to court earlier than anticipated, the administrator issues a letter that authorizes the delivery of the accused back to court. The administrator contacts the court clerk at the court, who adds the information to the list. Duty counsel will notify counsel if the accused has retained counsel or, alternatively, will take instructions.

TREATMENT ORDER
Ontario Court of Justice

CANADA *Section 672.58*
PROVINCE OF ONTARIO
Toronto
(Region)

WHEREAS (hereinafter referred to as the "Accused") (*name of accused*) has been charged with the following offence(s) (*charges*)

AND WHEREAS the accused was found unfit to stand trial on (*today's date*) by (*name of Judge or Justice*)

AND WHEREAS the prosecutor has applied for a treatment order pursuant to section 672.58 of the *Criminal Code*

AND WHEREAS the Court is satisfied on the basis of testimony of a medical practitioner that:

i) a specified treatment should be administered to the accused for the purpose of making the accused fit to stand trial within a period not to exceed 60 days;
ii) without the treatment the accused is likely to remain unfit to stand trial;
iii) the risk of harm to the accused from the treatment is not disproportionate to the benefit anticipated to be derived; and
iv) the treatment is the least restrictive and least intrusive that could be provided for the purpose.

AND WHEREAS the following person or persons have given their consent as required by s. 672.62:

- ☐ ____________________ the person in charge of the hospital where the accused is to be treated or
- ☐ ____________________ the person to whom responsibility for the treatment of the accused has been assigned by the court.

I HEREBY DIRECT the treatment of the accused is to be conducted by/at (*name of person or service by whom or place where treatment is to be administered*) for a period of _____ days (*Not to exceed 60 days*)

I HEREBY DIRECT that the specific treatment to be administered to the accused be as follows:

I HEREBY DIRECT that during the time of the treatment the accused is to remain: (Check applicable option)

- ☐ in custody at ____________ and shall return to 102 court (*place where accused to be detained*) on ________ at __________ or such earlier date specified by the Administrator of the hospital. (*return date*) (*time*)
- ☐ out of custody, on the following conditions: (*set out conditions, where applicable*)

Dated at the *City of Toronto* this ______________________ (today's date)

______________________________ Signature of Judge or Justice as the case may be

"Keep Fit" Order (Section 672.29)

This form is not contained in the *Criminal Code*. It is the creation of one of this book's authors, Richard Schneider. It covers the provisions of section 672.29 of the *Criminal Code*, which allow for accused who obtain a verdict of fit to stand trial to be hospitalized until the completion of their trial in order to preserve fitness. It is to be used to preserve fitness only *after the issue has been tried.*

CANADA
PROVINCE OF ONTARIO
Toronto
(Region)

Section 672.29

WARRANT OF COMMITTAL
Detention of Accused in Hospital Until Completion of Trial (672.29)

To the peace officers in the said region, and to the keeper (administrator, warden) of the ____________________ (prison, hospital or other appropriate place where the accused is currently detained)

This warrant is issued for the committal of: (hereinafter called the accused) (*accused name*)

Whereas the accused has been charged that (set out briefly the offence in respect of which the accused was charged)

And whereas the accused, upon a trial of the issue, has been found *FIT TO STAND TRIAL* and there are reasonable grounds to believe that the accused would become unfit to stand trial if released.

It is therefore Ordered, pursuant to the provisions of section 672.29 of the *Criminal Code* of Canada, that you, ____________________ in her Majesty's name, take the accused in custody and convey the accused safely to the ____________________ (*hospital*) and there deliver the accused to the Administrator with the following precept:

I do therefore command you the said Administrator to receive the accused In your custody in the said hospital and to keep the accused safely there until the completion of the accused's trial or such earlier time as may be Ordered.

Dated at the *City of Toronto* this ____________________ (today's date)

____

Signature of Judge or Justice as the case may be

Hospital Pending Review Board (Section 672.46(2))

This form is not contained in the *Criminal Code*. It is the creation of one of this book's authors, Richard Schneider. The following form covers the provisions of subsection 672.46(2) of the *Criminal Code*, which permit the court to place an accused, upon the verdict of either unfit or not criminally responsible on account of mental disorder, in hospital pending the accused's hearing before the Ontario Review Board, rather than returning the accused to jail.

CANADA

Section 672.46(2)

PROVINCE OF ONTARIO
Toronto
(Region)

WARRANT OF COMMITTAL
Detention of Accused in Hospital Pending Disposition of the Ontario Review Board (672.46(2))

To the peace officers in the said region, and to the keeper (administrator, warden) of the (*prison, hospital or other appropriate place where the accused is currently detained*)

This warrant is issued for the committal of: (hereinafter called the accused) (*accused name*)

Whereas the accused has been charged that (*set out briefly the offence in respect of which the accused was charged*)

And whereas the accused, upon a trial of the issue, has been found

Check One

- □ UNFIT TO STAND TRIAL
- □ NOT CRIMINALLY RESPONSIBLE ON ACCOUNT OF MENTAL DISORDER, and a Disposition has not been held pursuant to the provisions of section 672.54,

It is therefore Ordered, pursuant to the provisions of section 672.46(2) of the *Criminal Code* of Canada, that you, in her Majesty's name, take the accused in custody and convey the accused safely to the (*hospital*) and there deliver the accused to the Administrator with the following precept:

I do therefore command you the said Administrator to receive the accused in your custody in the said hospital and to keep the accused safely there until a hearing has been held by the Ontario Review Board and a Disposition made.

Dated at the *City of Toronto* this ______________________ (today's date)

____

Signature of Judge or Justice as the case may be

Disposition: Detention in Hospital (Section 672.54(c))

This form (Form 49) is contained in the *Criminal Code*. It is used where the court makes a disposition (for either an unfit or a not criminally responsible accused) pursuant to the provisions of section 672.54(c). This form, along with a "New Accused Information Sheet" filled out by the Crown, is sent to the Review Board within forty-eight hours. Note that any disposition of the court (other than under section 672.54(a)) is reviewed by the Review Board within ninety days.

FORM 49
(Section 672.57)
WARRANT OF COMMITTAL
DISPOSITION OF DETENTION

Canada,
Province of
(*territorial division*)

To the peace officers in the said (*territorial division*) and to the keeper (*administrator, warden*) of the (*prison, hospital or other appropriate place where the accused is detained*).

This warrant is issued for the committal of A.B., of __________, (*occupation*), hereinafter called the accused.

Whereas the accused has been charged that (*set out briefly the offence in respect of which the accused was charged*);

And whereas the accused was found*

- ☐ unfit to stand trial
- ☐ not criminally responsible on account of mental disorder

This is, therefore, to command you, in Her Majesty's name, to take the accused in custody and convey the accused safely to the (*prison, hospital or other appropriate place*) at _______, and there deliver the accused to the keeper (*administrator, warden*) with the following precept:

I do therefore command you the said keeper (*administrator, warden*) to receive the accused in your custody in the said (*prison, hospital or other appropriate place*) and to keep the accused safely there until the accused is delivered by due course of law.

The following are the conditions to which the accused shall be subject while in your (*prison, hospital or other appropriate place*):

The following are the powers regarding the restrictions (*and the limits and conditions on those restrictions*) on the liberty of the accused that are hereby delegated to you the said keeper (*administrator, warden*) of the said (*prison, hospital or other appropriate place*):

* Check applicable option.

Dated this ____ day of _________ A.D. _______, at ________ .

____

(Signature of judge, clerk of the court, provincial court judge or chairperson of the Review Board)

Disposition: Discharge Subject to Conditions (Section 672.54(b))

DISPOSITION

This form is not contained in the *Criminal Code*. It is the creation of one of this book's authors, Richard Schneider. Parliament did not include a form for the making of a disposition where the disposition is not a custodial one. Where the accused is to be discharged absolutely (section 672.54(a)), no form is required; however, where the accused is to be discharged subject to conditions (section 672.54(b)), the following form may be used to record the disposition.

CANADA
PROVINCE OF ONTARIO
Toronto
(Region)

Section 672.54 (b)

DISPOSITION
Accused Out of Custody

WHEREAS (hereinafter referred to as the "Accused") (*name of accused*) has been charged with (*set out briefly the offence in respect of which the accused was charged*)

And whereas the accused, upon a trial of the issue, has been found

Check One

- ☐ UNFIT TO STAND TRIAL
- ☐ NOT CRIMINALLY RESPONSIBLE ON ACCOUNT OF MENTAL DISORDER,

and a hearing has taken place pursuant to the provisions of section 672.47(1) of the *Criminal Code* of Canada and it has been determined that the least onerous and least restrictive Disposition is that the accused be discharged subject to conditions, it is Ordered that: [*list terms of Discharge*]

THIS IS THEREFORE TO COMMAND you, ____________________, in Her Majesty's name, to comply with the terms of this Disposition and, upon Notice, to appear before the Ontario Review Board as directed.

Dated at the City of Toronto this __________________ (today's date)

____

Signature of Judge or Justice as the case may be

Table of Cases

Index

NOTE: The following terms in the index are represented by acronyms: Fitness to stand trial = FST; Difficult self-represented accused = DSRA; Figure = F; Table = T

About the Authors

Hon Richard D Schneider, PhD, LLM, CPsych is a justice of the Ontario Court of Justice, a deputy judge of the Territorial Court of the Yukon, chair of the Ontario Review Board, and an alternate chair of the Nunavut Review Board. He is also an adjunct professor in the faculties of law and medicine at the University of Toronto. Prior to his appointment to the bench, Justice Schneider was a criminal defence lawyer, a clinical psychologist, and counsel to the Ontario Review Board. He has published extensively in the area of mental disorder and the law.

Hy Bloom, LLB, MD, FRCP(C) is a forensic psychiatrist and lawyer who assesses individuals who have mental illnesses and outstanding criminal charges. He is a founding member of the PSILEX Group, Consultants in Behavioural Sciences and the Law. He is also a part-time staff member in the Complex Mental Illness/Forensic Services Program at the Centre for Addiction and Mental Health, an assistant professor in the Department of Medicine at the University of Toronto, an assistant clinical professor in the Department of Psychiatry and Behavioural Neurosciences at McMaster University, and adjunct faculty at University of Toronto's Faculty of Law. Dr Bloom has published on a number of topics in psychiatry and the law.

Printed and bound by CPI Group (UK) Ltd, Croydon, CR0 4YY
15/09/2026
14962402-0003